AF541620

SOCIO-PSYCHOLOGICAL CORRELATES OF VOCATIONAL ASPIRATIONS

By

Dr. H.M. Shailaja
Reader
Deptt. of Education
Karnataka University
Dharwad, Karnataka

&

Dr. Rajeev P. Gundale
Lecturer
J.S.S.'s Shree Manjunatheshwara
College of Education
Dharwad, Karnataka

DISCOVERY PUBLISHING HOUSE PVT. LTD.
NEW DELHI-110 002

First Published-2010

ISBN 978-81-8356-642-1

Published by:

DISCOVERY PUBLISHING HOUSE PVT. LTD.
4831/24, Ansari Road, Prahlad Street
Darya Ganj, New Delhi-110002 (India)
Phone: 23279245, 43764432 • Fax: 91-11-23253475
E-mail: parul.wasan@gmail.com
info@discoverypublishinggroup.com
Website: www.discoverypublishinggroup.com

Printed at:
Sachin Printers
Delhi

Preface

The study of vocational aspiration has attracted the attention of educators more than the psychologists. We are still very much in the dark as to the characteristics of the individual who makes a wise selection of objective as contrasted to the barren or unrealistic chooser. Our professional ignorance of what constitutes a "good" choice explains part of our failure to identify the characteristics of the adequate vocational planner. Among all levels of intelligence, individuals show a wide difference in their capacity to set vocational goals, reasonable in the light of their potentialities. Such individual differences need to be explored. In the past there has been too little attention to the phenomenological study of choice and a resulting tendency to regard vocational choice as whimsical and devoid of significance, particularly when the choice was regarded as irrational. There is a continuing need to study the psychological factors in relation to occupational aspirations. It is also a common observation that social factors also play a vital role in occupational aspirations.

Educators generally agree that major variables affecting classroom performance are academic achievement motivation and personality adjustment. The occupational application of psychological theory to education has not typically eventuated in a theory of academic achievement motivation nor a unified and coherent body of information. As a result there is a little in the way of academic achievement motivation theory which is clearly of help to the classroom teacher or to education in general. And there is no doubt that adjustment influence daily living is seldom denial. It might be expected, then, that emotional stability or adjustment would be in some way related to the occupational aspirations. Based on the review of the aspiration literature in sociology, psychology and education, one expects variation in levels of occupational aspiration to correlate with measures of social status. The controversial findings of personality in relation to occupational aspirations need a carefully designed study to clarify the extent to which an individual's personality plays a part in the relationship of aspirations. On the whole, the students' achievement motivation, their personality and social background may help the counsellors in understanding their vocational planning counselees problems and to offer counselling assistance in a more effective way at this stage.

H.M. Shailaja
Rajeev P. Gindala

Contents

Contents

1

Introduction

Introduction

Everybody is destined to choose a vocation for one's basic need and it is imperative for the survival. However, an occupation for the sake of merely survival is a low rung concept. As Maslow's motivation theory holds the view that every one desires to depart for hither needs, so to excel in an opted occupation is a natural tendency. It is very difficult to discern the personal and professional growth, as these are deeply interwoven phenomenon. Any one lives one's greater part of life in chosen vocation. To live the life holistically and happily the occupation of an individual must be paired with love when a person enters in an aspired occupation, personal and professional progress goes hand in hand.

Occupation of an individual is considered as a major source of satisfaction in adult life and it links to the real world. It is the identity of an individual when a simple query is made about any one "who is he/she" the answer flows in terms of persons occupation. Therefore, the vocation of a person is not only the means of livelihood but also the way of life. In order to succeed in a chosen vocation a realistic and pragmatic approach is highly desirable. It has become exceedingly difficult to adjust for the poorly skilled and educated individual to face challenges of the modern society. Exorbitant advancement in scientific and technological field has exerted enormous pressure on individual to sharpen and substantiate the occupational competencies. Undoubtedly, the education imparted to a child, which is commensurate with the interest and abilities can prepare for the right vocation to meet the contemporary challenges. There is a great need to match the education imparted to the students with their endowed potential. As after certain standard of schooling, education is nothing but the preparation of an individual for the "World of Work". Vegetative growth in Academics without realistic vocational goal, which is not in accordance with one's abilities, interests and aptitude, can be responsible for the drop-out at the later stages.

Social and national progress can be augmented by means of productive education. Peace and prosperity has been perceived as a proliferation of productive society from time immemorial. The chaos among the educated youths is apparently visible as they are not able to secure economic better off. Growing stress to cope with galloping demands of efficiency is no more secrets, which is further growing exponentially.

Education for the sake of merely knowledge has become pseudo-phenomenon. The education without pecuniary value is a utopian concept. Nostalgia of general education without its appropriate appraisal has proven shallow, as an unskilled graduate working for meager wage is facing hardship in terms of growing monetary demands where as a garage technician who opts his occupation out of his interest and attitude is presently able to rise to the occasion of his financial needs and able to live a balanced life. Remarkable progress in one's career is not a matter of chance but the result of right preparation and planning at the right time. A real and comprehensive appraisal of one's aspiration, ability and aptitude has become mandatory requirement before choosing any vocation. It will not augur well for a person who chooses his profession inadvertently without self-appraisal. Rapid scientific and technological advancement, urbanization, industrialization and ever changing society have left no room for the traditional and stereotype education that could ensure the economic security of an individual. A happy and ecstatic life has umbilical relation to competency of one's profession. It will be a great humbugging and the tenets of the education will tacitly prove futile if one is not suitably prepared for his 'World of Work'.

There are some unequivocal questions before a person, who is intended to opt a vocation. Whether any one will thrive in any occupation? Whether all occupations are equally suitable for every one? Is there ample chance of culmination in the occupation opted for? These scientific queries are to be addressed well before take off.

The pupils at the pre-university stage are in the twilight zone and at the terminal stage. Concept of vocation crystallizes at this level so they have to prepare accordingly. There is a great need of suitable guidance in order to choose the right vocation, which is commensurate with the personality. A holistic approach is essential at this juncture to optimize the potential and analyze the psychological strength and weaknesses in terms of vocational success at the later stages.

In India, the need for vocational education was stressed in the Gandhian philosophy of basic education which propounded the principle that education should be work centred. This emphasis was reiterated by the University Education Commission (1949) chaired by Dr. S. Radhakrishnan, the All India Secondary Education Commission under the chairmanship of Dr. A. L. Muddliar (1953) and the Kothari Commission which advocated work experience. The need to establish operational linkages between the world of school and the world of work was mentioned in the National Policy on Education (1969). Subsequently, vocationalization of education was propagated by the Central Advisory Board of Education Committee on Education Structure in 1972. It also found a significant place in the review of the education system done by the Janata Party in 1977 and the Dr. Eshwar Bhai Patel Committee which suggested socially useful productive work (SUPW) and the state Education Ministers Conference in 1981. The repeated announcements of the protagonists of the scheme seem to have strengthened the idea of vocational education.

The National Policy on Education (1986) envisaged diverting 10 per cent of students at the plus-two level to the vocational stream of education by the end of the Seventh Five-year Plan and 25 per cent to the vocational stream at the end of Eighth Five-year Plan, with substantial financial assistance from the

Central Government. In accordance with the priority accorded to vocational education in the National Policy on Education, a centrally-sponsored scheme of Vocationalization of Secondary Education was launched in February 1988. The main objective of the scheme was to enhance individual employability, reduce the mismatch between the demand and supply of skilled manpower and to provide an alternative for those pursuing higher education. Under the Ninth Five-year Plan the government envisaged an increase in the labour force up to 450 million. It also plans to provide employment to 443.6 million workforce during the same period. One of the daunting challenges facing the Ninth Five-year Plan is to accelerate the growth of employment opportunities to absorb the increase in the labour force. The emerging structure of employment is marked by a high level of underemployment, increasing casualisation, emergence of low productivity jobs and underutilization of educated persons.

The objective of vocational education is to prepare students for vocations and enable them to enter the world of work with the necessary skills. For this reason, after completing 10 years of general education, the student sets about acquiring new practical knowledge of technical processes, regulating manual operations and also certain knacks and tricks of the trade. Last, but not the least, the student must develop civic attitudes.

In our country, education is still a privilege. The path each student takes differs depending on the stage of dropping out and individual circumstances. However, most school dropouts should learn a vocation which would open the door to a technical college from which they can go on to institutions of higher education. Others can proceed from 10 years of schooling to two years of supplementary schooling after which they would be qualified to embark on a course of higher education. And should any one's studies fall to proceed smoothly, his fate should not be sealed. He should be given an opportunity for making up for the lost time in vocational training institutes of adult education classes. He, too, should be able to attain the level of education of which he is capable. Partially skilled jobs like domestic helpers, dry cleaners, gardeners, seamstresses, store clerks, assistant cooks, printing workers and skilled jobs such as fitters, grinders, electricians, building painters, garage mechanics, post office workers, etc. are among the possibilities. They ensure everyone the chance of a career even when individual circumstances are unfavourable.

The planned development of the national and state economy requires an exact calculation of the demand for skilled workers with various specializations and for technologists and engineers of various kinds. There is, therefore, an enhanced need for career guidance centres to provide information on various careers available and their importance to the community. There is also need to introduce poly-technical instruction (regular visits to factories) to help in the preparation for a career by giving the pupils an opportunity to become acquainted with individual specializations.

To strengthen vocational education, it is suggested that the core curriculum should include important components. Fragmentation of Secondary education into academic and vocational streams should be avoided. Secondly, schools should offer vocational courses in varying combinations with academic subjects. Thirdly provision should be made for further education in vocational subjects for students taking up vocational courses at the Higher Secondary stage, leading to direct job placement or self-employment. Fourthly, vocational courses should be reorganized as relevant to the number of vocations in both organized and unorganized sectors particularly in rural areas.

The majority of students leaving the portals of the institutions after completing their higher secondary education are neither well acquainted with the employment avenues nor do they have any information regarding the scope of job opportunities. In addition to it many of them are not conscious of their own suitability in relation to the job requirements. Those who are keen to continue education do not necessarily make a choice of subjects and courses which may be in line with their special aptitude and capabilities.

The introduction of the system of professionally oriented education at the Higher Secondary level during the fifties created a practical field for a significant improvement in the standards of instruction. This system aims at directing the students to choose a field of study consistent with his aptitude and abilities right at the school level. This system with greater choice of subjects for the students is an attempt to prepare educand at an early stage for a particular profession rather than leaving this choice after the completion of studies.

Study of ever-growing range of jobs and career opportunities must be a background for choosing a career area. Study in this area gives a basis for intelligently choosing a future work role that allows one to use his talents, develop his interests, and enjoy making a contribution to society and move up a career ladder through continuous learning. Fortunately there are many choices available and the more one knows about the present and future workload and himself, the better he can prepare for and choose an occupational area where he will be happy and successful.

Every occupational area has work that ranges from the less complex to the very theoretical. Therefore, if one is interested in medicine, electricity, construction or art, there is work to be done if one prepares. Many of these jobs require early planning and preparation. At present the teachers and institutions know that one cannot get a good job unless one has a minimum of education and a saleable job skill. Whatever a young person's interests and abilities, there is a place for one if one plans and prepares for it.

It is said that one's occupation is the watershed down, which the rest of one's life flows. If an individual is to lead his life happily one should be happy with work. If one is to be happy with work, one should choose an occupation that would give satisfaction. For every young child, the world of work may appear remote. But as one grows and goes through the pressures and processes of socialization the 'world of work' comes into one's focus. Certain ideas about work take shape during the pre-adolescent years. The process of vocational development is further accelerated in competitive societies like ours by the educational system, which is so designed, that the individual must make a beginning in the matter of occupational choice early in the high school days. The individual has to choose a particular curriculum and by so choosing one would be preparing oneself for certain types of employment and all the same denying himself certain other types of occupational openings in the 'world of work' thus restricting one's aspirations.

Choosing a career goal is one of the most important decisions one may ever have to make. Also for many of the pupils the Higher Secondary school stage is the terminal stage of education. It is an important phase in their lives because at the conclusion of this period they are on the threshold of the 'world of work'. The amount of education one receives and the career one chooses will go a long way towards determining one's chances for steady employment in the future. The students at this juncture have to learn more about themselves, what are their interests, abilities and aspirations. Here 'aspirations' refer to an individual's goal or expectations or wants in regard to the welfare of one's future whereas 'occupation' is a particular kind of productive property known as person's occupation, by which it means the kind of job one holds.

The Concept of Vocation

Dictionary of Education (1959) means "vocation" as "A calling, as a particular occupation, business or profession". As per the new *Oxford Encyclopedic Dictionary* (1978), vocation means "Divine call to sense of fitness for, a career or occupation". *Dictionary of Psychology Fourth Edition* (1988) views the meaning of vocation as "The manner in which one earns his living or in religious writing a call to the religious life".

The word "vocation" is derived from the latin "*vocare*" which means "to call". The concept of vocation as a "calling" dates back some 2000 years before the Common Era when some religious figures who were called of a divine power to perform special work normally the propagation of religion. Luther and John Calvin came out with reform of such notion and affirmed that any work, which was done for the glory of God, for the betterment of others, was a vocation, a calling from God.

Luther changed the religious "calling" concept of work and proclaimed as "There is just one way to serve God to do most perfectly the work of one's profession." In the words of Tilgher the "so long as work is done in a spirit of obedience to God and of live for one's neighbour, every variety of labour has equal spiritual dignity each is servant of God on earth" (Tilgher, 1962).

In the modern period, the concept of vocation has become more general and secular.

Nelson (1963) writes :

> "Obviously – and by a process much investigated in recent decades by historians, economist and sociologists – this reformation rediscovery of the vocation of every man was the basis of our whole modern approach to daily work. In American or any other society deeply stood in protestant presuppositions. Long after the Deity has been ushered out of every day commerce and professional life, people push on here with a vocational intensity unknown in nay culture. With all its glory and tragedy, its mighty works and its ulcers and ruthless competition, this motive of work is in our history a Protestant affair, deeply grounded in past theological claims which have been largely forgotten today."

Vocation is longing by every one in order to survive and live happy life. Everybody craves for vocation with variation in its intent and purpose.

Parks (2000) writes :

> "I have observed among some of the most talented, many who simply have been lured into elite careers before anyone has invited them to consider the deep questions of purpose and vocation."

A vocation is an occupation in which a person is specially gifted or "called" for the work and in this way vocation is not only the set of work but a way of life. Morse and Weiss (1955) observe "most common positive reasons for working". Working keeps one occupied gives one an interest: working keeps an individual healthy, is good for a person and the kind of work is enjoyable.

Fowler (2000) defines vocation as "vocation is the response a person makes with his or her total self to the address of God and to the calling to partnership."

Vocation term is more scientific for a person to opt a vocation one requires interest and aptitude irrespective of his families' profession whereas an occupation is a job, which is occupied for the earning (Sharma 2003).

The term 'vocation' can be perceived as the occupation chosen and engaged for longer period of time due to its cangues of one's ability, interest and affiliation.

The principal usage in the social sciences follows closely the common usages which take an occupation to denote an employment, business, or calling. The term occupation can be defined as the kind of work performed by the individual regardless of the industry in which this work is performed and of the status of employment of the individual.

The British 1951 Census of population used the classification of occupations compiled in 1950 in which the term occupation is defined as follows:

> The occupation of any person is the kind of work which he or she performs, due regard being paid to the conditions under which it is performed; and those alone determine the particular group in an occupation classification to which the person is assigned. The nature of the factory, business or service in which a person is employed has no bearing upon the classification of his occupation, except to the extent that it enables the nature of his duties to be more clearly defined. This will perhaps be made clearer by an example. A career driver may be employed in a ship-hard, an engineering work or in a building construction but this has no bearing upon his occupation and all crane drivers should be classified with the same occupational group.

Particular kind of productive property is known as a person's occupation by which is meant the kind of job one holds. 'Occupation' is significant because of its profound influences on all other aspects of a person's life. Lynd (1929) concluded from his study of Middletown thus:

> "It is after all this division into working class and business class that constitutes the outstanding cleavage in Middletown. The mere fact of being born on one or the other side of the watershed roughly formed by these two groups is the most significant cultural factor tending to influence what one does all day long throughout one's life".

"An individual's occupation", states Ginsberg (1933), "is generally a fair index of his mode of life and educational attainments, the sort of people whom he would meet on equal terms, the range of individual from among whom he would normally choose his pattern in marriage and so forth".

Edwards, (1965) the Census Bureau's life long student of occupational trends observes:

> "The most nearly dominant single influence in a man's life is probably his occupation. More than anything else, perhaps a man's occupation determines his course and his contribution in life. Indeed there is no other single characteristic that tells so much about a man and his status – social, intellectual, and economic – as does his occupation. A man's occupation not only tells for each work day what he does during one-half of his waking hours but it indicates with some degree of accuracy the manner of his life during the other half – the kind of associates he will have, the kind of clothes he will wear, the kind of house he will live in, an even, to some extent, the kind of food he will eat. And, usually it indicates in some degree, the cultural level of his family".

The Concept of Aspiration

The first study of '*Anspruchsniveau*", translated somewhat inadequately as the "level of aspiration", grew out of the Gestalt – inspired experiments on both the effects of forced stopping of tasks before their completion and on the nature of psychological background preceding spontaneous breaking off and spontaneous resumption of a task. Such considerations led to the realization that feelings of pleasure or displeasure with the task, arising from the feeling of failure or success associated with the obtained performance, determined the subsequent behaviour (of breaking off or resumption) and the attitude of the subjects to that task or similar tasks. This approach to the problem revealed that different individuals depending on their different standards interpreted the same objective performance score differently. Thus feelings of failure and success were dependent almost entirely on the individual's standards of performance or his 'goals' of performance in a given task and situation, rather than on the objective task – instructions.

Hoppe (1930) then attempted to study the reciprocal relationship between goals and feelings of failure and success i.e., how the latter affected the height of goals and how the height of goals determined whether a given performance level would be interpreted as failure or success. It must be borne in mind that the experience of failure and success is not strictly bound to particular performances so that a given objective achievement is not psychologically the same experience at different times for the same individual nor for different individuals at the same time. Largely in qualitative terms, the height of the individual's goal or "aspiration level" was ascertained by Hoppe (1930).

The Theoretical Framework

Aspiration has been accepted as one of the important variables of personality. In describing a person's level of aspiration we are in fact describing the person. It is inalienably an expression of the self of the subject's future or past orientation, his confidence in himself, his fear of failure, his optimism or pessimism, his ambition and his courage to face reality.

Webster's Dictionary (1976) defines aspiration as a "strong desire for realization (as of ambition, idea or accomplishment)", whereas *Oxford Dictionary* (1972) defines it as "pure upward desire for excellence – the steadfast desire or longing for something above one".

Encyclopedia of Religion and Ethics (1971) describes it as "worldly ambition or desire". It is said to be :

> "the power inciting to a spiritual progress, an inward impulse by which men are urged to the development of their highest nature and true ends as spiritual being".

English and English (1958) have defined it as "an ardent desire to accomplish what one sets out to do".

Hoppe (1941) defines 'aspiration' as "a dynamic psychological factor which will operate in the production of feeling of success and failure". Further aspiration is differentiated into realistic and idealistic as realistic levels do but idealistic do not have behavioural relevance (Stephenson, 1968). Therefore aspiration refers to the conscious desire and expectation of an individual coupled with the deliberate striving for the achievement of goal.

In the opinion of Hoppe (1930) level of aspiration represents a person's expectations, goals, claims or his future achievement in a given task. He further stresses that the 'experience of performance' as a success or failure does not depend upon its objective goodness alone but also on the level of aspiration reached. Subjects tend to lower or raise future goals depending on their success and failure with previous goals. Experiences of success and failure do not attend tasks which are too easy or too difficult. Hoppe has concluded that level of aspirations are chiefly determined by two sets of opposing principles in the individual: (a) ego-forces which tend to set high goals even at the cost of failure (b) pleasure principles which seek success thus lowering the aspiration level.

Frank (1935) defines it as "the level of future performance in familiar tasks which an individual, knowing his level of past performance in that task explicitly undertakes to reach". By level of past performance is meant the goodness of the individual's past performance, as he knows it.

Frank (1935) concluded that the presence of ego-involvement (i.e., the degree of the person's involvement in the quality of his performance) as indicated by criteria of self-competition and awareness of social pressure is correlated with divergence of level of aspiration. The aspiration may be higher or lower than the performance when ego-involvement is present but not equal to it.

In Lewin's (1944) views level of aspiration is the difference between how a person expects or aspires to perform on a given task and how actually does he perform (the level of aspiration always being slightly above his level of performance. If he succeeds in fulfilling his expectations, the level of aspiration rises if he fails the level of aspiration falls (Verman and Calvin, 1974).

Trow (1941) opines that aspiration is quite similar to a person's fantasy choice.

Crites (1969) also expressed similar views and reports that in vocational selection the first stage is aspiration, which is not in touch with apparent reality though it may have visionary reality. Aspiration has been considered by.

Eysenck (1972) as the level of possible goal (score) an individual sets himself in his performance.

The term 'aspiration' is used most of the time when a decision or desire is usually out of context with reality and it is appropriately determined by fantasy level, which has, minimum experimental (concrete reality) component attached to it.

The use of the term 'aspiration' has been made use in different fields, (Eysenck, 1947; *Encyclopedia of Religion and Ethics*, 1971). In the sociological field, the term aspiration is used as an index of upward social mobility (Critics, 1969); in the clinical psychology aspiration (when entirely out of touch of reality) may be taken as an indicator of conflict and maladjustment (Eysenck, 1947). In religion aspiration is used to express the level of desire to attain *'nirvan'/ moksh* whereas in Ethics it is used for realization of higher ideals (*Encyclopedia of Religion and Ethics*, 1971). In educational and vocational guidance the term aspiration has been frequently used to denote the fantasy level connected with the future goals. A number of studies have tried to correlate it with various personality variables (Flugel, 1945; Eysenck, 1947; Heckhausen, 1963; Bhargava and Dhir, 1980).

Development of Aspiration

In a given culture the individual while attaining his adulthood identifies himself with various groups viz., 'participating groups' comprising of family and professional colleagues and 'reference groups' consisting of other individuals whose standards one tries to identify. Through this process of identification one perceives a sense of distinction (status) and the standards of participating and reference groups set in him the level of his aspirations (Cantril, 1950). The Need Achievement theory also throws light on the development of aspiration while describing "Career Striving Process", Rayner (1978) states that:

> "the individual develops 'Step-path Scheme' in career striving process".
>
> He further adds thus:
>
> "children from a very early age try out career roles such as doctor, nurse, policemen, fireman etc., although realistic striving for one of them does not begin until after a whole series of 'identities' have been explored and either some initial differentiating competence has been developed and/ or appropriate extrinsic motivation is aroused for one 'career path' than another. Thus in various ways and to various extents; children and adolescents learn about the adult world of work, 'occupation or careers'. Parents, grand-parents, relatives, friends, folk images, teachers and the modern society particularly mass media heroes are sources of information on vocations and provides role models for the

acquisition of the appropriate behaviour and expected consequences of career related activity where 'appropriate' is seen in terms of the societal perspective of later adult striving in acceptable avenues of pursuit".

According to him the structure rather than the content of knowledge about career striving may be the most critical factor. The perception of this 'structure' concept may provide information regarding his level of striving vis-à-vis the level of his aspiration in the world of work. The researchers Jucknat (1937) and Heckhausen (1963) in this field showed that the development of level of aspiration was affected by momentary achievement, long standing achievement, confidence, seriousness of the situation, the presence as well as prestige and behaviour of on-lookers, success/failure and also by other extrinsic and intrinsic factors. Describing topologically this development is viewed as being affected by objective field barriers – besides social and personal barriers. Social barriers are in the form of prohibition, customs and personal barriers may be dislikes, scruples etc. (Lewin, 1944).

Meaning of Vocational Aspiration

It is a vocational attainment that an individual wishes to achieve in his immediate future.

It is a compromise between interests and expectations of being able to enter various occupations. It is a rational decision making situation which entails a series of progressive delimitations of alternatives which are eliminated during the process due to factors both within and outside the individual. These determinants may be intra personal (e.g., needs and values of the individual) and interpersonal (e.g., the influence of peers and others) and extra personal (economic factors).

Vocational aspirations are aspects of behaviour which are internally derived manifestation through directed and selected choices within the environment and influenced by psychological and socio-environmental factors.

Man responds to his environment by active degree of aspiration or aversion by movement towards or a way from flue exciting stimulus. In social life, aspirations about one's education and occupation play a major role in shaping one's destiny of life.

Roe (1956) points out that in our culture there is no single situation which is so capable of satisfying the basic psychological needs as in an occupation.

Roe (1957) states that the early family experience of acceptance, avoidance and emotional concentration influence orientation of the child towards things or people, and predispose him toward certain major occupation groups.

Occupational aspiration is defined as orientation towards occupational goal (Haller and Miller, 1971).

As pointed out earlier the term level of aspiration has been applied in the 'vocational choice field' by various psychologists and sociologists, 'Occupational aspiration is usually means what the individual considers to be the ideal vocation for him. Defined in this way aspiration is quite similar to if not identical with a person's fantasy choice' (Trow, 1941). As elicited by interviews and open ended question as "what would you do, if you could do what you really wanted to do? (Crites, 1969). In occupational aspiration, the individual expresses as to what ones wants or wishes to do irrespective of the limitations imposed by reality.

In a democratic set up, an individual has the fundamental right to adopt the occupation he aspires for the most but owing to various social, cultural and personal factors, his aspirations seldom materialize. In spite of this, the process of his aspiring for certain occupations continues.

Occupational aspiration is "a goal directed attitude which involves conception of the self in relation to particular level of the occupational prestige hierarchy" (Chadha, 1982.)

Occupational aspirations are the desires, thought of and verbalized by young individuals at Higher Secondary school level that when they grow up this or that is what they wish to engage in as work. In many areas, Higher Secondary school students lack the clarity of reasoning why they would like to take to certain occupations.

According to Crites (1969), vocational aspiration means what the individual considers to be ideal vocation for him.

Aspirations are the target a person sets for him to achieve which creates a 'desire' or 'will' in him. Formation of a strong desire and ambition motivates individual to strive hard to achieve that goal. Such motivation is keenly required if one has to succeed in life. If one goes through the education on a preferred vocation, he can get job satisfaction from the vocation and the individual shall be well placed. Aspiration adds to the efficiency of the person by exhibiting the best in him on the job. Therefore, before providing for education for a vocation, there is a need for planners to try to know which vocations are aspired by the students.

Methods of Measuring Vocational Aspirations

Vocational aspiration has been measured in term of levels – high, middle and low. For its measurement several occupational classificatory methods were evolved. In the beginning these classificatory methods were based on 'economic activities' and they were generally one-dimensional (Edwards, 1943). Further, two dimensional Roe evolved occupational classificatory method during 1954; where the system contained 6 levels based on factors like responsibility, capacity and skill required by various occupations. Later on, Super (1957) added one more dimension of 'Enterprise' and offered three dimensional classificatory system. Shah and Bhargava (1973) have devised a scale which measure general level of aspiration by providing Goal discrepancy and attainment discrepancy scores. Grewal (1973) has also constructed a scale "Occupational Aspiration Scale" on the basis of Haller and Miller's scale (1971).

Vocational Aspiration as Differentiated From Vocational Preferences, Choices and Interests

Vocational aspiration, preference and choice are considered to be on the same continuum known as 'process of vocational choice' aspiration and choice being on either side of this one-dimensional continuum shown as under-

Aspiration ———Preference———Choice———

This process marches from 'fantasy towards realism' which is the final act of vocational choice. The distinction among them is clearly understood from the type of questions used to elicit responses as indicated below, taken from Gilger (1942) and Trow (1941).

S. No.	Questions	Measures
1.	Gilger, (1942) What kind of work do you feel you are best prepared to do at present?	CHOICE
2.	What vocation or life work do you want most of all to undertake?	PREFERENCE
3.	If you were financially able and free to choose without restriction, what kind of work would you like to prepare for?	ASPIRATION
1.	Trow, (1941) What kind of job do you think you will probably be able to do when you are through school?	CHOICE (Probable Occupation)
2.	If you could be sure to get the education and training that you would need, what kind of job would you choose?	PREFERENCE (Possible Occupation)
3.	People sometimes think about what they would like to be although they do not really believe it could ever come true. If by some magic you could be anything you want, what would you like to be?	ASPIRATION (Fantasy Occupation)

It is clear from the above that the vocational aspiration is quite distinct from choice which is formulated solely in terms of the wants and wishes of individuals, irrespective of the limitations imposed by reality. "When an individual express a preference, he ranks two or more occupations along some continuum of desirability of thinking. When he makes a choice, he ranks two or more occupations along a continuum of his estimated chances of actually entering them. Moreover, in expressing a preference he indicates what he would like to do and in making choice he predicts what he probably will do" (Crites, 1969).

In brief, vocational choice can be termed as what the individual predicts to do in future and vocational preference can be termed as to what he would like to do. In vocational aspiration the individual expresses as to what he wants or wishes to do irrespective of the limitations imposed by reality. The three variables are distinct to the extent they differ in representing the reality-oriented selection of occupation. They are the same in nature as they all involve the selection of an occupation regardless of the basis for the selection. The vocational choice is considered to be more realistic than either vocational preference or vocational aspiration and the vocational preference is relatively more realistic than the vocational aspiration.

Crites (1969) has proposed a schematic diagram showing the developmental stages of vocational aspiration, preference, choice and interest. On the horizontal axis the 'age' is demonstrated whereas on the vertical axis the reality orientation is depicted as none, some and considerable.

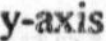

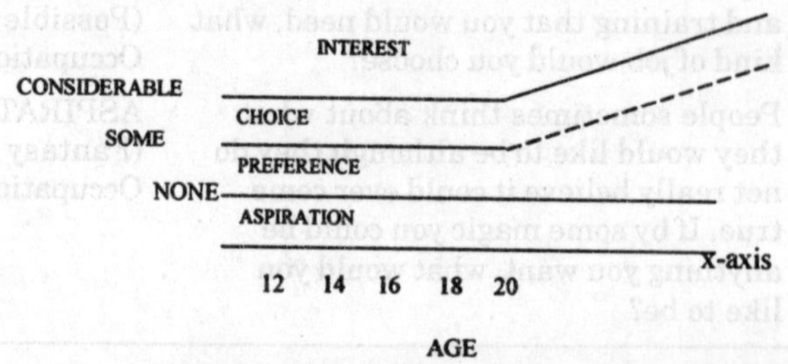

Fig. 1.1. A conceptual scheme for the vocational choice process and related variable during adolescence - Crites, 1969

The vocational aspiration, preference, choice, and interest are differentiable approximately at age range of 15-16 and not before that. However, on vertical axis reality orientation might be present, but many a time it is not possible for the child to really distinguish between vocational aspiration, preference, choice and interest. No matter how a question is asked, he will always be expressing his aspired vocation, which has high social value judged by him or transmitted to him through extrinsic and intrinsic factors constantly influencing him through their intersectional process. That is why, probably, the researches conducted on adolescent subjects of High school revealed no significant difference in them, (Empey, 1956; Kahl, 1953; Sewell, Haller and Straws, 1957; Wilson, 1959; Perrone, 1964).

Vocational aspiration is purely determined by fantasies whereas vocational choice is more reality based and, therefore, no one has formulated any theory specifically for vocational aspiration alone. The theories of vocational choice are, however, discussed by Crites (1969), Bailey and Stadt (1973) and career striving theory by Raynor (1978) and their description automatically includes the process of crystallization of choice and the choice is crystallized on the parameters of age and reality orientation.

Variables of the Study

Personality

Allport (1937) called personality one of the most abstract words in our language and listed 50 distinct meaning that were derived from fields as diverse as theology, philosophy, sociology, law and psychology. Although there is some disagreement among contemporary personality theorists about the meaning of personality but there is agreement what people generally do is influenced by stable characteristics that is their personality. He defined personality synthetically as "Personality is the dynamic organization within the individual of those psychological systems that determine his unique adjustments to his environment".

Angyl (1941) views "Personality is to be regarded as the total organism which includes the social self and other factors which bind the individual into sapper individual relationships".

For Murphy (1947) "Personality is a structured whole definable in terms of its own distinctive structural attributes in an organism environment field, each aspect of which stands in dynamic relation to the others."

Eysenck (1953) defines "Personality is the more or less stable and enduring organization of a person's character, temperament, intellect and physique which determines his unique adjustment to the environment."

McCrae and Costa (1989) viewed personality as enduring emotional, interpersonal, experimental, attitudinal and motivational styles that explain behaviour in different situation.

Hogan (1991) opines that personality has two-fold meaning which must be discern properly. The first is a social reputation of an individual which refers to the way an individual is perceived by others; it is the personality from observer and public perspective which can be verified. Second one refers to the structures, dynamics, processes and propensities that explain why a person behaves in a characteristic way; it is private and must be inferred. An individual's characteristic patterns of thought, emotion, and behaviours together with the psychological mechanisms-hidden or not-behind those patterns Funder (2001). Personality and vocational success are intimately related.

Accordin⁻ to Super and Crites (1962) :

"Psychologists interested in vocational guidance and personal work seem to have found the concept of personality as a patterning of traits most helpful in their work, for discussions of emotional or personal adjustment and of personality traits abound in the literature, and attempts to measure both general adjustment and specific traits and to ascertain their significance for vocational success have been humorous."

Individual's personality is the key factor in understanding the potential of success and progress in particular vocation. Researchers and practitioners in industrial and organizational psychology have long been intrigued by potential for measure of personality to describe, explain, and predict the behaviour of individuals at work, Jeff (2003).

Aspiration and personality traits are interwoven to each other. An individual difference in personality is one of the important causes of variation in vocational aspirations.

Personality traits and vocational aspirations are important because they influence numerous outcomes associated with work and life success. One common thread that links personality traits and vocational aspiration is that they influence behaviour through motivational processes. That is, they influence choices individual make about which tasks and activities to engage in, how much effort to exert on those tasks and how long to persist with those tasks (Mount *et a*l. 2005).

Personality of the individual may affect his vocational aspiration. A social and an extrovert in all probability would make a successful public relations officer but not a scholar or a librarian. Similarly, a quest and an introvert would be unhappy if placed on the job of a salesman.

Every job can be described in terms of the personality characteristics it requires for the person to happy and satisfied in it. For example, good teachers are usually social, communicative, self confident, self-sufficient and aggressive. Bankers, dentists, and musicians are more conservative self-contained and less aggressive.

Prediction of the most suitable career for an individual is based on the numerous profiles of successful individuals in various jobs. The profile of the individual wanting guidance can be compared with those who have already been successful in that particular field. The similarity and divergence between their personal qualities is a reliable guide for prediction of a career for the individual tested. Studies of reliability of these predictions have proved that young people changing a particular career have interest profile markedly similar to those of the successful persons in that particular line.

Achievement Motivation

The study of achievement motivation in the field of vocational psychology is of vital concern for the researcher and theories as well. Achievement motivation has got significant impact on economic advancement of the society.

McClelland (1961) suggested that achievement motivation may explain economic differences between societies.

Economic growth of a society is dependent on the existence in that society of a high level of need for achievement among people playing key role in the economy (Vroom, 1964).

McClelland (1965) found that n-Ach predisposes people to seek entrepreneurial jobs, the same was corroborated by Andrews (1967).

Singh and Kaur (1987) studied that n-Ach in association with economic interest and preferences for activity tended to promote achievement oriented behaviour. Human motivation derives its origin from the seminal work by Murry (1938), he views that personality is a configuration of some basic psychogenis needs or motives which can be understood basically a lack of something vital to the organism.

Achievement motivation is the acquired tendency and one of the most important social needs (Newcomb 1964).

According to Lindgren (1973) "n-Ach relates to accomplishment, mastering, manipulating and organizing the physical and social environment overcoming obstacles and maintaining high standards of work competing through striving to excel one's previous performance as well as reveling and surpassing others and the like."

Achievement motive is defined by Atkinson (1958) as a disposition to strive for success and/ or the capacity to experience pleasure contingent upon success.

Borady (1983) defines achievement motivation as a desire to do well in competition with some standard of excellence.

n-Ach is a characteristic which has to be considered as an integral pat of an individuals personality make (Tiwari 1984).

According to International Encyclopedia of Psychology (1996) Achievement motivation can be understood simply as the tendency to strive for success or the attainment of a desirable goal, which implies.

(*a*) It involves an inclination on the part of the individual this includes a consideration of the individuals personality and how that personality influences a motivational state given the presence of certain environmental factors.

(*b*) It involves A task oriented behaviour that can be evaluated and

(*c*) Task orientation involves some standard of excellence that may be either internally (by the person) or externally (by other imposed).

Social Status

The social level of the family appears to exercise the most potent influence of all. The level and quality of education available and aspired to as well as the level of work aspired to and accessible are greatly affected by the education of the family and social contacts. Upper and middle class parents tend to have higher educational and vocational aspirations for their children than do lower class parents. Thus, their children have higher aspirations either as a result of pressure from the parents or as a result of internalizing parental pressure or both. If their intellectual endowment is good, their higher level of aspiration may be achieved. But if intellectual endowment is not commensurate with level of aspiration conflict will arises; the individual will not be able to have an integrated self concept, and vocational maladjustment is likely to follow. At times, however, the reverse is true. Among very affluent families, the level of educational and vocational aspirations may be low, and a person with good abilities may not be sufficiently motivated to concentrate on studies and strikeout a vocational path for himself, thus may fail to actualize his potentialities.

The New Pattern of Education in India

The adoption of the common pattern of 10+2+3 for schools and colleges has been a significant reform introduced/implemented in the Indian system of education. This pattern of education was followed more than 50 years and carries on it the imprint of the deliberations of many national level Committees and Commissions.

10+2+3 Pattern of Education in India – A Brief Historical Retrospect

The structural reform was first recommended by the Calcutta University Commission (1917-19), popularly known as, the Sadler Commission. At that time, the pattern of 10 to 12 years of intermediate stage plus 2 years of undergraduate stage was prevailing in the country. Further, it is interesting to note that the matriculation examination conducted at the end of 10 to 12 years of schooling by different universities were regarded as equivalent to each other in all parts of the country. The Universities also held the intermediate examination.

The Commission examined in depth the content of education at the intermediate and the undergraduate stages and came to the following conclusions:

1. That the intermediate stage was really a part of the school course and that the students at this stage could be more effectively taught by school methods than by those which were appropriate at the university stage; and
2. That the standard of undergraduate education was so poor that the first degree in India was not really comparable to the first degree in the advanced countries.

The Commission, therefore Recommended that:

(i) The dividing line between the University and the Secondary courses is more appropriately drawn at the intermediate examination than at the matriculation.

(ii) The duration of undergraduate course for the first degree should be increased to three years;

(iii) A board of Secondary and Intermediate Education should be established for the purpose of reorganizing High school and intermediate education on the lines recommended by it and for holding the matriculation and intermediate examinations. The Universities would thus be left to their proper sphere, namely the provision of undergraduate and post-graduate education and the holding of examinations for the first, second or research degrees; and

(iv) Instruction in Arts, Science, Medicine, Engineering Education, Agriculture and Commerce be provided at the intermediate stage.

The recommendation made a great impression on the Indian educational thought and, for a time, it appeared to be on the verge of acceptance on all India bases. But ultimately it was implemented only in one province, the U.P., and that too, in a mutilated form. Steps were not taken to increase the duration of the first-degree course from two to three years. Further no effective steps were taken to vocationalize the intermediate stage.

The University Education Commission (1948-49) under the Chairmanship of Radhakrishnan took up the discussion of the problem once again. After examining the problem from all points of vies, the Commission recommended that:

(*i*) The total duration of school course should include the present intermediate stage and should be over in a period of 12 (10+2) years in total;

(*ii*) The University course should begin after the intermediate and not after the matriculation;

(*iii*) In each province, a large number of well equipped and well-staffed intermediate colleges with classes IX to XII and VI to XII be established; and

(*iv*) The undergraduate course is lengthened to three years.

It is thus clear that the Commission came to the conclusion that it was necessary to adopt the uniform pattern of 10+2+3 for school and college classes.

The Commission also felt that:

(*i*) The pattern would make it possible to vocationalize the Secondary stage of education as to divert students into different walks of life at the end of Secondary school and thus reduce pressures on University admissions; and

(*ii*) The lengthening of the undergraduate course to three years, preceded by an intensive preparation at the earlier stage of two years, would result in a considerable improvement of standards in Higher education.

Unfortunately, no steps were taken to implement these recommendations:

The problem came up for consideration once again when the Secondary Education Commission (1952-53) was appointed under the chairmanship of Dr. A. L. Mudaliar.

The Commission recommended that:

(*i*) Secondary education should commence after 4 or 5 years of primary education and should include:

(*a*) The middle or senior basic or junior secondary stage of three years; and

(b) The Higher Secondary stage of four years;

(ii) The present intermediate stage should be replaced by the Higher Secondary stage which should be of four years duration, one year of the present intermediate being included in it;

(iii) For those who pass out of the High school there should be provision for a Pre-university course of one year, during which period the scheme of studies should be planned with the regard to the needs of the degree of professional course to be taken up by the students; and

(iv) The diversified curriculum should begin in the second year of High school stage.

As a result of these recommendations, then the prevailing intermediate course of two years was broken up into two parts and the first year was either added to the school stage or converted into a Pre-university course of one year and the second year was added to the first degree to create the three year degree course. This pattern was implemented in most of the parts of the country excepting Kerala, U.P., M.P., and the Delhi Union Territory.

The Conference of Vice-Chancellors (1962), the All-India Council for Secondary Education (1963), the Conference of State Education Ministers (1964) all recommended a 12-year course of schooling before admission to a 3-year degree course as the goal towards which the country must move.

The entire position was reviewed once again by the Indian Education Commission (1964-66). It found that, as a result of the decisions taken after the Report of the Secondary Education Commission, there were at least four different patterns of schools and colleges in the country. They may be stated as follows:

(i) Kerala was the only state where the pattern of 10+2+3 had been adopted with the two year stage being located in Junior Colleges;

(ii) The pattern of 10+2+3 prevailed only in Uttar Pradesh where as ten-year school was followed by a two-year intermediate course and a two-year course for first degree.

(*iii*) The pattern of 11+3 prevailed in the Delhi Union Territory and the State of Madhya Pradesh where an 11-year Higher Secondary school was followed by a three-year course for the first degree; and

(*iv*) The pattern of 10 (or 11 or even 12 in some cases) +1+3 was followed in the other states where a school stage of 10 to 12 years was followed by a year of pre-university course and a three year course for the first degree (alternatively, the pre-university year was often added to Secondary schools which were designated as higher Secondary).

The Commission examined this situation from all points of view and came to the conclusion that :

(*i*) On sound academic considerations, it would be highly desirable to adopt the uniform pattern of 10+2+3 for school and college classes in all parts of the country; and

(*ii*) The school stage should consist of 12 years (10+2); and

(*iii*) Every effort should be made to vocationalize the Higher Secondary (+2) stage so that ultimately, 50% of the enrolments at this stage should be in the vocational courses.

The proposals of the Education Commission found general support in the country.

Even before the Report of the Commission was submitted, the National Integration Committee appointed by the Ministry of Education, under the Chairmanship of the Late Dr. Sampurnanand recommended that, from the point of view of National Integration, the uniform pattern of 10+2+3 should be adopted for school and college classes in all parts of the country. This recommendation was also supported by the committee of Educationists and student leaders appointed under the directive of the National Integration Committee and also by several conferences of students' organizations.

The Central Advisory Board of Education also unanimously supported the proposal and expressed the view that it should be implemented on a priority basis and that, at any rate, the programme should be completed in all parts of the country by the end of Fifth Five-year Plan. The resolution of the Government of India on the National Policy of Education (1968) also supported the uniform adoption of this pattern.

The pattern 10+2+3 has since been introduced in almost all parts of the country.

Philosophy and Functions of the Pattern

The Education Commission of India (1964-66) emphasized that there is a direct link between education, National Development and prosperity and stated that this can be vitalized only when the national system of education is properly organized, both qualitatively and quantitatively. According to the Commission, a well-designed national system of education should help to :

(*i*) Increase productivity,

(*ii*) Achieve social and national integration,

(*iii*) Accelerate the process of modernization and

(*iv*) Cultivate values – social, moral and spiritual.

Keeping this in view the commission recommended the adoption of 10+2+3 pattern of school and college classes in all parts of the country along with the important changes to be introduced in respect of curriculum, teacher education, teaching methods and evaluation system.

The National Policy statement on education issued in 1968 said 'a radical reconstruction of education on the broad lines recommended by the Education Commission, is essential for economic and cultural development of the country, for national integration and for realizing the ideal of a socialistic pattern of society.'

It may be pointed out here that the first ten years, covering the elementary and lower Secondary stages, provide an undifferentiated and broad-based course of general education with provision for work experience for all without any diversification of studies to promote harmonious development of the pupils-intellectually, physically and emotionally to the optimum.

At the end of class X, two distinct streams are to be introduced one preparing intensively the students with academic aptitude for university education and the other preparing them for some vocation in life which would be terminal in character and also for different vocational course leading to graduation in those vocations. It is also felt that the enrolment in courses of a vocational or terminal character would be as high as 50% of the total, thus reducing pressure on university admissions.

From the psychological point of view, a student entering the college is expected to be 18 years of age or more. It is only then he can be adequately prepared for entering upon a course of higher education and also be mature enough to study on his own and to profit by the methods of teaching which are appropriate to the college stage. This necessarily implies a total duration of at least 12 years for the school stage, because the age of admission to the school system is generally six years.

The standards in higher education will also improve as the students going in to the university stream will not be better prepared and more mature.

The three year degree course would be a definite improvement on the existing two years course for the first degree. With longer duration, it will be possible to meet the demands of specialization as well as of a broad-based general and interdisciplinary education and to make adequate provision for practical experience field work and project oriented studies. The introduction of problem-oriented interdisciplinary courses at the Masters Degree level would also be greatly facilitated with the adoption of 10+2+3 formula.

It may be added here that the goals of national integration, training for democratic living, cooperativeness, cultural and religious tolerance can be fully emphasized in the courses of languages and social sciences and find ample scope in community service.

10+2+3 Pattern of Education in Karnataka—A Brief Historical Retrospect

In the year 1970-71, the pattern of 10+2+3 was prevailing in the Karnataka State. The one-year pre-university course was provided in degree colleges as well as in selected high schools which were upgraded into Higher Secondary schools. These Higher Secondary schools were under the administrative control of the Directorate of Public Instruction. However, the responsibility of framing the syllabus, prescription of text-books, and conduct of examinations remained with the concerned universities. That is, the students in Higher Secondary schools were taking the pre-university examinations conducted by the respective universities.

In accordance with the national policy in education (based on the recommendations of the Education Commission, 1964-66), the Karnataka State Advisory Board of Education recommended the introduction of two year pre-university course in the State from the academic year 1971-72, keeping in view the twin objectives viz., (i) that it has to be terminal course to a large number of students, and (ii) that it has to be a preparatory course for the university education including the professional streams. Pursuant to the recommendation of the State Advisory Board of Education, Government constituted an ad-hoc Committee under the Chairmanship of the Education Minister to draft a bill and frame the syllabus for the proposed course.

The Ad-hoc Committee recommended that the two year pre-university course should be under the control of a separate Board. It also recommended the setting up of a curriculum co-ordination committee to formulate the draft regulations, course of study, syllabi and scheme of examinations.

On the recommendation of the Ad-hoc Committee, Government constituted the Board of Pre-University Education in December 1970. It was felt that the introduction of the two year pre-university course common to the entire state under a separate agency would;

(*i*) Ensure free mobility of students from one university area to another;

(*ii*) Simplify selection to professional courses;

(*iii*) Relieve universities of what is essentially pre-university work and enable them to concentrate on the improvement of standards at graduate and post-graduate levels; and

(*iv*) Help to upgrade academic standards in view of the addition of one year to the total span of education.

The board at its meeting held in February and March 1971 considered the draft regulations, course of study, syllabus and the scheme of examinations governing the two year pre-university course, prepared by the Curriculum Co-ordination Committee, in the light of comments and suggestions received from the heads of institutions and finalized the same.

The two-year pre-university was introduced in the State from the academic year 1971-72. All the Higher Secondary schools teaching one year P.U.C. were permitted to have the first year of the two year P.U.C. during 1971-72 as a transitory measure. Only 312 out of 380 Higher Secondary schools started the 1 year of the two year P.U.C., 190 colleges were teaching one year P.U.C. during this period. Further, on the recommendations of the Inspection Committees and with the approval of Government, 23 private managements started junior colleges with first year of two year P.U.C. during the period. The formation of the Board marked the beginning of the third type of institutions, which offered exclusively the +2 stage, and these were called independent junior colleges, controlled, supervised and administered directly by the Board of pre-university education.

Diversification at the +2 Stage

With a view to make the +2 stage terminal in character for those who would like to enter life, the following vocational subjects were introduced from 1973-74.

1. Typewriting.
2. Short-hand.
3. Theory and Practice of Banking.

4. Office Practice and Procedure (Business and Government).
5. Income tax and Sales Tax Procedure.
6. Business Law and Public Administration.
7. Insurance and Costing.
8. Fine Arts, Agriculture, Education, Technology.

A separate Director of Vocational Education is established to administer the implementation of various vocational courses in selected institutions. With the establishment of this Directorate, the responsibility of conducting the examination for the candidates offering vocational courses has also been transferred to the New Directorate. Thus there are now two Directorates conducting the P.U.C. Examination, P.U. Directorate for general candidates and vocational Directorate for candidates offering vocational courses.

Need for Guidance in Institutions

Guidance and counselling services are becoming more and more important as the society and its various institutions are growing in complexity. The society and all its institutions are built of individuals as their units as mansion is built of bricks. The strength and solidarity of the society and its institutions are therefore contingent upon the strength of these individual units. Strength and solidarity of these individual units constitute the foundation of a strong nation. Hence, the optimum development of each of these units should be the most cherished goal of every nation. Guidance and counselling contributes to the achievement of this goal.

Coming to the vocational point of view, every one of us knows that our educational system has grown haphazard. While humanities and the liberal arts are subjects most frequently offered and taken, both in the college and Universities they were the oldest and relatively inexpensive areas of knowledge taken because they require no specified intellectual equipment. Hence, thousands of young-men educated in these liberal are arts without jobs.

Our student population reaches the university level, having made up their mind broadly about the courses that they may have a decision, which in almost all cases, is taken by unthinking and unsympathetic parents and relatives with an eye on a more lucrative profession. It is a great tragedy when a potential poet becomes a chemical engineer. Many a mute inglorious Milton is languishing in the dark engineering world. For the best development of individuals and growth of society, the process of herding youths into educational disciplines unconnected with their aptitudes must be checked through a scientific process of guidance and counselling.

Ours is highly complex and rapidly changing world of work. The changing requirements in industrial jobs, altered market conditions for professional manpower, the development of paraprofessional occupations and many other labour market trends are making occupational selection more difficult than ever. The young students in Secondary schools, colleges and universities must be informed about various available jobs and openings and the requirements, responsibilities and the nature of work involved in them so that they could measure themselves up to them and develop and crystallize their occupational goal. They should be helped in making meaningful occupational selection. They must be prepared for an entry into them to have a fulfilling and rewarding career.

The majority of students in our school, colleges and universities are the first generation learners. They have no one with an experience of college or university education background in their family to guide them in the choice of career. With a right to the best education available and a wide range of jobs open to them, these students need mature help in making a judicious occupational choice. This shows the need of adequate guidance and counselling arrangement in our schools, colleges and universities.

The process of vocational development covers almost the entire span of life of an individual. It begins quite early in one's life and continues till sometimes after retirement. In this process, the individual passes through growth, exploration, maintenance and decline. Guidance services are provided at the schools, colleges and universities to help the students in the process of vocational development by making it possible for them to gain knowledge about themselves their abilities, interests and needs and knowledge about the world of work. Their transition from education to work can be facilitated by providing them opportunities for self exploration as well as exploration of the world of work while they are still in an educational institution.

There is an indispensable need of vocational guidance facility to be extended in the schools, where students identify themselves with teachers and peers. Every school must have expert counselors to meet the impressing needs of the youths.

Many researchers and Theorists in the field have felt the imperative and immediate need of guidance programmes in the school that not only encompasses career aspects of the students but also channelizes the energy of clients for emotional integration to all kinds of achievement.

Highland (1998) advocates that career guidance should become part of a teacher's agenda to improve opportunities for students. Teacher can help students plan alternative career paths as contingencies, implement work-based learning programmes and provide information on vocational possibilities. School counselors are required the blue print of world of work.

Jarvis and Keeley (2003) emphasize. As schools, the work place and career development change, so does the need for school counselors to demonstrate leadership in helping students prepare for the future. A blue print of life/work design provides a foundation for integration and infusion of carter building and career management competencies into school Counselling programmes to effectively prepare students for the future. Vocational guidance the formal process through which an individual makes informed vocational decision. It is a part of vocation guidance programme vocational Counselling may be included formally or informally in a school curriculum (career Education, regular school curriculum vocational Education). A formal programme of testing (i.e., personality, psychological, vocational Aspiration, skill and aptitude tests) are normally made part of the Vocational Guidance process.

Cassell (1998) emphasizes the need of guidance in the school for every student. The average student beings high school (9th grade) when he/she is 14 years of age and the major purpose for high school, then is preparation for life. Success in a democracy always includes economic security and the ability and desire to make a living (a job success). In order to succeed for pupils and schools, there is an immediate and imperative need for a tentative job career plan for each and every student. It is common observation that while guidance services thrive and form and integral part of the educational system in the advanced countries, they exist in only nine percentage schools in India (NCERT, 1992). To avoid maladjustment in the life as a whole an early comprehensive guidance is inevitable for every individual. School is the best agency in this regard which can squarely meet the imperative need of vocational guidance and career counselling for each and every student who is in the threshold of vocational planning at +2 level.

One of the most important aims of education is to equip children for earning their livelihood in future. Education at the +2 stage is vital in our educational system because as it serves as training ground for young boys and girls in choosing their future courses. A wise choice of the subject and the career will avoid maladjustment and will increase an individual's chances for success and happiness in life. The rapid strides in scientific and technological advancement have bestowed on mankind several advantages but not without the accompanying problems. The number of vocations has learning to the world of work. It is by providing guidance services in schools and colleges that the youth could be helped enormously. The need for guidance is recognized and stressed by various committees and commissions appointed by the Governments both at the centre and in the states. However, it must be admitted that vocational counselling is still in the infant stage in India and other developing countries. The Governments at the centre and in the states are planning to introduce guidance services only in the Secondary schools. Information about the process of vocational development and the dynamics of occupational aspirations would be of immense value of those who will be administering guidance services.

The most accepted definition of 'Guidance' today is "a process of helping an individual to help himself, to know his needs, assess his potentialities, develop life purposes, formulate the plans of action and proceed to realize these under the most favourable conditions provided by the environment (Jones, 1961).

Counselling service aims at getting to learn about the personality of an individual and then attempting to remove the blocks or hurdles in the way of individual's further growth. To clarify the concept of counselling, the factors or aspects covered under guidance and counseling is to be listed. They are:

(*i*) Adjustment of all types,

(*ii*) Educational problems,

(*iii*) Personal and Social development and

(*iv*) Vocational problems.

Now-a-days more attention is paid to the conservation of human resources. Human resources are very valuable and the country's prosperity and advancement depend upon their proper utilization which means the matching the man with machine for the maximum utilization of the individual's capacities. Counselling helps the individuals in this process. There is a felt need in channelising the counselee's hidden potentiality into useful skills and developing and directing their activities. This is regarded as the absolute necessity for flowering of individual's personality. To bring about the desired changes or to achieve this objective of personality development, counselling service has to play a Keyrole (NCERT, 1968). According to Chopra and Chopra (1967), if we have to utilize our human resources effectively immediate attention will have to be paid to the organization of vocational guidance services in our schools.

Counselling service aims at getting to learn about the personality of an individual and then attempt to remove the blocks or hurdles in the way of individual's further growth. A study conducted by Venkatarami Reddy (1978) on vocational choices proved that the teachers' influence was less significant when compared with that of peer group. The researcher pleaded for introducing vocational counselling in schools.

The changing trend of the educational activities aims at relating education to the needs, life and aspirations of the individuals. In simple words, counselling is to help in the possible selection of courses meeting the individual's and individual make a decision and a vocational choice, plan a future and build a career, prepare for it, enter upon and progress in it. Every individual is not fit to take up any and every job. Round pegs should be fitted into round holes and square pegs into square holes. Professional adjustment is essential for having success in life as well as for bringing prosperity to the nation. It is possible only through the right choice of the job suiting one's abilities, interests and aptitudes which needs guidance at the earlier age by competent persons. Guidance services can help a lot in this direction by imparting valuable information. The most accepted definition by Super (1951) on vocational guidance is "the process of helping a person to develop and accept an integrated and adequate picture of himself and of his role in the world of work, to test this concept against reality and to convert it into a reality with satisfaction to himself and benefit to society."

Need and Importance of the Study

The study of vocational aspiration has attracted the attention of educators more than the psychologists. We are still very much in the dark as to the characteristics of the individual who makes a wise selection of objective as contrasted to the barren or unrealistic chooser. Our professional ignorance of what constitutes a "good" choice explains part of our failure to identify the characteristics of the adequate vocational planner. Among all levels of intelligence, individuals show a wide difference in their capacity to set vocational goals, reasonable in the light of their potentialities. Such individual differences need to be explored. In the past there has been too little attention to the phenomenological study of choice and a resulting tendency to regard vocational choice as whimsical and devoid of significance, particularly when the choice was regarded as irrational. There is a continuing need to study the psychological. There is a continuing need to study the psychological factors in occupational aspirations. It is also a common observation that social factors also play a vital role in occupational aspirations.

Failure in one occupation has a greater demoralizing effect on an individual. In the crucial period of adolescence many formative forces related to psychological and social factors affect the growing individual. The urgent need of greater understanding of the factors, which influence the occupational aspirations of young people, prompted this study.

Though there are innumerable influencing factors, the present study is concerned with academic achievement motivation, personality and social status of urban and rural students. A review of the available literature reveals that there are a few studies that investigated the relationship between the above important variables and an occupational aspiration of Indian youth, but the research in this area is not exhaustive.

The adolescent pupils belonging to different geographic localities such as the metropolitan, urban and rural areas would be exposed to different environmental and situational conditions that provide varied stimulation and learning experiences. The limited and restricted stimulation and opportunities for growth in the rural environments may handicap the individuals in certain significant ways. In contrast the urban environment is expected to offer richer and wider learning experiences. So it is possible that individuals hailing from different localities may be expected to show significant differences in their occupational aspirations.

Educators generally agree that major variables affecting classroom performance are academic achievement motivation and personality adjustment. The occupational application of psychological theory to education has not typically eventuated in a theory of academic achievement motivation or a unified and coherent body of information. As a result there is a little in the way of academic achievement motivation theory which is clearly of help to the classroom teacher or to education in general. And there is no doubt that adjustment influence daily living is seldom denial. It might be expected, then, that emotional stability or adjustment would be in some way related to the occupational aspirations. Based on a review of the aspiration literature in sociology, psychology and education, one expects variation in levels of occupational aspiration to correlate with measures of social status. The controversial findings of personality in relation to occupational aspirations need a carefully designed study to clarify the extent to which an individual's personality plays a part in the relationship of aspirations. On the whole the students' achievement motivation, their personality and social background may help the counsellors in understanding their vocational planning problems and to offer counselling assistance in a more effective way at this stage.

Therefore, there is a need to study occupational aspirations of students at Pre-university stage level as majority of them usually drop out at this stage and seek employment assistance. So the investigator is promoted to explore the relationship of occupational aspirations with some selected social and psychological variables of the students studying in +2 stage of Dharwad district.

Genesis of the Study

Throughout the life, an individual constantly makes decisions whether to listen to one radio programme or another, whether to vote for one candidate or another, whether to make along short or no vacation, whether to buy a Maruti, Santro, Zen etc. Whether it is a matter of deciding what to have for breakfast or deciding what college to enroll in the common characteristic is that a man must make a choice from among certain range of alternatives.

Getting right down to it, however, there aren't many really "big" decisions that have to be made in a mans lifetimes decisions which involve very long commitments which influence chances for living full, rich, satisfying lives which influence a mans thoughts, feelings and actions for years to come. One of these "big" decisions is marriage- whether to marry and if so, to whom. Another is choosing one's life work-whether to work at this job or that. It is plan that the selection of a particular kind of work has important implications both for the individual and for the total society. It means individuals occupational decision has important implications both for society and for his future life activity and satisfaction. Behind every decision about occupations many factors play an important role, one of the important factor is individual's vocational aspiration.

An interesting area for research in vocational education is development of vocational aspiration among students. This is of value for educational planning, curriculum designers, career guidance personnel and educational administrators. Vocational aspiration influence vocational maturity and vocational choices in later life which interns affect job satisfaction and optimization of job performance.

The study of vocational aspiration seems to have attracted the attention of educators more than psychologists. Indian society is still very much in the dark as to the characteristics of the individual who makes a wise selection of objective. The professional ignorance of what constitutes a "good" choice explains part of the failure to identify the characteristics of the adequate vocational planner. Among all levels of intelligence, individuals show a wide difference in their capacity to set up vocational goals, reasonable in the light of their potentialities, such individual difference need to be explored.

The vocational fields, which are considered on a hierarchical basis, seem to be misleading. An individual, for example, may have genuine aspiration for medical profession despite his low intellectual abilities. According to literature and general view his choice behaviour would be considered as quite unrealistic. On the other hand this individual having genuine interest in the medical line may profit more if he is placed in this field. He may not prove to be suitable for as high a position as that of a medical specialist with 3 or 4 years of training after MBBS or a medical technologist, laboratory technician, pharmacist, but he may do well in the job of a vaccinator, basis health worker, sanitary inspector. Similarly in the engineering profession an individual with interest in the line but with low intelligence may not be considered fit for the position of an engineer, overseer, draftsman but may be suitable for an assignment of a fitter, turner, moulder, sheet metal worker, radio-mechanic, welder etc. Thus the 'field' as a whole cannot be classified in hierarchical order. These vocational fields are rather independent and within each vocational field area an individual may opt for a very high or a very low occupation. Therefore, it is of immense practical value to evaluate the subjects achievement motivation, personality, the social background of the individual in addition to his verbal future vocational plans to assist them and also their guardians in the vocational planning process. If an individual opts for a vocation of which he never thought or for which he has little liking or interest he may make himself vocationally misfit.

Adolescence is an ideal time to study the career development of young men/ women. It is during adolescence that many changes occur that strongly influence the development of career preferences and aspirations. Puberty and emerging sexuality, including a growing interest in hetero-social relationship, create an intensification of gender role identity. Greater autonomy and independence contribute to the process of identity development. Hence, there is a large scope for educational researches to explore this field. The present is therefore undertaken to study the vocational aspirations of the students.

Statement of the Problem

The problem selected for the present investigation is as follows:

"Socio-Psychological Correlates of Vocational Aspirations".

Objectives of the Study

The present study has been undertaken with the following objectives.

1. To study the relationship between vocational aspirations of Pre-university students and their achievement motivation.
2. To study the relationship between vocational aspirations of Pre-university students and personality traits with its factors :
   (*a*) Reserved and outgoing,
   (*b*) Less intelligent and more intelligent,
   (*c*) Affected by feeling and emotionally stable,
   (*d*) Phlegmatic and excitable,
   (*e*) Obedient and assertive,
   (*f*) Sober and happy-go-lucky,
   (*g*) Expedient and conscientious,
   (*h*) Shy and venturesome,
   (*i*) Tough minded and tender minded,
   (*j*) Vigorous and doubting,
   (*k*) Placid and apprehensive,

(*l*) Group dependent and self sufficient

(*m*) Undisciplined self-conflict and controlled

(*n*) Relaxed and tense.

3. To study the relationship between students belonging to different social status groups and their vocational aspirations.
4. To study the relationship between sex and vocational aspirations.
5. To study the relationship between locality and vocational aspirations.
6. To study the relationship between different type of Pre-university college (Government/ Aided/Unaided) and vocational aspirations.
7. To study the relationship between different medium of instruction (English/ Kannada) and vocational aspirations.
8. To study the relationship between students belong to different categories.

Limitations of the Study

1. The study is limited only to selected Pre-university colleges of Dharwad district of Karnataka State.
2. Other psychological factors like aptitude, attitude, interest are not considered for their relationship with vocational aspirations.
3. The sample of the study is confined only to Pre-University students of different categories of colleges.

Overview of the Study

The book is organized in five chapters. The first chapter reveals, introduction, the concept of vocation and aspiration, theoretical framework of the study, development of aspiration, need for guidance and counselling in the school, Need and importance of the study, genesis, statement of the problem, objectives of the study, limitations and it is concluded with overview of the study.

Second chapter deals with review of related literature of vocational aspiration in relation to achievement motivation, personality, social status, gender, locality, and type of school.

Third chapter explains the methodology adopted for the present study. The chapter includes the operational definitions, research design, variables of the study, hypotheses, tools used, population and sample of the study, data collection and statistical techniques to analyse the data.

In the fourth chapter analysis and interpretation of data are presented.

In the fifth chapter the summary of the study, findings, educational implications, recommendations and suggestions for further study is presented.

2

Review of Related Literature

Introduction

In the earlier chapter an attempt was made to introduce the present study and to establish the need for such an investigation. The present chapter is designed to bring to light a few related empirical and conceptual studies having relevance to the problem under investigation.

Review of related literature is a valuable guide to define the problem, recognizing its significance, suggesting promising data, gathering devices, appropriate study design and also sources of data. Only those studies that are plainly relevant, competently executed and clearly reported are included in the review.

Theoretically speaking, in a democratic set-up an individual has the fundamental right to adapt any vocation the individual aspires the most but owing aspirations seldom materials. In spite of this the process of one's aspiring for certain occupations continues from childhood to adulthood but still in adolescent period one is considered, psychologically, to be living in a world of 'fantasy', as far as future career plans are concerned. The fantasy starts weaning off as one grows in age. Possibly it may be due to greater development and sharpening of reality orientation or maturation. One's vocational thinking is, thus reckoned to be influenced by these factors and the interaction effect of various psychological and sociological variables. It will therefore be worthwhile to review as to how and to what extent the above factors affect the vocational aspirations of the adolescents.

The studies related to the present problem are reviewed under the following five headings:

1. Vocational aspirations in relation to personality - 1989
2. Vocational aspirations in relation to Achievement motivation -1995
3. Vocational aspirations in relation to Socio-economic status - 1993
4. Vocational aspirations in relation to Gender - 2004
5. Vocational aspirations in relation to Locale -2005

Personality

Gruen (1945) studied the aspiration of subjects and their adjustment and found that maladjusted adolescents were most sensitive to failure, less stable and more unrealistic in their aspiration as compared to well adjusted adolescents. He further reported that frustration was found to disturb that there was a relationship of adjustment with vocational aspiration.

Small (1953) compared job concept fantasies of better and poorly adjusted adolescents boys and found that they differed to the extent to which they reflected the environment involvement or environment avoidance with regard to job requirements. In most of their fantasies of first choice which were most realistic the better adjusted boys expressed needs for order, achievement, reorganization and affiliation integrative with their social expectations. In contrast the poorly adjusted boys and significantly stronger needs for inward pains and tension discharge which reflected their inadequate relationship with social realities and inability to compromise.

Porter (1954) made an investigation on vocational plans and preferences upon emotional adjustment. Emotional adjustment measured by a single index was not found to be significantly related to vocational plans.

Chown (1959) investigated the personality factors in the formation of occupational choice. It was found that girls with low confidence scores office work while the boys with high sociability scores favoured office work.

Reddy (1972) examined the Adjustment and Aspiration of scheduled caste and non-scheduled caste students. The study was conducted on 400 students of IX standard from Bangalore city. The sample was drawn based on stratified random sampling technique. The tools used were Bell's Adjustment Inventory Educational and Vocational Aspiration Scale and Socio-Economic Status Scale. The collected data were analyzed by t-test for testing the hypothesis. The findings revealed that educational aspirations were found to bring about variations in the adjustment of students in the area of home and health and also in total students with high educational aspirations were found to be maladjusted in total and also in the area of health, students with low educational aspirations were found to have more adjustment problems than the high group. Similarly how vocational aspirations were found to be more maladjusted than the high vocational aspirations. Hence it can be concluded that there exists a significant relationship between aspirations and adjustment also.

Gupta (1973) studied the occupational choices of 18-20 years old students and found that personality characteristics influenced the occupational choice. Boys and Girls exhibited significant differences in their occupational choices.

Brown (1973) found that delinquent and non-delinquent students differed significantly in their occupational aspirations. Non-delinquents preferred higher occupations than the delinquents.

Andrew (1973) in his study on personality and vocational choice supported Holland's premise that people search and environments and vocations that are compatible with their personalities. These findings indirectly showed relationship of adjustment with vocational choice behaviour.

Mathur (1974) investigated into the causes of frustration in adolescence in relation to the levels of aspiration. Kuppuswamy's socio-economic status scale. Jalota's Mental Ability Test, Sexena's Personality Inventory and Questionnaire were administered on a sample of 772, IX standard students to study causes of frustration in relation to aspiration. Causes of frustration were found due to home, health and socio, personal areas. All types of frustration and levels of aspiration were not found to be related except home frustration and level of educational aspiration.

Krishna and Ansari (1975) investigated the influence of certain personality factors on occupational choices among college students. The findings revealed that there was significant difference between the students having high and low personality traits.

Bitney (1975) analyzed the relationship of occupational choice with selected personality characteristics and found significant relation between personality type and vocational aspirations.

Gaur and Mathur (1978) tested the hypothesis that high and low occupational aspirations would be correlated with such personality characteristics as emotional stability assertion and intelligence. The results indicated that occupational aspirations correlated with emotional stability, confidence, self control and tension in boys. The correlation traits included for girls were intelligence, outgoing personality and seriousness.

Chadha (1979) A study conducted on vocational aspirations in relation to their personality adjustment by Chadha (1979) concluded that aspirants of various vocational fields did not differ on Sinha and Sinha's adjustment scale except for social adjustment (a sub-scale on it). In the social adjustment, aspirants of outdoor, artistic and administrative vocational field were found to be poorly adjusted as compared to other fields of vocations. The results of the levels of vocational aspiration were comparable to the results as obtained through the field-wise analysis. Thus, it leads to the conclusion that vocational aspirations by and large are not determined by the subjects scores of adjustment scale.

Majoribanks (1985) examined the proposition that for children of different personality types there were variations in relations among measures of ability towards occupational aspirations. The results indicated that there was personality group difference in the amounts of variation in children's aspirations associated with their ability.

Quereshi and Bhargav (1989) conducted a study on "Adjustment Problems of Female Adolescents Belonging to Realistic and Non-realistic Zones of Aspiration Level". The major objective of the study was to investigate the adjustment problems of adolescent girls belonging to realistic and non-realistic zones of aspiration level. The major hypothesis of the study was both the groups belonging to the realistic and non-realistic zones of aspiration level differ on various adjustment problems. The sample of the present study consisted of 100 undergraduate adolescent girls of Firozabad city belonging to the age group from 17 to 21 years. In the realistic group 56 and non-realistic group 44 adolescent girls were included in the study. The tools used for data collection were (1) Level of Aspiration Measure developed by Shah and Bhargav (1987) (2) Adjustment Inventory for College students standardized by Sinha and Singh (1971). The t-test was used to analyze the data. The major findings of the study were : (1) Non-realistic group was found to be more maladjusted than realistic group in the area of health and educational adjustment whereas realistic group was found to be more maladjusted in the areas of social and emotional adjustments but they were found to be poor in their health and educational adjustment. (3) On the contrary, girls belonging to realistic zone of aspiration level expressed poor socialization and emotionally unstable behaviour but they were found comparatively better in their health and educational adjustment (4) As regards home adjustment, both the groups did not show any significant difference.

Achievement Motivation

Motivation is a major variable which affects on classroom performance of children. The term achievement motivation is employed here to explain certain behaviours when we observe people frequently expending considerable energy to do something well or to do it better than some one else. The study studies conducted on achievement motivation are not exhaustive some studies conducted in the past are worth referring to.

Minor and Neel (1958) made a study on occupational preference in relation to achievement motive and found a significant positive relationship between occupational preference and achievement motive. The subjects with high 'n-achievement' tended to be less realistic in their occupational preferences.

Mahone (1960) made a study on fear of failure and vocational aspirations. The results revealed that the men in whom need achievement was dominant more frequently had realistic aspiration whereas the men dominated by anxiety more frequently were unrealistic. They either set their vocational aspiration very low or very high but usually they set their aspiration very high for their ability.

Singh (1963) in a study of the relationship between personality and vocational choice, Singh (1963) found that there was a significant positive relationship between the achievement motive and level of occupational preference.

Morris (1966) conducted a study on 'Personality for risk taking as a determinant of vocational choice'. An extension of the theory of achievement motivation'. His study showed a relationship of risk-taking tendencies with vocational aspirations.

Study on achievement motivation by Singh (1970), Arnoff (1971) and Aubrey (1971) showed relationship of need achievement with occupational selection and advancement.

Bloom (1972) studied the relationship between achievement motivation and occupational choice of adolescent girls. It was confirmed that girls with high achievement motivation wanted to be both home makers and job doers while those with low achievement motivation wanted to be home makers only.

Prenter and Steward (1972) conducted a study on "Educational and Vocational Aspiration of New Zealand Adolescent Girls in Relation to Achievement Motivation" and found out significant relationship between aspirations and achievement motivation.

Tseng (1972) conducted a study on comparisons of selected familiar personality and vocational variables of high school students and drop outs. The conclusion was that the school drop-outs who had the low level of achievement motivation and lower accuracy in perceiving the occupational prestige hierarchy showed lower occupational aspirations and chose occupations of types which were of lower level of different responsibility and prestige.

Krishna and Ansari (1975) studied the influence of n-achievement on occupational choices among college students. The findings revealed that high n-achievers preferred teaching, social welfare, business, administration, agriculture and judicial work. Low n-achievers preferred teaching, business, agriculture and social welfare.

Liting (1975) conducted a study on personality race and social class determinants of occupational goals. He held that for women there was no identifiable relationship between occupational aspirations and the motivational variables.

Ory and Helfrich (1978) studied the career selection of 68 female and 63 male college students. The important findings were (1) disproportionately more men than women aspired to professional career and (2) professional career aspiration had higher achievement motivation than non-professionals.

Chadha (1979) conducted a study on vocational aspirations in relation to need achievement on urban and rural sample. McClelland Thematic Apprecption Test (NCERT adaptation 1966) was used to collect the data. Duncan's multiple range test was used to determine the significant of mean difference of variables obtained by the aspirants of different vocational fields. He concluded that the urban and rural samples differed in their vocational aspirations. The hypothesis of positive relationship between need achievement and level of vocational aspiration could not be sustained.

Williams and Woodward (1983) made an attempt to study factors related to career aspirations and found that subjects with high career aspirations had a high need for dominance and strong personal growth needs.

Chadha (1983) studied the vocational aspirations of 713 Indian tenth graders. The results indicated that 37 subjects had unrealistic vocational aspirations for their future careers. Low vocational aspires obtained significantly higher scores on the need for achievement only.

Saxena (1985) studied need achievement in relation to level of aspiration. The study was carried out to achieve the following major objectives :

(i) to find out the nature and extent of relationship between need achievement and level of aspiration

(ii) to study the sex difference in need achievement and level of aspiration

(iii) to test the significant difference between the mean need achievement scores of group having high level of aspiration and

(iv) to establish regression equations for need achievement using level of aspiration as predictor.

Random sampling procedure was used to select 300 male and 300 female students of class IX and X standard students of Agra City. The tools used were (a) Achievement Motivation Test by Prayag Mehta and (b) Level of Aspiration Test (non-verbal) by Shah and Bhargav. Under the descriptive method of research differential and correlational techniques were used to carry out the study which was *ex-post-facto* in nature. The researcher followed different statistical methods to analyze the collected data. The important findings of the study were as follows :

(1) No significant relationship was found between need achievement and level of aspiration.

(2) Boys and girls differed significantly with regard to their level of aspiration.

(3) Groups having high level of aspiration and low level of aspiration (total), boys and girls having low level of aspiration, boys having high level of aspiration and boys having low level of aspiration and girls having high level of aspiration and girls having low level of aspiration did not differ significantly regarding need achievement.

(4) Boys and girls having high level of aspiration differed significantly regarding need achievement.

Dabir (1986) made an effort to study the relationship between motivation, socio-economic status and aspirations of IX, X and XI graders in Nagpur District. The hypothesis examined were:

(i) there is an interaction between achievement motives and vocational aspirations.

(ii) hierarchy of motives leads to hierarchy of vocational aspirations.

(iii) some motives may form a cluster/ patterns and function collectively to determine vocational aspirations.

The sample of the study comprised of 1080 students. The tools used were the Occupational Aspiration Scale (OAS) by Grewal, Achievement Motivation Inventory by Preyag Mehta and SES scale prepared by the investigator. Statistical techniques used to analyze the data were co-efficients of correlation. Partial correlations, multiple regression equations and cluster analysis. The major finding was that there were positive and significant values of relationship between vocational aspirations and achievement motivation.

Gopal (1987) conducted a study on aspiration, motivation and achievement on rural and urban children belonging to scheduled caste and tribe. Data were collected from villages located in four different districts and urban areas in Karnataka state. Studies showed that aspirations were modest or high but achievement was low. Rural Harijans were having more occupational aspirations than urban Harijans. Occupations which had the scope to make higher levels of contribution to the family pursue were considered as more important by rural children.

A study on career and life style aspirations of gifted Canadian Secondary school males was conducted by Anne (1988) to obtain a description of the career expectation of a sample of intellectually gifted female secondary school students in Ottawa, Ontario in Canada. The sample consisted 140 gifted female students. The career factor check-list showed that subjects perceived the strongest effect on their career choices to come from an individual factor including need to achieve.

A study by Majumdar (1990) revealed as to what extent academic motivation of the college students in Calcutta was affected by their vocational aspirations. The findings however, revealed that, vocational aspirations of the students do affect their academic motivation significantly and a closer study of the mean academic motivation scores of both boys and girls revealed that girls possessed higher academic motivation than the boys.

Lim (1991) determined a structured equation model which links three exogenous variables (academic achievement motivation is one) and two criterion endogenous variables (career aspiration and career maturity) and examined the casual relationship between these criterion endogenous variables in the determined mode with the target population of Korean male high school students. For this purpose 693 high school juniors were sampled in 14 general or vocational high schools. Data were collected using the questionnaire comprising seven scales to assess the variables specified in the research model. Selected important findings were: (1) the most meaningful and significant casual paths in the general sample model included Householder's occupation. Location of the school and Academic ability parental influence career aspirations: Householder's occupation, location of school and Academic ability parental influence General self concept career maturity and (2) in the general sample model, career aspiration proved to causally affect career maturity, while no significant relationship between those endogenous variables was found in the vocational sample mode.

The study by Anniamma and Kunhi Krishnan (1995) explored the relationship between achievement motivation and level of aspiration among 40 post-graduate women students. The tools used were achievement values and anxiety inventory, achievement motivation test and letter cancellation test. Results indicated that the concepts were positively related and lèvel of aspiration was dependent on the tasks used to measure it.

In general it may be said that the studies reviewed in this section could established the fact that achievement motivation is a potential factor which influences vocational aspirations of the individuals.

Socio-economic Status

The social status is the place of an individual in society. This is generally determined by various factors such as occupation, educational qualification and economic status of an individual enjoyed in the society. There are number of studies from India and abroad showing influence of this important factor on the vocational aspirations of the children.

Although social status is generally recognized as an influence on the lives of people, a few attempts have been make to measure its effects on such specific areas of vocational planning. Of the many objectives and semi-objective scales for ascertaining status, almost all include occupation as one of the indices of status. In many instances, it is the sole index. Centres (1949) states that the occupation seems generally agreed upon as the most satisfactory single index.

Studies by Davis, (1963); Miller and Haller, (1964); Tayer (1966); Writz (1966); Wytic, Hutchins et.al., (1967); Brook et.al., (1974) Carolli and Petrucsi (1978); Harvey and Kerin (1978) Chadha (1979) and Chopra (1984) showed positive relationship between the youths level of occupational aspirations and various measures of social status of the family. Parental background was found to be related to occupational aspirations (Peace, 1975; Head, 1978; Chanda et.al., 1983). However, Mehta, *et. al.,* (1984) did not find any relationship between these two variables.

The study made by Carp (1949) on high school boys to observe as to what extent they were realistic about occupation revealed that 29% of the preferred occupations at the same level as those of their fathers and 24.9% preferred occupations above the level of their fathers.

Porter (1954) studied 100 high school senior boys in relation to the prediction of their vocational plans and found that their fathers occupation was significantly related to their vocational plans. A high degree of consistency between what the high school senior boys preferred to do what they planned to do and what they actually did after six months was seen. A large number of high school senior boys had definite vocational plans. And as a group the high school senior boys were found to select a wide range of occupations. Their selection showed considerable variation with regard to the prestige level of the occupations chosen.

Jenson and Kirchner (1955) on the basis of their investigation of urban males over the age of 25 concluded that sons tended to follow their fathers general type of occupation. If not, the sons preferred jobs of higher occupational level than their parents.

Empey (1956) conducted a study on social class and occupational aspiration and concluded that lower class youth had limited their occupational aspiration level to the class horizon and that lower class youth had the same lofty occupational aspiration as those of upper strata. These findings pointed out that lower class youngsters aspired for occupations at different status levels than those from the higher strata.

Grounce (1957) based on his research on perception of occupation, stated that lower status individuals concentrated on those occupations which occupied lower positions in the occupational ladder.

Sewell William H., *et al.*, (1957) conducted a research on social status and educational and occupational aspirations among the more than four thousand Wisconsin high school seniors in all parts of the state to test the hypothesis in respect of level of occupational aspirations of youth and their families where the effects of intelligence were controlled. In the end, it was concluded that among both high schools boys and girls there was significant association between the level of occupational aspirations and the social status of their families.

Schoenfeld (1959) conducted a study on choosing career in relation to their socio-economic status and found that the female whose parents belonged to upper status had chosen their future career better than those belonging to lower status. This was not true in the case of males.

Uzzel (1961) investigated the influences of occupational choice and found that models in occupations played a significant role in occupational choice.

Reisman (1962) attributed correlation to educational and occupational achievement values that are presumed to be directly influenced by the family's position in the status structure.

Geschwender and Form (1962) found that the children of manual workers tended to depend on peer groups and on other male member of their family as they packed ideology of opportunity coming from their parents. They further observed that 8% of subjects (N = 595) stated that their parents had no aspiration for them. Perhaps for most of manual workers it is normal not to expect great upward mobility.

Steimal and Suziedelis (1963) also suggested the possible influence of parents education in the evolution of vocational preferences of the children based on their research on perceived parental influence and inventoried interests.

Miller and Haller (1964) in their study on "A measure of level of occupational aspiration", found a correlation of 0.37 between socio-economic status of the family and occupational aspiration of the respondents.

Studied by Bennet and Gist (1964) and Hodgkins and Porr (1965) on occupational aspirations found that the different social classes did not differ significantly in their occupational aspirations but they differed in their plans i.e., what they expected to achieve.

Gibbons and Lohnes (1964) in their study found moderate correlation (r = .50) for eight and tenth standard subjects between RVP (Readiness for Vocational Planning) and socio-economic status. However, the cross-cultural study of SES and vocational aspirations among aboriginal tribes of Baster by Misra (1975) could not lend support to it. This might be due to special cultural attributes of his sample.

Hauson (1965) studied IX grade girls' vocational choices and their parents occupational level and concluded that the pupils preferences were significantly higher than the fathers vocations.

Werts (1967) investigated a sample of 70,015 male college freshman and concluded that the boys preferred their fathers occupations in most of the cases. This was true in the case of boys whose fathers held scientific occupations, medical careers and teaching professions.

Calvin (1969) studied relationship of occupational aspiration of youth to selected variables in two Mississippi countries and found that all students had relatively high occupational aspirations except Negro students of the low socio-economic country. The study pointed out that low aspiration in one goal area tended to influence low aspiration in another goal area but high aspiration in one goal area did not provide any conclusive evidence. The perception of opportunity was positively and significantly related to occupational aspiration.

An attempt was made by Mahatma (1969) to find out the vocational interests of tenth class students. His sample consisted of 240 students from two districts of Rajasthan. The study revealed that the students' highest concentration was on scientific area and the lowest on social service. The socio-economic status of the parents was insignificantly related with the vocational interests of boys.

A study of vocational aspirations by Kamala (1970) threw light on the vocational aspirations of girls. It was found that the girls level of occupational aspiration was slightly higher than the level of occupations they planned to enter. Many of them realized their financial and other limitations, turned down their aspirations and planned to enter the careers which appeared to be within their reach.

Camp and Rothney (1970) found that parents of all socio-economic levels were interested in the development of their children and took action when specific suggestions based upon the knowledge of children were provided.

Orleans (1970) based on his research on "Family Interaction, Personality Development and Vocational Choice in Adolescent Males" stated that the vocational preference patterns reflected the social mileau of the subjects.

Srivastav and Palo (1970) conducted a study on "Occupational Choices of High School Boys in relation to their fathers occupational level" and found that the subjects preferred occupations at a level higher than their fathers.

Passi (1970) studied the relative importance of the aspired vocations among Higher Secondary boys and girls of rural and urban areas to pinpoint certain vocational aspirations opted by girls or boys exclusively and to see if residential status had its bearing on such aspirations. The study was carried on a total sample of 600 boys and girls of IX, X and XI grades belonging to both rural and urban areas. Data concerning sex, grades, residential locality and measures of vocational aspirations were collected with the help of an open-end questionnaire. The findings revealed that there was a definite hierarchy in the vocational aspirations among boys and girls of rural and urban residents existed with maximum emphasis on the vocations of doctors, teachers, engineers and professors. The sample reported certain aspired vocations out of which some were exclusively clustering around the sex variables (nursing, telephone operator, research for girls and military, mechanic, naval services for the boys) similar picture was presented by the rural and urban residents. Boys were found more divergent than girls in their outlook towards vocational aspirations. Likewise, the rural residents showed greater divergence than their counterparts living in urban areas. Vocational aspirations differed significantly with respect to the variables of sex and residential status of the students.

Tseng (1971) studied social class and occupational aspirations using Halland's OAS (Occupational Aspiration Scale) and found that subjects from lower and lower-lower socio-economic groups had significantly lower occupational aspirations and more distorted perception of occupational prestige hierarchy than subjects from middle class.

Shah *et al.* (1971) conducted a study to examine the influences of socio-economic status on the vocational aspiration of the students. The sample consisted of 5,201 students of X standard from 52 high schools. The data obtained were analysed and the findings of the study disclosed that socio economic status had its influence on vocational aspirations.

Reddy (1972) based on his research "A Study of Vocational Needs of Secondary School Pupils in relation to their Occupational choice and other variables" concluded that the occupational choices of the subjects were significantly related to the occupational level and the level of education of their parents.

Vignod (1972) investigated the relationship between occupational choice and parental occupations and found that the higher the socio-economic status of the child, higher was his level of the expected occupation than wished occupation. Moreover, socio-economic status was found to be negatively related to the discrepancy between expected and wished occupation.

Schoenfeld (1972) conducted a study on choosing career in relation to their socio-economic status and found that the females whose parents belonged to upper status had chosen their future career better than those belonging to lower status. This was not true in the case of males.

Klemmack and Edwards (1973) assessed how women acquired stereotyped occupational aspirations. It was found that the degree of faminity of occupational aspirations was an indirect function of family background.

Picou (1973) studied Black-White variations in a model of the occupational aspiration process. The study was confined to 582 white and 333 Black rural high school seniors. The results showed that fathers occupation and education were related to the occupational aspirations of white. Family income was related to occupational aspirations of Black.

Picou and Curry (1973) conducted a study on female adolescents' occupational choices and concluded that socio-economic status was positively and significantly related to occupational choice.

Thakur (1974) attempted to determine the relationship of social variable with occupational aspirations of rural youth in India. It was concluded that occupation of the father was positively associated with occupational aspirations of the school going adolescents.

Hypothesising that there would be significant relationship between socio-economic status and the occupational aspiration levels. Mathur and Gaur (1974) studied 202 male and 29 female tenth graders in Delhi. The results indicated that higher socio-economic status was significantly associated with their occupational aspirations.

Brook, *et al.* (1974) also obtained the results indicating that the occupational aspirations for the child were related to the socio-economic status of the family to which he belonged. The correlation between parents and the child's aspirations were the highest for the 5th grade subjects of white parents' irrespective of socio-economic status and for the Black parents of higher socio-economic status.

Teachan (1974) while studying the effect of sex and socio-economic class on expectations of success among Black students observed no difference in socio-economic level.

Desai (1974) studied the aspirations and value preferences of rural, urban and overseas students in making occupational decisions. The findings strengthened the observation that occupational identities of parents who had different socio-economic background, had important bearing on the occupational decision making.

Anderson (1975) conducted a study on "Anxiety, Risk and socio-economic class in relation to occupational preferences" and found that socio-economic status was significantly related to occupational preference.

Sibbison (1975) studied occupational preferences and expectations of rural high school males and females and found that occupational preferences were related to parental educational and occupational attainment. The aspiration levels of females were lower than those of males.

Reilly (1975) conducted a study to find out the influence of socio-economic status on vocational choice. The subjects were 373 students of eight grade. It was concluded that vocational choice was influenced by socio-economic status of the students.

Pappas and Anthony Vincent (1975) studied occupational aspirations of 6558 North Mississippi post-elementary pupils drawn from 23 schools. The findings suggested important relationship for level of occupational aspiration with socio-economic variables of fathers education, mothers' education and socio-economic status level of family as determined by occupation of head of household. Females appeared to suffer from minority problems of under aspiration.

Mishra (1975) has conducted a study on A cross cultural study of status and vocational aspirations among aboriginal tribes of Bastar. The study aimed of understanding a cross cultural study of the status and vocational aspirations among the tribals of Bastar and examining the hypothesis that the fathers vocational status and the vocational status of the community were the determinants for a subjects vocational aspirations.

The sample included 258 tribal and non-tribal school children from the whole district of Bastar. This included 20 upper-class boys, 25 upper class girls, 18 lower class boys, 13 lower class girls and the remaining boys an girls were form various aboriginal tribes. Their ages ranged from eight to twenty years. All relevant data were collected through scheduled interviews.

The t-test, F-test, product moment coefficient of correlation, ANOVA, ANCOVA and chi-square test were the various statistical technique used for data analysis.

The major findings were:

(*i*) Fathers vocational status did not influence the vocational aspirations of the subjects, except in the case of upper caste females and lower class females were the effect of fathers vocational status on the aspirations of subjects appeared significant.

(*ii*) Significant differences in the vocational status as a correlate of vocational aspiration were found between tribal and non-tribal, upper caste and tribal, lower caste and tribal and male and female groups. On the other hand, tribal males and tribal females were found more or less similar.

(*iii*) The trend analysis indicated a general trend in VAs irrespective of any influence of the vocational status of the subjects suggesting a great possibility of influences from introduced standards from other groups.

(*iv*) No differences of distribution of VAs could be seen under different community groups.

(*v*) The upper caste and the lower caste did not appear to differ in their distributions of VAs whole the upper caste were found to differ from other community groups in their VAs the lower caste subjects also differed from other community groups except those of Raj and Dhur Gouds, Muras of Jagdalpar and Bhatras.

(*vi*) Raj and Dhur Gouds were highly acculturated and socio-economically distinct from Muras and Bhatras and were comparatively distinct in their aspirations from the lower caste non-tribals.

Esslinger (1976) explored the role of educational and family characteristic sin the occupational aspirations of XII grade girls. The following conclusions were drawn:

(1) 90% of the subjects gave preference to white color occupations.

(2) Occupational choice was related to the level of parents occupation.

(3) Majority of the subjects indicated realistic occupational choice.

Thaj *et al.* (1976) studied occupational aspirations and socio-economic study of 300 advantaged and disadvantaged high school students. A SES measure and a translated version of occupational aspirations of the Adivasi and scheduled caste children revealed that the socio-economic status and the occupational aspirations of the Adivasi subjects were the lowest.

Mclaughlin, *et* al. (1976) conducted a study on socio-economic status and the career aspirations and perceptions of senior girls in high schools with a sample of 1,036. A questionnaire was used to collect the required data. The findings reported by them were :

(*i*) socio-economic status was positively related to activities, grades and was inversely related to security concerns and career plan certainly.

(*ii*) subjects saw professionals and parents as particularly important career influencers. Subjects belonging to low socio-economic status attributed most value to counselors.

(*iii*) All groups aspired to minimum career competence.

(*iv*) All groups strongly preferred the traditional roles of teachers and social worker.

Socio-economic status had relationship to women's aspirations similar to those for men. Women of low socio-economic status appeared particularly receptive to counselling for aspiration rising.

Harvey and Kervin (1978) in their study on "The Influence of Social Stratification Occupational Aspirations of Adolescents" concluded that subjects from a higher socio-economic stratum had the desire to obtain prestige occupations while lower socio-economic subjects tended to prefer jobs with lower status.

Rodman, *et al.* (1978) studied social class and parent's range of aspirations for their children. Interview data from 436 Black parents in Detroit and Michigan were used to test the hypothesis that a lower class status was related to a wider range of aspirations. The hypothesis was supported for several measures of the range of educational and occupational aspirations.

Ogawa and Tanak (1979) in their investigation on "The influence of fathers' occupation on sons' occupational choice" showed that more sons hoped to enter the occupation of their fathers.

Gautam (1981) made a study with an objective of knowing the relationship between vocational preference and their parents' occupational background of Higher Secondary students. One hundred and thirty students randomly selected from three institutions constituted the sample. Along with socio-economic status scale, a form - Occupational Choice Record (OCR) was used to collect the required data. He found that the relationship between the school students occupational choices and their parents occupations was complex and inconsistent. In the case of some occupations like military and medicine it was highly positive while in the case of others it was negligible or even nil. On the whole it appeared that the occupational choice of the pupils was more influenced by their parents, socio-economic status.

Nelms *et al.* (1982) investigated the impact of socio-economic status on job choice of 128 high school students. The results indicated that socio-economic status was not a factor in job choice. It was also found that world of work gain scores did not influence job choice.

Occupational levels and ranges of aspiration were studied in relation to home background parents educational and occupational levels of Shoeib (1982). The sample of the study (N=405, 159 boys and 246 girls) was obtained from final year preparatory school classes in Tanta (Egypt). The statistical procedures followed in studying the data were cross tabulation using chi-square test and paired 't' test. The result indicated that (i) significant relationships were obtained between pupils levels of occupational aspiration and each of such variables in home background as parents level of education and parents occupational class and (ii) significant relationships were obtained between pupils ranges of occupational aspiration and fathers level of education.

Toong (1982) vocational aspirations in relation to creativity personality achievement and socio-economic status of high school students.

The main objectives of the study was to answer the questions :

(i) whether the high school students aspired differently in relation to different fields and levels of vocation.

(ii) Whether vocational aspirations of students were realistic or unrealistic.

(iii) whether significant differences existed between realistic and unrealistic aspirants for vocations in respect of creativity, personality achievement and socio-economic status? and

(iv) whether creativity, personality, achievement and socio-economic status taken separately accounted for significant differences among group significant difference among group aspiring for different fields and levels of vocations?

A sample of 1039 students of class nine was selected on the basis of multi-staged randomization of clusters from 12 urban higher secondary schools of three districts headquarters of Punjab.

The students were administered the following tools:

The Torrance Test of Creative Thinking (1966), the Jalota (1972), Group Test of General Mental Ability Raven's (1960) standard progressive Matrices, the Cattell (1967), High school personality Questionnaire Hindi version, the Chadha (1979) Vocational Aspiration Blank, and the Chadha (1979) Classificatory System of Occupation. The percentage of total score obtained by students in the eighth grade public examination was taken as the measure of achievement.

The findings of the study were:

1. The highest percentage of students aspired for the teaching and welfare field, the lowest percentage of students aspired for artistic fields,.close to which was also the percentage of students aspiring for literary field.
2. The highest percentage of students (47.65 percent) aspired for level-II vocations and level-I vocations ranked third with 24.83 percent aspiring for it.
3. Although the highest percentage of students in the field of engineering and health aspired for high level vocations and in the teaching and welfare field the highest percentage of students aspired for low level vocations. Yet the percentage of students aspiring for medium level vocations in these fields was significantly higher than the percentage of students aspiring for low level vocations in the field of engineering and health and high level vocations in the field of teaching and welfare.
4. The significant percentage difference was observed between realistic and unrealistic aspirants for vocations.
5. On verbal fluency, flexibility, originality and verbal creativity total, significant mean differences were observed between ten, one, four and two parts of comparisons for groups aspiring for eleven fields of vocation.
6. The significant mean differences were observed between nine, five, three and four of the pairs of combinations out of 55 possible comparisons for groups aspiring for eleven fields of vocations on figural fluency flexibility, originality and figural creativity totals respectively.
7. The aspirants for an artistic field obtained higher scores on all verbal and figural creativity measures barring,

verbal originality, which the aspirants for the health field got higher scores as compared to aspirant for other fields of vocation.

8. The levels by field analysis on verbal creativity measures revealed significantly mean differences among the aspirants for different levels within three vocational fields, namely health, administrative and clerical and protective fields out of eight vocational fields.
9. For fields taken conjointly significant mean differences were shown among levels on figural fluency, flexibility and originality.
10. The level of fields approach showed significant mean differences among the aspirants for vocational levels within five vocational fields, viz., Engineering, health, administrative and clerical services and outdoor, out of eight fields of vocations.
11. The mean differences obtained on personality factors revealed that out of 14 personality factors only eight (B, D, E. F, G. H, Q3 and Q4) significantly differentiated between 11, two, one, 13 and five and one pair of combinations out of 55 possible pairs of comparisons for groups aspiring for different fields of vocations.
12. For the fields taken conjointly, the students who aspired for level-I vocations differed significantly, with higher scores on personality factors B and C from those who aspired for level-II vocations. But the aspired for level-II vocations achieved significantly higher scores on personality factor P and J than the aspirant for level-I vocations.
13. The levels by field analysis showed that all personality factors except the personality factor Q4, differentiated significantly among groups of students aspiring for vocational levels within the four fields only engineering, health, administrative and clerical and service.
14. In respect of achievement, significant mean differences were elicited between ten pairs of combination out of

55 possible comparisons for aspiring for different fields of vocation.

Indowu and Dere (1983) conducted a study on occupational aspirations of high school seniors in Nigeria in relation to their socio-economic status and showed that higher the socio-economic status higher would be the aspiration level of subjects.

A study on aspirations of Negro and White students by Gist and Bennet (1983) showed that there was no great difference between the occupational aspiration of Kansas city Negro and white students, even when socio-economic status and IQ were held constant.

A study was conducted by Chopra (1984) on "Occupational aspirations of the adolescents from different socio-economic levels". The sample consisted of 598 boys under the age range 15-16 years randomly selected from 12 boys schools in Lucknow district. The data obtained were analyzed to compare the occupational aspirations of the students both by an absolute and a relative standard. The findings reported by him were: when an absolute standard was used, the students from the higher occupational groups aspired for comparatively higher occupations. However, when a relative standard was used it was observed that students from the lower occupations also showed the desire for upward occupational mobility and aspired for occupations higher than those in which their fathers were engaged.

Westaway, *et al.* (1984) investigated the relationship between vocational aspirations and socio-economic status. The sample consisted of 120 white 15-16 years old females in Johannesburg, South Africa. The result indicated that socio-economic status was the most important predictor of high vocational aspirations.

Ugwuh (1984) in his study on anlaysis of career choices in Nigeria found that 160 students had preferences for professional careers regardless of their family income.

Uplaoankar (1985) conducted a study on education and occupational aspiraitons of college students. The results showed that students with higher levels and urban background had higher educational status.

Marjoribanks (1985) collected data from Australian children at age 11 and again at age 16 from 5122 subjects to examine occupational aspirations in relation to their social status. The findings suggested that social status acted as an allocation factor such that low social status inhibited associations between early school attitudes and later aspirations.

A study of Dabir (1986) on the relationship between socio-economic status and aspiration showed that the relationship between socio-economic status and vocational aspirations was predominant.

Sungoh, Sherwin (1988) A survey of the educational and vocational aspirations of the Doordarshan viewing pre-university students in Shillong.

The study surveys the educational and vocational aspirations of those pre-university students of Shillong who viewed various Doordarshan telecasts. The study is undertaken on the assumption that television viewing would influence the educational and vocational aspirations of plus two level students.

The major objectives of the study were:

(*i*) To find out the educational aspirations of those pre-university students of Shillong who were exposed differentially to television programmes.

(*ii*) To find out the vocational aspirations of those pre-university students of Shillong who were exposed differentially to television programmes and

(*iii*) To find out the correlations between the educational and vocational aspirations of the viewers between their educational aspirations and socio-economic scores and their vocational aspirations and socio-economic status scores.

The methodology of the study was – population consisted of 4,100 pre-university students studying in 14 colleges, out of which a representative sample of 1,100 students was chosen using the stratified random sampling technique. An attitude scale to measure the attitude towards vocationalization of education was constructed using the Likert method. The split-half and test-retest reliability coefficients and content and criterion validity as well as percentile norms have been calculated and reported. Mean, SD and 't' test were used to find the significance of mean differences between the various groups.

Major findings of the study were:

There was no significance difference in the attitude towards vocationalization of education between pre-university male and female students; rural and urban students, commerce and science students; but the difference was significant between tribal and non-tribal students; commerce and arts students and arts and science students.

Sundararajan and Rajasekhar (1988) in their study on "Occupational aspirations of Higher Secondary students" concluded that parents income was found to influence the level of occupational aspirations of the students.

Arora (1988) Educational and vocational aspirations of students of class XII preparation of an interview schedule. Through a pilot study an interview schedule was developed to assess the educational and vocational aspirations of students of class XII against their socio-economic background. The interview schedule was tried out and its final version was used in further research work of assessing the educational and vocational aspirations of class XII students. The interview schedule was tried out in four senior secondary schools of Delhi. Based on the feedback obtained, the interview schedule was circulated among 130 training colleges. For the study, data were collected from 300 students (110 boys and 190 girls). The sample included both high and low achievers and was carried out using the interview schedule. In order to analyze the data bi-variate tables were prepared.

Major findings of the study were:

1. The percentage of boys obtaining marks above 75 per cent was greater than that of girls.
2. Out of 19 per cent of the students whose fathers were post-graduate, about one percent obtained marks above 75 per cent.
3. None of the boys whose fathers were doctors, engineers or teachers obtained marks less than 45 per cent.

4. About 60 per cent girls of the science stream belonged to the income group between Rs. 10,000 and Rs. 20,000 and out of these 31.26 per cent girls aspired to join the medical course.
5. The sex-wise degree of importance of reasons motivating students to pursue higher education was also studied. The reasons regarded most important by boys were :
   (*i*) a desire to cultivate the right interest, attitudes, morals and intellectual values.
   (*ii*) to improve prospects of employment.
   (*iii*) to come into contact with learned people in their area of interest.
   (iv) to develop power of mind.
   (*v*) to seek new knowledge.
6. The reasons regarded most important by girls were :
   (*i*) a desire to cultivate the right interests attitudes, morals and intellectual values
   (*ii*) to seek new knowledge.
   (*iii*) to develop power of mind.
   (*iv*) to have a good social life.

Rhee (1989) described the occupational aspirations of Korean female adolescents. The purpose of the study was to determine the family background variables of Korean female adolescents in relation to traditional versus non-traditional occupational aspirations. The sample comprised at 1.320 junior and senior high school girls in Seoul, Korea. The findings revealed that socio-economic status of the family was a variable related to the occupational aspirations of female adolescents.

Sundararajan and Bai (1990) conducted a study on socio-economic status and the occupational aspirations of the higher secondary leavers.

The major objectives of study were:

1. To find out if there was any differences in the socio-eçonomic status (SES) of the Higher Secondary Boys and Girls.
2. To find out if there was any difference between the SES of the Urban and the Rural students.

3. To find out if there was any difference in the level of the Occupational Aspirations (OAS) of students with low SES and high SES.
4. To find out if there was any difference in the level of the Occupational Aspirations of Boys and Girls
5. To find out the relationship between the SES and the ORAs of the students

Researchers framed the following hypotheses for the study:

1. There is no significant difference in the SES for the Higher Secondary boys and girls.
2. There is no significant difference in the SES of the Higher Secondary students studying in the urban and the rural schools.
3. There is no significant difference in the OAS of students with high SES and the low SES.
4. There is no significant difference in the OAS of the Higher Secondary boys and girls.

Random sampling technique was used in the selection of the sample. Eight higher secondary schools were chosen at random and 510 second year higher secondary students were again chosen on the same principle. This sample, consisted of the following sub samples: boys = 290 and girls = 220, Urban students = 320 and rural students = 190, students with high SES = 300 and students with low SES = 210. The researcher used the following tools in their study – the Socio-Economic status scale developed by Beena Shah (1927) and the Occupational Aspirations Scale developed by Grewal (1984). The statistical techniques were used are the means and the SDs of the SES and the OAS scores were calculated for the different sub samples and the test of significance was used to find out the significance of the difference between any two means of the sub samples.

Important findings of study were:

1. There was a significant difference in the SES and the OAS of the higher secondary boys and girls.
2. There was significant difference in the SES of the higher secondary students studying in the Urban and the rural schools.

3. There was significant difference in the OAS of the students with high SES and those with low SES.
4. The relationship between the SES and the OAS of higher secondary students was positive but negligible.

Shailaja (1992) conducted a study on the Interaction effect of Intelligence, SES and Sex on Occupational Aspiration of IX Standard pupils of Bangalore City. Results of the study indicated that social factors were greatly important in the vocational development and career planning of an individual. The concept that boys have Occupational Aspiration of higher level in comparison to girls was not found true. It was also observed that Intelligence and SES influences Occupational Aspiration.

The purpose of the study conducted by Kesiezic (1992) was to explore and identify the significant factors influencing the occupational choice of students from standard 10th to 11th grades in Nagaland. An extensive questionnaire was developed and administered to 213 students from three different types of schools. A follow-up interview with selected cases of students had been carried out for a more intensive investigation into their socio-economic background. The collected data were analyzed using both quantitative and qualitative approaches. On the basis of information provided by the students, the social and economic backgrounds of the families were divided into two levels of income groups. The pattern of students' occupational choice was also categorized into higher and lower aspirations and compared with their parents socio-economic status. The findings of the study revealed that the most significant factors influencing the occupational choice of students in Nagaland were parental educational attainment, parental occupational status, field of employment and geographic vocation. On the basis of these results the researcher concluded that these socio-economic factors may have a significant influence on occupation choice of youngsters.

Current literature on career aspirations and expectations suggests a correspondence between socio-economic status and occupational expectations. The research by Gresham (1993) was able to reveal the impact of socio-economic status on the difference between aspirations and expectations with a sample of 377 college freshmen, the hypotheses that were investigated indicated that socio-economic status would be important in predicting the differences between occupations and expectations. Support for the hypotheses was revealed and implications for counselling and further research were discussed.

The study by Shipp (1997) explored the role of several constructs in influencing the development of career aspirations overtime; viz., the personal attributes i.e., gender, socio-economic status cited in Gottfredson's (1981) developmental theory of occupational aspirations and the structure of opportunity presented in Astin's (1984) socio-psychological model of career choice and work behaviour. While findings confirmed the importance of many of Gottfredson's variables in determining career aspirations, they disputed Gottfredson's choice of socio-economic status as one of the primary determinants of the zone of acceptable occupational alternatives and it might be better represented by sex-type and ability level than by sex-type and prestige level as Gottenfredson proposed. The findings indicated that demographic variables were the best predictor of career aspirations overtime. The findings of their investigation was that individuals from a low socio-economic status background aspired to high prestige.

Mahale (1999) conducted a study on the adolescent's Vocational Aspirations and Economic Status of the family. It conducted that the economic condition of the family is one of the main deciding factor whether it can or cannot provide adolescents to achieve higher education in accordance to their vocational aspirations.

Khobragade has conducted a study on vocational aspirations and interests of SC/ST students of regional College of Education Bhopal. The major objectives of the study were:

1. To know vocational aspirations and interests of the SC/ST students of class X of Bulsar District.
2. To know vocational aspirations and interests of the SC/ST students of educated and uneducated parents.

3. To know vocational aspirations and interests of the SC/ST students and parents of economically higher and lower strata.
4. To know vocational aspirations and interests of high and low intelligent students of SC/ST categories.
5. To know impact on aspirations and interests of parents occupations/professions on students of these categories.
6. To study effect of family circumstances of these students in making selection of the suitable vocations.
7. To study the factors effecting vocational choices of the SC/ST students from their surroundings.

To achieve above objectives the investigator found survey sampling method suitable for his study.

The sample selected was exclusively from rural tribal schools. The total student population being 600 out of this sample, SC boys constituted 196 and SC girls 184, whereas ST boys numbered 116 and ST girls constituted 104. The total schools from where sample was collected, were 14 in number.

The tools employed for the required data were self prepared questionnaires, intelligence tests, readymade tools, SES scale to achieve the objectives stated and formulate major hypothesis, previous year students achievement record, interview schedule etc.

The responses obtained were scored and evaluated based on the instructions supplied in the Manual used for the purpose. The raw scores obtained were finally converted into final scores and tabulated. The necessary procedures were followed for further results. The data gathered was classified and subjected to computation, analysis, and interpretation of the results and finally conclusions were drawn based on the findings.

Major findings of study were Analysis indicated ST boy students had less adequate facilities (physical and transport) at their homes compared to SC boy students and this has significantly affected performance in the examination and this had consequently affected selection of their vocations/professions.

In the case of both SC/ST girl students, the analysis yielded more or less similar results as observed in case of SC/ST boys.

The study in area viz., vocational aspirations and interests, it has been observed that there has been certain influencing factors, viz., home, school surroundings, SES of students have the bearings on vocational choices. Similarly vocational maturity also found its place in vocational aspirations and interests of the students.

Most of SC/ST girl students showed disinterest in extra-curricular and co-curricular activities. They spent leisure time in helping their parents in domestic work. They felt shy in exposing themselves in out of school activities.

They seemed to be more concerned with their immediate environment and adaptability which has been the major asset. Very less number of boys and girls of these communities were fully aware of the vocational avenues available in the vicinity.

The analysis of the result confirms that higher achievers showed vertical mobility by preferring challenging subjects for future prospects and aspired for engineering and medicine and to become scientists. Their second priority being teaching profession. The lower achievers have shown lower vertical mobility and preferred to be primary teachers.

Sundararajan and Chandra (1993) have conducted a study on "The occupational aspirations of the higher Secondary students of the matriculation schools in Salem town".

The major objectives of the study were:

(*i*) To find out whether there is any significant difference among the occupational aspirations of students whose parents have different educational levels.

(*ii*) To find out whether there is any significant difference in the occupational aspirations of students whose parents monthly income varied and

(*iii*) To find out whether there is any significant difference in the occupational aspirations of students on the basis of their sex.

Researchers framed the following hypothesis for the study:

1. The students whose parents are graduates do not have a better level of occupational aspiration than those whose parents are literature but not graduates.
2. The students whose parents are graduates do not have a better level of occupational aspiration than those whose parents are illiterates.
3. The students whose parents are literates but not graduates do not have a better level of occupational aspiration than those whose parents are illiterates.
4. The students whose parents monthly income is Rs. 2,001 or above do not have a better level of occupational aspiration than of those whose parents monthly income is from Rs. 1,001 to Rs. 2,001.

By the random sampling two matriculation schools from the Salem town were chosen and all the 255 higher Secondary +2 students studying in these selected two schools were involved in this study.

This sample consists of the following sub-samples:

(A) Parents educational level Graduated (96), literates but not Graduates (87) and illiterates (72) = total 255.

(B) Parents monthly income Rs. 2001 and above (103), Rs. 1001 to Rs. 2001 (82) and upto Rs. 1000(70) = total 255.

(C) Sex – Girls (115) and Boys (140) = total 255.

The researchers used the occupational aspiration scale (OAS) constructed and standardized by Grewal (1984).

Statistical Technique

The occupational aspiration scores of the students belonging to the three educational levels of their parents were arranged into frequency distributions and their Mean and SDs were calculated. Then the test of significant was used.

The occupational aspiration scores of the study belonging to the three income levels of their parents were arranged into frequency distributions and their Means and SDs were calculated. Then the test of significance was used.

Important findings of the study were:

(*a*) The more educated the parents are the better is the level of the occupational aspiration of their children.

(*b*) The more affluent the parents are the better is the level of occupational aspiration of their children.

(*c*) Girls have a better level of occupational aspiration than the boys.

Schustack (2001) conducted a study on Career Decision-making in a Social-culture Context: Understanding Vocational Aspiration and Choice Among Female First-Generation College Students.

This study examined the first-generation students those individuals who are the first in their family's history to pursue post-secondary education represent an important emerging segment of the student body at our nation's colleges a group that is entering college in ever-increasing proportions. This qualitative study examined the vocational decision-making processes of 15 female first-generation juniors and seniors at a public college near Boston. Massachusetts. Participants from three racial groups (African-American, Latina and white) were selected through random sampling, and data was collected via in-depth interviews, observation, and document review.

Two overarching questions framed this study, which is based on prior sociological research about family structure, culture and social identity, and career development. First, this study examined participants' perspectives about how their social networks, aspirations, and perceived needs influenced their occupational choices. Second, this study investigated the processes through which participants identified and used resources to make vocational decisions.

This study revealed three categories of major findings:

(1) Social networks across different contexts do play an important role in educational persistence and in the identification and development of career plans among female first-generation students.

(2) Most of the patterns and processes revealed by this study did not vary by racial or ethnic group. Within each of the three racial groups, however, students' lives varied substantially as did their attitudes, expectations, and styles of social adaptation.

(3) Overall three elements unified this diverse sample. First, all participants reported strong beliefs in the benefits of obtaining a college education. Second, a majority of participants maintained strong interpersonal connections while preserving their self-reliance and autonomy. Finally, students were adept at cultivating social and information resources to support their educational and vocational goals.

Recommendations for education policy and future research in higher education and career development are included.

Some studies showed that socio-economic status was not found to be significantly related to the occupational aspirations of Secondary schools. Stephenson (1955) conducted a study on occupational aspirations of ninth graders and found that occupational aspirations were relatively unaffected by social class.

A multiple regression analysis was used by Howell *et.al.* (1989) to examine aspects of adolescent career development by investigating the relationship of socio-economic status on occupational aspirations. Data was collected from 215 twelfth grade students. Results indicated that parental influence was a significant predictor of occupational aspirations.

Mehtha, *et al.* (1987) studied the influence of occupational aspiration of adolescents. The population consisted of adolescent boys and girls studying in class IX in urban and semi-urban areas. The data were collected through a questionnaire which was prepared by the project team to assess vocational plans of the students. This study reported that the career aspirations of boys were not influenced by socio-economic status.

Bigler and Liben (2003) conducted a study on "Race and the Workforce: Occupational Status, Aspirations, and Stereotyping Among African American Children".

This study examined whether African American children's perceptions of occupational status and their own vocational interests are affected by racial segregation of the workforce. Children (N = 92) rated familiar occupations with respect to status, desirability, and stereotyping. Children also rated novel jobs that had been depicted with African American, European

Americans, or both African and European Americans. As predicted, for familiar jobs, children's judgments were linked to their knowledge of racial segregation of these jobs. In addition, novel occupations that had been depicted with African Americans were judged as lower in status than the identical occupations that had been depicted with European Americans, demonstrating a causal influence of workers' race on children's judgments. Children's age and socio-economic background moderated their occupational judgments.

Gender

Hault and Smith (1978), Gaur and Mathur (1978), Kriedberg et.al. (1978) and Vendewiele *et al.* (1985) reported that there was no relationship between occupational aspirations and sex, while some studies of Powell and Bloom (1962); Donald A. Davis (1962); Nelson (1963); Glady (1968); Passi (1970); Vincent (1975); Zookryk (1975); Pillai (1977); Gottfredson, Linda (1981); Mathur *et al.* (1987); and Jenkins (1989) reported significant relationship between these two factors.

Arnstein (1953) administered on inventory of 136 occupaitons to 14-15 years pupils to study occupational preferences of Israel children. The results revealed that the boys preferred technical work whereas girls preferred social and educational occupations.

Rezler (1963) in his study on occupational values and choices of young Indians, noticed that engineering was the most liked vocation among boys and teaching and medicine among girls.

Knill (1964) conducted a study on occupational aspirations of Northern Saskatchewan students and concluded that boys and girls differed in their vocational choices. Ethnic differences slightly influenced the occupational aspirations.

In a study on vocational choices of ninth class students with 60 boys and girls, Jain (1965) found that the boys chose a greater variety of jobs than girls. A majority of the boys chose engineering while many of the girls chose medicine.

Clark (1965) studied vocational aspirations of culturally disadvantaged boys and girls. 30% of the boys and 85% of the girls expressed their preference for professional and white collar occupations.

A study was conducted by Byati (1966) with 100 secondary school leavers (both boys and girls) belonging to two schools of Nathdwara to find out their vocational preferences. The choices of the group as a whole in order of preference were: Medical, technical, literary and household work. Out-door activities and sports were the two least liked areas. Girls were interested in technical and craft work. The three most favoured areas of interest of the boys in order or preference were scientific, medical and technical work and those of the girls were medical, scientific work and literature.

Grewal (1987) conducted a study to find out the relationship between Educational choices and vocational preferences of secondary school students in relation to environmental process variables. The sample of 127 boys and twenty six girls from the urban schools and 126 boys and fifty girls from rural schools all in the age group of fourteen to twenty-one was randomly drawn from higher secondary schools of Bhopal and Indore. Index of vocational environment and vocational preference inventory adopted from Haller and Miller's Occupational Aspiration Scale. (1971), the Educational Vocational Plans Questionnaire and Joshi's General Mental Ability test were administered. The IVE had the validity co-efficient of 0.57 and internal consistency co-efficient of 0.93. The findings were as follows:

(*i*) Boys differed significantly from girls in their levels of vocational preference.

(*ii*) Significant relationships were found between vocational environments of home, community and level of vocational preferences.

(*iii*) Home environment was more favourably perceived in comparisons to that of the school and community.

Looft (1971) attempted to find out the Sex difference in the expression of Vocational Aspirations by Elementary school children. Sample consisted of 53 boys and 33 girls of Parochial School first and second graders. The following questions were put:

(*b*) What they wanted to be when they grow up?

(*c*) What they thought they would really do when they grow up?

While answering to the first question, boys indicated a total of 18 different occupations most frequently foot ball players (9) and policeman (4). Girls nominated only 8 occupations. Most frequently nurse (14) and teacher (11), one girl indicated that she wanted to be a doctor. 23 boys and 14 girls changed their initial responses when 2nd question was put. Results indicated that sex differences in vocational aspirations developed early in childhood and reflex traditional sex-role expectations.

Vasantha (1970) conducted a study on vocational preferences and administered it to 1,000 pre-degree students. Her findings were:

(*i*) The range of vocational preference was narrow concentration of choices being in four vocations – school teaching, engineering, medicine and college teaching.

(*ii*) Mot of the boys chose engineering while the girls chose teaching.

(*iii*) Teaching was preferred by the highest percentage of students for the total sample.

The narrow range in the vocational preferences was attributed to lack of information in general.

Gaur (1974) studied the factors affecting Occupational Aspirations of the students Socio-economic status scale devised by Jalota *et al.* (1969) was used to collect the required data. Results indicated that sex had significant influence on the occupational aspiration of the students.

Rao and Pal (1973) administered a job value and an occupational preference test to 8th grade boys and girls and 11th grade boys of rural Delhi. The most preferred occupational values were social service and fame' power was the least preferred. Girls attached significantly more importance than did boys to leadership, interest and security. Medicine and teaching were the dominant occupational preferences for both boys and girls. preference for agricultural jobs and sales positions was very low.

Singer (1974) investigated sex differences in job preferences. The subjects were 55 females and 75 male undergraduates. Though there were differences between sexes on the job preferences. These differences were not related to sex stereotypes. Both the sexes preferred jobs where they could learn, achieve something worthwhile and work with congenial persons.

Reilly and Janet (1975) conducted a study to determine whether it was statistically possible to differentiate eighth grade students into four occupational areas according to specific personal data including sex of the subjects. The subjects for the study were 373 eighth grade students (202 females, 171 males) drawn from four middle schools. It was concluded that (i) selected variable such as sex of the subject was related to the vocational choices of eight grade students, (ii) the strong influence of the sex of the subject variable reflected the fact that sex stereotyping in occupations was a common phenomenon.

Hewitt (1975) asked 128 Dutch children aged 6-8 years to indicate their vocational aspirations. The results suggested that sex-role expectations for adult occupations were acquired very early. Boys aspired to a greater variety of vocations than girls.

Berman (1975) et.al. examined the effect of sex on the discrepancy between educational as well as occupational goals and expectations among 812 urban college youth from varied social class backgrounds. Contrary to expectations, sex characteristic did not affect mobility discrepancies. However, when level of aspiration was controlled, differences did emerge among high occupational aspirations aiming to be executives or major professionals. Moreover, sex differences in level of aspirations along with the importance of this variable in explaining goals expectation discrepancy suggested that the effects of discriminatory practices operated through the mechanism of limiting the educational and occupational objectives which young people set for themselves.

Gupta (1975) studied status values of professions on vocational preferences of school pupils and concluded that boys chose vocations with higher status values than the girls.

Bennette (1964) in his study found sex differences in occupational preferences and prestige and concluded that males learned to prefer prestigious occupations while females learned to avoid them.

Reilly (1975) probed into the influence of sex of sibling on vocational choice. Sex of the subject was related to vocational choice. It was found that there was sex-stereotyping in occupations.

A study on occupational choices in relation to sex difference was carried out by Levine (1976). According to his findings, sex was a major factor which influenced occupational attainments.

Konle and Piliavin (1976) studied sex differences in vocational aspirations of kindergarten children. The findings indicated that there were significant differences between the sexes on the vocational aspirations.

Pappas (1976) conducted a study on occupational aspirations of North Mississippi post-elementary pupils and stressed that there were deficiencies in the socialization of women and Blacks concerning the 'World of Work'. Females had lower aspirations.

Burlin (1976) found the influence of sex-role values in the occupational aspirations of women in his study on female occupational aspirations.

Yaegel (1977) observed that females were found to be significantly more certain about their vocational choice than males in his study on 'certainty of vocational choice'.

Abiri (1977) conducted a sample study of Nigerian adolescents' academic and occupational aspirations. The pattern of the occupational aspirations of 1.254, I, II and V year grammar school boys and girls in13 grammar schools in Ibadan, Nigeria was studied by means of a questionnaire, it was found that although there were age and sex related differences. The pupils were largely unrealistic in their occupational aspirations. Some professions appeared to have exercised excessive pull on the pupils while others were inadequately chosen. It was concluded that there is an urgent need for Guidance and Counselling Services in Nigeria Grammar Schools.

Significant sex differences were found in the study which was carried out by Becker and Murff (1978) on career decision.

Hoult and Smith (1978) in their study on sex differences in the number and variety of vocational choices and aspiraitons, examined 646 children and found that males listed a greater range of choices and preferences than females.

Marini and Greenberger (1978) examined the sex differences in occupational aspirations for 2.495 of XI graders. The following conclusions were drawn: (i) Boys aspired and expected higher levels of occupational attainment than girls, (ii) Boys occupational aspirations and expectations were characterized by greater variability than those of girls.

Head (1978) conducted a study on the determinants of occupational expectations of urban Black high schools students and found that sex role orientation had an important influence on occupational plans of boys and girls.

Thomas (1978) in his study on "differences in vocational preferences among Black and White high school students" established that significant differences did not exist between sexes and vocational preferences.

Parsons *et al.* (1978) studied career aspirations in college women and reported that women with high career aspirations were satisfied with their lives, confident of their career plans and were non-traditional in their vales and behaviour.

Ory and Hulfrich (1978) examined the sex differences in the career selection of 68 female and 63 male college students and concluded that disproportionately more men than women aspired for professional careers.

Margaret (1978) conducted a study to find out the sex differences in the determination of adolescents aspirations. Because the aspirations and expectations of adolescents were predictive of subsequent adult attainment, they were important mediating factors in the process by which individuals of the two sexes come to occupy different educational and occupational positions in adulthood. Adolescent boys aspired to a higher level of education than girls, and the occupational choices of the two sexes were highly sex-stereotyped. Although sex differences existed in the process by which both educational and occupational aspirations were formed, they were greater with respect to occupational than educational aspirations.

Clealeck (1979) in his study on vocational aspirations of male and female high school students pointed out that female subjects aspired for less demanding occupations than males.

Gaskel (1980) investigated that sex role ideology and aspirations of high school girls and found that sex stereotyped aspirations were seen in girls choosing nursing, telephone operator and boys preference to military, mechanic services etc., as their vocations. This study revealed that sex influence the aspiration of an individual.

Matheny *et al.* (1980) in their study on vocational goals in adolescence held that females were interested in domestic, artistic and social pursuits; while males were interested in manual, arts and outdoor pursuits.

Moracco *et al.* (1981) showed that males had higher vocational aspirations than females, in their study on occupational aspirations of a select group of military men and women.

Dunne *et al.* (1981) studied the occupational aspirations of 962 female and 861 male rural X, XI and XII graders and found that females showed significantly higher occupational aspirations than males.

Shaha (1982) conducted a study on determinants of occupational aspirations and expectations and found that males had higher career plans than females.

Currie (1982) studied the sex factor in occupational choice and declared that females chose teaching, nursing and therapy while males chose teaching, accounting and engineering.

Farmer (1983) studied career making plans for high school youth with 1234 pupils of IX and XII grades and found that females aspired to higher level careers than males.

Erab (1983) conducted a study on "Career preferences of early adolescents: sex differences" and found that boys were more interested in high technical careers while girls were interested in tradition areas such as service and organization.

Kenkal and Gage (1983) studied the restricted and gender typed occupational aspirations of young women and reported that both elementary and high school females aspired to gender appropriate occupations.

Kenyan Primary School Children's Vocational Aspirations and their perceptions of sex roles were studied by Maritim, Ezra (1984). Subjects were 120 males and 83 females in III, V and VII grades; aged between 9-19 years. Two hypotheses were tested:

(*i*) Males would aspire to a greater variety of vocations that are not available within their village community than females.

(*ii*) Both males and females would perceive themselves and the opposite sex in different social and professional roles. Both predictors were supported by the data.

The variety of vocational aspirations increased with increasing grade level among boys but not among girls. In addition, sex differences were associated with types of careers, task assignments and roles that were perceived as desirable and valued for both śexes. The findings were discussed in terms of the availability of career models for rural children, differential upbringing, task assignment and cultural norms pertaining to male-female desirable and valued roles in Kipsigis.

A study by Mehta *et al.* (1985) on occupational aspirations indicated that there was a strong indication of sex differences on level of occupational aspiration in favour of girls among both semi-urban and urban students.

Khan (1985) conducted a study on educational and vocational aspirations of Hindu and Muslim school students and found that in both the communities a higher percentage of boys than girls aspired for higher level jobs.

Lee (1985) in his study on gender comparison of occupational choice among rural adolescents indicated that females regardless of ethnicity, aspired and expected to attain higher level occupations than males.

Abra,s. et.al. (1985) studied the impact of sex on siblings on occupational aspirations on 50 males and 31 females of 16-18 year old and found large sex differences in their occupational ambitions.

Marjoribanks (1985) conducted a study with an objective to identify the influence of sex on occupational aspirations. Findings disclosed that occupational aspiration was influenced by gender.

The research by Winterbottom and Nancy (1988) investigated how high school females as compared to males think about careers. The sample consisted of 500 students in grades IX through XI in a sub-urban middle class high school in Northern New England and hour long interviews with a sub-sample of 12 senior females and 12 senior males. The researcher collected the required data through 28 item questionnaire and interviews. The findings of their investigation were: females and males choose different fields (most females in traditions, sex stereotyped areas) and they offered different reasons for such choices. Though both considered money and skills first in choosing a field, females valued money only slightly more than the other factors such as the opportunity to care for others with the people with whom they will work and the opportunity to combine work with home and family.

A study was carried out by Howell *et al.* (1989) to examine the aspects of adolescent career development by investigating the relationship of gender to occupational aspirations. Results indicated that gender was a significant predictor of occupational aspirations.

The primary purpose of the study by Hall *et al.* (1989) was to determine if college students selected occupational preferences on the basis of sex. The sample consisted of 198 college students. ANOVA was used for statistical analysis. The findings of their investigation were: There were significant differences among the groups on the occupational preference, selection pattern of males and females. The pattern of responses appeared to indicate that men and women selected occupational preferences based on their sex, using Halland's typology of occupational classification. There also appeared to be a sex biased occupational preference in selection patterns on the status scale.

Shoeib (1989) conducted a study with a purpose to investigate occupational aspirations of Egyptian Preparatory school pupils in relation to sex. It was reported that both levels and ranges of occupational aspirations of the pupils in the first year of preparatory schooling were independent of the pupils sex.

Pratt (1989) conducted a study on aspirational stability and its relation with sex through longitudinal study. The analysis of the data led the researchor to conclude that there was no significant difference between males and females.

Read (1989) conducted a study on occupational choices of high school students in relation to their gender. The major conclusion drawn from this study entailed the potential significant interaction of gender variable in the career choice process.

The study of Rhee (1989) was to describe the occupational aspirations of Korean female adolescents. The investigation led to the conclusion that Korean female adolescents occupational aspirations were still sex-stereotypical as almost three quarters of them aspired to female dominated occupations.

Sharma (1990) made an attempt to study sex differences in the vocational aspirations of Tibetan students. The sample comprised of 150 (98 male students and 52 female students). Survey method was employed. Majority of the students had fairly high vocational aspiriatons and there was significant difference in the aspirations of male and female students.

The study conducted by Tsering and Sharma (1990) was an investigation into the vocational aspirations of the contemporary Tibetan youth. The main objective of this study was to find out the sex differences in the vocational aspirations. The sample comprised of 180 students i.e., 90 boys and 90 girls between classes IX to XII. Survey method was employed by using questionnaire developed by the researcher. The findings revealed that there was considerable sex difference in the students vocational aspirations. The boys had a greater range of vocational choice compared to the girls.

No significant gender differences were observed by Rogell *et al.* (1991) when they conducted a study on occupational aspirations in relation to sex on 198 high school seniors.

The main purpose of the study conducted by McWhirter *et al.* (1993) was to test the model of the career development of Mexican, American girls. Three models predicting career commitment, level of aspirations and planned schooling respectively were tested on a sample of 280 girls using path analytic technique. Predictor variables consisted of socio-economic status, academic achievement and gender role attitudes. Results indicated that the initial models of career commitment was plausible in the sample and post hoc exploratory analysis yielded a plausible mode of level of aspirations.

Aniself *et al.* (1999) found that from a rational action perspective, one might predict that the occupational aspirations and expectations of Canadian youth would have declined between the 1970s and the 1990s as the youth labour market deteriorated. Whether or not such a shift in the level of occupational goals was observed, a late modernity analysis would predict that social class, gender, and urban-rural residence would become less prominent determinants of aspirations and expectations, in contrast to a social structural prediction of continued strong structural effects. Analysis of baseline data from five longitudinal studies of school-work transitions conducted in Canada during the 1970s, 1980s, and 1990s lead us to reject the rational action argument - a decline in occupational aspirations and expectations was not observed. Instead, male occupational goals remained largely unchanged while female occupational ambitions rose. Social class continues to have strong independent effects on occupational goals, which appear to be mediated, to a considerable extent, through the streaming of high school students into academic or non-academic programmes. Gender continues to influence specific occupational aspirations and expectations, while rural youth continue to report somewhat lower occupational goals. The persistent structural effects on aspirations and expectations provide strong support for the social structural hypothesis.

Gillock (1999) identified that gender distribution of jobs remains vastly disproportionate, especially among minority groups: Women continue to be overrepresented in traditionally female occupied jobs and underrepresented in high-status, high-paying occupations. Literature on gender distribution of careers and factors affecting career choice remains sparse where ethnic minority females are concerned. The present study attempts to fill this gap and focuses on adolescent females from Mexican American backgrounds. Descriptive findings indicate the general male dominance of females' career aspirations. Compared to females aspiring to highly female-dominated careers, females aspiring to highly male-dominated careers were more acculturated, earned higher grade point averages (GPAs) and higher achievement scores in science and social studies, and held higher educational aspirations and expectations, and a greater number of this group evidenced a clear understanding of the steps needed to achieve career goals. Findings are discussed in terms of their contradiction of previous findings and Mexican cultural norms.

Leve and Deckard (2002) conducted a study to find out relationship between adolescent vocational aspirations, attachment to parent, and gender role traditionality using a longitudinal sample of 351 children (approximately 50% female). Data was collected at age 14/15 and age 17/18. Two hypotheses were examined: (1) attachment security was expected to correlate positively with higher vocational aspirations, (2) higher gender role traditionality was expected to relate to lower vocational aspirations for girls and higher vocational aspirations for boys. In a simple correlation analysis, boys' attachment at age 14/15 showed a significant positive relationship to higher vocational aspirations at age 17/18. No significant relationship between attachment and vocational aspirations was found for girls. A hierarchical regression analysis on the gender role traditionality hypothesis showed trends toward significance for both females and males, suggesting that further research is needed in this area.

Gómez (2003) the study examines the relationship between gender, parenting, and adolescents' academic outcomes in Mexican-origin immigrant families. Self-report survey data were collected from adolescents attending three high schools in Los Angeles. Correlation and multiple regression analyses were conducted on the 273 adolescents (M = 15.5) whose parents were both born in Mexico. Girls reported higher academic motivation and educational aspirations. Substantial support was found for the positive relationship between mothers' and fathers' behaviors (ability to help, monitoring, support) and adolescents' academic motivation. Substantial support was found for the relationship between mothers' and fathers' educational level, and educational aspirations. Generation status was not related to the academic outcomes. Implications for researchers, practitioners, school personnel, and policy makers are discussed.

Hannahdenga (2004) conducted a study on "The Influence of Gender on Occupational Aspirations of Primary School Children in Cross River State."

The sample of this survey was 629 children randomly drawn from ten (10 primary school in Calabar Municipality. Primary six (6) pupils from six (6) public schools and primary 5 children from four (4) private schools were used. There were 350 girls and 270 boys in number. Their ages ranged from 10 to 14 years old. In each school, sixty two (62) pupils were sampled. The hat-and-draw method was used to select the number of boys and girls as sample. This method adopted gave ample chance for every child in the mentioned years of study to be selected for the study. The sample had the similar traits of the entire population of about 1,800 primary five (5) and six (6) pupils from a total number of schools.

The children's Occupational Aspirations Questionnaire (COAQ) was used. The first part solicited for children's personal data while the second part required the participants to rank 1, 2 and 3 occupations they would like to do when they grow up. A list of twenty occupations was given for children to choose their three desired occupations. The X 2 analysis was used to report the result at 0.05 level of significance.

Locale and Type of School

William Wattenberg (1955) quotes Robert and Garfield who made a questionnaire study of approximately two thousand boys and girls and found that many young people had job preferences although they eventually had to take whatever job the community offered. They observed that a boy or a girl growing in a metropolitan area had greater freedom to choose than a boy or a girl in an isolated village.

Smith (1960) investigated the occupational choices of rural Jamaican youth and found a big gap between occupational opportunities, expectations and aspirations.

On a sample of 26,000 city and rural junior high school pupils, Csirzka, Janes (1965) conducted a study on choice of profession and found significant differences in the occupational motives of subjects from the town and the villages but not between those from the city and the country.

Studying 9986 Wisconsin high school seniors belonging to urban and rural communities, Sewell and Orenstein (1965) found that the proportion of students choosing high status occupations was related to the residence of the community. The differences in the choices were the greatest for boys from low intelligence range and for those from high status families.

Stenic and Uhlig (1967) conducted a study on occupational aspirations of selected Appalachian Youth and found that rural youth had a significantly lower aspirational level than those from semi-urban localities.

Kulas (1974) studied the occupational aspirations of urban and rural graders and found that the urban students had more realistic aspirations than the rural ones.

Surinder Singh Chadha (1979) has conducted a study on A Study of Some Psychological and Social Factors as Related to Vocational Aspiration of Rural and Urban High School Children.

The major objectives of the study were (a) to find out whether there is any significant difference in vocational aspiration of the urban and rural subjects (b) to find out the difference between the vocational aspirations of urban and rural fathers for their sons. (c) the relationship of vocational aspirations of the sons and of the fathers for their sons with the variables of intelligence. Socio economic status, Need achievement, adjustment and reactions of frustration of urban and rural sons and (d) the cluster of variables which go together in the determination of vocational aspiration.

To fulfil the above aims the following hypothesis were proposed :

Hypothesis-1

(*a*) There will be differences in the fields of vocational aspirations of urban and rural subjects

(*b*) There will be differences in the levels of vocational aspirations of urban and rural subjects.

Hypothesis-2

(*a*) Levels of vocational aspirations of rural sons will be different from that of the aspirations of fathers for them.

For finding out the relationship of vocational aspiration with need-achievement, socio-economic status, adjustment and reactions to frustration the following hypothesis were proposed.

1. Subjects aspiring for higher levels of occupations will have higher need-achievement.
2. Subjects aspiring for higher levels of occupations will have higher socio-economic status of the family
3. There will be differences in the levels of vocational aspiration of the subjects scoring high and low on adjustment variable. The subjects with unrealistic aspiration would be maladjusted as compared with the subjects of realistic aspiration.
4. There will be no difference in the scores on reactions to frustration obtained by these who aspire for either high or low levels of occupations.

To achieve the objectives 713 tenth class boys of four urban schools and six rural schools constituted the sample. The schools were selected at random.

The researcher has used following tools to collect data :

(1) McClelland Thematic Apperception Test (NCERT Adaptation, 1966) for measurement of Need Achievement.

(2) Socio-Economic Status Scale (Phami and Dosajh, 1974) for measuring 'Socio-Economic Status.

(3) Adjustment Inventory for school students (Sinha and Singh) for measuring reactions to 'Frustration'.

(4) Vocational Aspiration Blanks were used for eliciting vocational aspiration of subjects as well as of their father's vocational aspiration for them.

Duncan's Multiple Range test was applied to observe the significance of differences in the various test scores obtained by the aspirants of different vocational fields separately for fathers and sons of urban and rural samples. The correlation matrices were prepared and elementary linkage analysis (McQuitty, 1957) was done to find out the clusters of variables that go together in determination of vocational aspirations. Correlations between level of vocational aspirations and measured psychological variables were worked to find out the determinants of vocational aspirations of the subjects and the fathers, separately for urban and rural samples.

Major findings of the study were: In the various fields of vocations no consistent pattern of significance of these variables was observed in urban and rural subjects and their fathers except for socio-economic status and social adjustment scores. The relationship between levels of aspiration and the measured variables was found to be of some significance. Scores on SES were found to be positively and significantly related to the levels of aspirations of urban and rural samples.

In the rural sample significant correlation was also found between social adjustment and levels of aspiration of sons. The fathers' aspirations however, were found to be related to the need achievement and need persistence scores of their sons. The adjustments of realistic and unrealistic vocational aspirations were also not found significantly different.

To sum up it may be said that the vocational aspirations of the urban and rural subjects were different. The unrealistic vocational aspiration group did not differ on adjustment scores. The SES and need achievement were found to be associated with levels of vocational aspirations.

The findings of Chadha *et al.* (1983) in their study on vocational aspirations showed that urban boys had a wider range of occupational aspirations than the rural boys. Urban pupils had the opportunity of contacting a variety of people.

Sundararajan and Rajasekhar (1988) made an attempt to find out if there was any significant relationship between the locality and the sex of the higher Secondary students and their occupational aspirations. The sample consisted of 442 students from urban and rural areas. The Occupational Aspiration Scale (OAS) constructed and standardized by Grewal (1984) was used. The important findings of the study were: (i) the urban students had a better level of occupational aspirations than the rural students and (ii) the boys did not have better level of occupational aspiration than that of girls.

Nagar (1991) A study of vocational aspirations of educated girls in Gorakhpur division and facilities available to them.

This study attempts to explore group of women who even today are educationally and vocationally disadvantaged specially those belonging to rural areas.

The major objectives of the study were:

(*i*) to study the vocational aspirations of educated girls belonging to various educational levels.

(*ii*) to study the vocational aspirations of rural and urban educated girls.

(*iii*) To study the effect of socio-economic status on the vocational aspirations of educated girls

(*iv*) To study the effect of intelligence on the vocational aspirations of educated girls and

(*v*) To study the facilities for vocational preparation available to rural and urban educated girls in Gorakhpur division.

The sample comprised educated girls of Gorakhpur division, who were chosen based on the stratified random sampling technique. The tools used to collect data included a vocational aspiration blank, socio-economic status scale by Kuppuswamy and a questionnaire. The collected data were treated using percentages, mean, SD and chi-square test. Major findings of the study were:

(*a*) There was a consistent pattern of relationship between the intelligence level and socio-economic status.

(*b*) As the educational level increased the socio-economic status and intelligence profile showed on upward trend. Location, too, exerted on influence.

(*c*) Level of educational did influence the vocational aspiration of girls at different levels of education. Also the other vocations aspired for differed with educational levels.

(*d*) A significant difference in the vocational aspiration of urban and rural respondents showed a higher preference for household vocations urban counterparts preferred the scientific area.

(*e*) A persual of the results of vocational choice also highlighted only a few vocational areas such as scientific, artistic, household, executive.

Research evidence shows that the level of occupational aspiration is influenced by geographical location. Miller and Haller 1964; Passi, 1970; Donald 1971; Desai, 1974 and Reddy, 1978 and Grewal 1980 reported that occupational aspiration had significant relationship with vocational environment. Chand et.al. (1983) also reported urban-rural differences in occupational aspiration. Although most of the researches show that geographical location influenced the level of occupational aspiration there is some evidence to the contrary also.

Sundararajan and Kalavathi (1990) have conducted a study on the occupational aspirations of the Higher Secondary girls in the city of Madras. The major objectives of study were:

(*ii*) To find out whether there is any significant difference among the occupational aspirations of students studying in different types of schools.

(*iii*) To find out if there is any significant difference among the occupational aspirations of the students whose parents have different educational qualifications and

(*iv*) To find out whether there is any significant difference among the occupational aspirations of the student whose parents belong to different income groups.

Researchers framed the following hypothesis for the study:

1. The students studying in the Government Higher Secondary schools do not have better occupational aspirations than those studying in the corporation Higher Secondary schools.
2. The students studying in the Government Higher Secondary schools do not have better occupational aspirations than those studying in the matriculation Higher Secondary schools.
3. The students studying in the matriculation Higher Secondary schools do not have better occupational

aspirations than those studying in the corporation Higher Secondary schools.

4. The students whose parents are either graduates or post-graduates do not have better occupational aspirations than those whose parents are professional degree holders.
5. The students whose parents are either graduates or post-graduates do not have better occupational aspirations than those whose parents are literates but not graduates.
6. The students whose parents are either graduates or post-graduates do not have better occupational aspirations than those whose parents are illiterates.
7. The students whose parents monthly income is from Rs. 1,001 to 2,000 do not have better occupational aspirations than those whose parents monthly income is Rs. 2001 and above.
8. The students whose parents monthly income is from Rs. 1,001 to 2,000 do not have better occupational aspirations than those whose parents monthly income is upto Rs. 1,000.
9. The students whose parents monthly income is Rs. 2,001 and above do not have better occupational aspirations than those whose parents monthly income is up to 1,000.

Random sampling technique was used in the selection of the sample.

The researcher used the Occupational Aspiration Scale (OAS) constructed and standardized by Grewal (1984). The same was translated into Tamil and used in this investigation. The means and the standard deviations of the occupational aspiration (OA) scores the various sub samples were found out and the test of significance was used (t-test).

Important findings of the study were:

(*i*) There was no significant difference among the girls studying in the government, corporation and the matriculation higher secondary schools in respect of their level of occupational aspirations. Thus the first three null hypothesis formulated in this study were retained.

(*ii*) There was no significant difference between girls whose parents were either graduates or post-graduates and those girls whose parents were professional degree holders in respect of their level of occupational aspirations. Thus the null hypothesis is retained.

(*iii*) Significant difference was found in the level of occupational aspirations of girls whose parents were either graduates or post-graduates and whose parents were literates but not graduates. Therefore the null hypothesis is rejected and it was concluded that the girls whose parents are either graduates or post-graduates had a better level of occupational aspirations than the girls whose parents were literates but not graduates.

(*iv*) The null hypothesis six was rejected and it was concluded that the girls whose parents were either graduates or post-graduates had a better level of occupational aspirations than the girls whose parents were illiterates.

(*v*) The null hypothesis seven was retained

(*vi*) The null hypothesis eight was retained.

(*vii*) The null hypothesis nine was rejected and it was concluded that the girls whose parents monthly income was Rs. 2,001 and above have a better level of occupational aspirations than those whose parents monthly income was up to Rs. 1,000.

Shah and Bhargava (2000) conducted a study on the Vocational Aspirations of Home Science Students. The study revealed that almost equal percentage, that is, little less than 50% of the respondents were under the category of highly aspired or less aspired to take up vocations. Majority of the respondents aspiring for jobs wanted to do so to become economically independent. Only one third of the respondents who aspired for a vocations were fully confident to get their aspired job.

Calvin W. (2005) the study was to examine the occupational aspirations, immediate plans, and future expectations of Level

III students from selected rural and urban areas of Newfoundland and Labrador. This study also examined student perceptions of barriers to post-secondary education and factors that influenced their career plans.

Individual questionnaires were administered to 104 Level III students attending five different Senior High schools located in rural communities within the Green Bay area, and 67 Level III students attending a Senior High school located in the province's largest urban center and capital, St. John's. Data analysis was completed using the statistical program, SPSS. Descriptive statistics that included frequencies, percentages, and crosstabs were used along the chi-squared analysis to summarize findings and compare differences.

Student occupational choices were consistent with findings reported in earlier studies. Although most students, particularly males, made gender stereotypical choices, their choices overall were in growth areas that hold promise for future employment. Approximately three-quarters of the students planned to pursue post-secondary education immediately following high school graduation. Most students expected to be employed full-time outside the province in five to ten years after high school graduation.

The most commonly perceived barriers to post-secondary education were: not knowing what program to do, lack of academic qualifications, and the high cost of post-secondary education. Community attachment was not considered a barrier to post-secondary education by most rural students.

Most students perceived that their parents played the most significant role in influencing their career plans followed by friends and academic ability. Females felt their mothers were more influential on their career plans while males perceived their fathers as being more influential. It is recommended that government, post-secondary institutions, school, and community agencies partner together in more deliberate and direct ways to educate students about the labour market, its trends, and future occupations, and to guide them more effectively in their career planning process. It is also recommended that parents be empowered through such partnerships to provide informed and adequate career guidance to their children.

Hodgins and Parr (1965) and Mehta *et al.* (1984) did not find urban-rural differences in the level of expected occupation.

The present review gives a broad synaptic view of the status of research in vocational aspirations in India and abroad. And the review in the area of Achievement motivation related vocational aspirations, personality related to vocational aspirations, SES related to vocational aspirations has helped the investigator in defining the research problem, drawing sample, study hypotheses, in selecting appropriate tools and statistical techniques for the analysis of the study.

The present review also indicates a number of gaps in the research efforts in the area of vocational aspirations.

The need for greater understanding of the factors which influence the vocational aspirations of high school pupils prompted this study. The review striking reveals that among many influencing factors, SES, personality, achievement motivation, parents influence and gender, medium of instruction, type of school seem to be good predictors of vocational aspirations of Secondary school students. Problems arising out of this state of affairs for the school going children that too X standard students who are going to for a course suitable to their vocational aspiration in the PUC course require an in-depth study.

3

Methodology

Introduction

In this chapter the details about the locale of the study, sampling design, data collection, scoring, design of the study, variables studied and the statistical techniques used in analyzing and interpreting the data are described.

The Problem

The problem selected for the present investigation can be restated as follows:

"Socio-Psychological Correlates of Vocational Aspirations."

Operational Definitions of the Terms Used

Although a number of definitions are put forth by different scholars, the researcher has selected only such those definitions which are operationally relevant to the present study.

Vocation : Vocation is a series of duties and responsibilities undertaken and related activities performed by an individual to accomplish a goal and/or for financial reward.

Aspiration : Aspiration is defined as a "strong desire for realization (as of ambition, idea or accomplishment)" (*Webster's Dictionary* 1976) and as "pure upward desire for excellence – the steadfast desire or longing for something above one". (*Oxford Dictionary*, 1972).

Level of aspiration represents a person's expectations, goals, claims, or his future achievement in a given task (Hoppe, 1941).

Vocational Aspiration: According to Crite (1969) vocational aspiration means what the individual consider to be ideal vocation for him.

Vocational aspiration is defined as "a goal directed attitude which involves conception of the self in relation to a particular level of the vocational prestige hierarchy" (Haller and Miller, 1971).

Achievement Motivation: Achievement motivation is defined as "the desire to excel regardless of social reward and the desire of winning or doing better than some one else" (McClelland, 1961).

Achievement motivation moves or drives an individual to strive to gain mastery of difficult and challenging situations or performances in the pursuit of excellence. It comes into the picture when an individual knows that his performance will be evaluated and that the consequence of his actions will lead either to success or failure and that good performance will produce a feeling of pride in accomplishment.

Thus, it is understood that achievement motivation is an urge to achieve success in one's life in the area of personal interest.

Personality: According to Allport (1962) "personality is the dynamic organisation within the individual, of those psycho-physical systems that determine his unique adjustment to his environment".

Personality is a very dynamic psychological concept it encompasses wider human behaviour. In the present study the personality considered as fourteen dimensions or traits viz., reserved vs. outgoing, less intelligent vs. more intelligent, affected by feelings vs. emotionally stable, phlegmatic vs. excitable, obedient vs. assertive, sobar vs. happy-go-lucky, expedient vs. conscientious, shy vs. venturesome, tough minded vs. tender minded, vigorous vs. doubting, placid vs. apprehensive, group dependent bs. self-sufficient, undisciplined self-conflict vs. controlled, relaxed vs. tense, which comprised the total personality of an individual.

Social Status: Social status means the position that an individual or family occupies by means of his/her parents education and occupation.

Status is a term used to designate "the comparative amounts of prestige, difference or respect accorded to persons who have been assigned different roles in a group or community" (Aaron *et al.*, 1970).

Since, pre-university college students are growing personalities and do not have social status of their own, their parents social status was considered for the present study.

Locality : In the present investigation, two localities viz., urban and rural are studied, 1991 census defines the terms urban rural as follows:

Urban: The urban locality constitutes an area where there is a municipality or corporation with a density of population of at least 400 per square kilometer. In addition to this, there should be a minimum population of 5000 and at least 75 per cent of the male working population engaged in non-agricultural pursuits.

Rural: A locality is considered as 'rural' which has definite surveyed boundaries with inadequate transport and communication facilities, which has no hospital, banks, government offices and recreational facilities.

Pre-University College: Pre-university college having classes PUC-I and II are called Pre-University Colleges.

Type of College: Type of college refers to the types of management of college. Colleges managed by the Government of Karnataka are categorised under government colleges and colleges managed by private managements are categorized as private colleges. In private colleges there are only two categories, those private colleges which are not getting aid by the government are called Unaided colleges and those private colleges which are getting aid from the government are called Aided colleges.

Medium of Instructions: Pre-University colleges which are using Kannada as their medium of instruction are called Kannada medium colleges. The pre-university colleges which use English as their medium of instruction are called as English medium colleges.

Research Design

In the present investigation descriptive survey research method was employed.

Variables of the Study

Independent Variables

1. Personality: Personality with 14 dimensions

FACTORS

A. Reserved, Detached, Critical, Cool (Sizothymia)

B. Less Intelligent, Concrete Thinking (Lower Scholastic Mental Capacity)

C. Affected By Feelings, Emotionally Less Stable, Easily Upset, Changeable (Lower Ego Strength)

D. Phlegmatic, Deliberate, Inactive, Stodgy (Phlegmatic Temperament)

E. Obedient, Mild, Conforming (Submissiveness)

F. Sober, Prudent, Serious, Taciturn (Desurgency)

G. Expedient, Evades Rules, Feels Few Obligations (Weaker Superego Strength)

H. Shy, Restrained, Diffident, Timid (Threctia)

I. Tough-minded, Self-reliant, Realistic, No-nonsense (Harrla)

J. Vigorous, Goes, Readily with Group Zestful, Given to Action (Zeppla)

O. Placid, Self-assured, Confident, Serene (Untroubled Adequacy)

Q2. Group-dependent, A "Joiner" and Sound Follower (group Adherence)

Q3. Undisciplined Self-conflict, follows Own Urges, Careless Of Protocol (Low Integration)

Q4. Relaxed, Tranquil, Torpid, Unfrustrated (Low Ergic Tension)

2. Achievement Motivation : Achievement motivation dimensions are:

(*i*) Long-term involvement.

(*ii*) Unique accomplishment.

(*iii*) Success in competition with standard of excellence.

(*iv*) Desire to excel regardless of social reward.

3. Social factors : includes educational and occupational status of parents.

Dependent Variable: Vocational aspirations

Moderate Variables

1. Sex (Male and female).
2. Type of management (Government/ Aided /Unaided).
3. Medium of instruction (Kannada/ English).
4. Birth order.
5. Locality (Rural/Urban).
6. Subjects selected (Arts/Science/Commerce).
7. Categories (GM/OBC/SC/ST/Cat-I).

Hypotheses

Based upon the discussion of the variables, the investigator intends to test the following hypotheses:

1. Male and female students of Pre-university college students do not differ significantly with respect to their vocational aspirations.
2. There is no significant difference between the students studying different subjects (Arts, Science and Commerce) of Pre-University College with respect to their vocational aspirations.
3. Students studying in Kannada and English medium of instruction of pre-university colleges do not differ significantly with respect to their vocational aspirations.
4. There is no significant difference between type of management (Government, Aided and Unaided) of Pre-university College students do not differ significantly with respect to their vocational aspiration.

5. There is no significant difference between different birth order (1-2, 3-4 and 5 and more than 5) of Pre-university College students with respect to vocational aspirations.
6. There is no significant difference between students belong to different categories (GM, OBC, SC/ST/Cat-I) with respect to vocational aspirations.
7. Students belong to Rural and Urban Pre-university Colleges do not differ significantly with respect to vocational aspiration.
8. There is no significant difference between the students belong to High and low achievement motivation of Pre-university college students with respect to vocational aspiration.
9. There is no significant difference between students belong to High and low social status of Dharwad district with respect to vocational aspirations.
10. There is no significance difference between students with High and Low Personality traits of Pre-university Colleges of Dharwad district do not differ significantly with respect to vocational aspiration.
11. Reserved, average and out-going students of Pre-university Colleges of Dharwad district do not differ significantly with respect to vocational aspirations.
12. Less intelligence, Average intelligence and more intelligence students of Pre-university Colleges do not differ significantly with respect to vocational aspirations.
13. Affected by feeling, Average and Emotionally stable students of Pre-university Colleges do not differ significantly with respect to vocational aspirations.
14. Phlegmatic, average and Excitable students of Pre-university Colleges of Dharwad district do not differ significantly with respect to vocational aspirations.
15. Obedient, Average and Assertive students of Pre-university Colleges do not differ significantly with respect to vocational aspirations.
16. Sober, Average and Happy go lucky students of Pre-university Colleges do not differ significantly with respect to vocational aspirations.

17. Expedient, Average and Conscientious students of Pre-university Colleges do not differ significantly with respect to vocational aspirations.
18. Shy, Average and Venturesome students of Pre-university Colleges of Dharwad district do not differ significantly with respect to vocational aspirations.
19. Tough minded, Average minded and Tended minded students of Pre-university Colleges of Dharwad district do not differ significantly with respect to vocational aspirations.
20. Vigorous, Average and doubting students of Pre-university Colleges of Dharwad district do not differ significantly with respect to vocational aspirations.
21. Placid, Average and Apprehensive students of Pre-university Colleges of Dharwad district do not differ significantly with respect to vocational aspirations
22. Group dependent, Average and Self-sufficient students of Pre-university Colleges of Dharwad district do not differ significantly with respect to vocational aspirations
23. Undisciplined self-conflict, Average and controlled students of Dharwad district Pre-university Colleges do not differ significantly with respect to vocational aspirations
24. Relaxed, Average and Tense students of Pre-university College of Dharwad district do not differ significantly with respect to vocational aspirations
25. There is no significant interaction effect of Achievement motivation (High and Low), Personality traits (High and Low) and Social status (High and Low) on vocational aspirations of students of Pre-university Colleges of Dharwad district.
26. There is no significant interaction effect of Achievement motivation (High and Low), Personality traits (High and Low) and Social status (High and Low) on vocational aspirations of Pre-university College male students of Dharwad district.
27. There is no significant interaction effect of Achievement motivation (High and Low), Personality traits (High and

Low) and Social status (High and Low) on vocational aspirations of Pre-university College female students of Dharwad district.

28. There is no significant interaction effect of Achievement motivation (High and Low), Personality traits (High and Low) and Social status (High and Low) on vocational aspirations of students of Pre-university College with arts subject of Dharwad district.
29. There is no significant interaction effect of Achievement motivation (High and Low), Personality traits (High and Low) and Social status (High and Low) on vocational aspirations of Pre-university Colleges students with science subject of Dharwad district.
30. There is no significant interaction effect of Achievement motivation (High and Low), Personality traits (High and Low) and Social status (High and Low) on vocational aspirations of students of Pre-university College students with Commerce subject of Dharwad district.
31. There is no significant interaction effect of Achievement motivation (High and Low), Personality traits (High and Low) and Social status (High and Low) on vocational aspirations of students of Pre-university College Kannada medium students of Dharwad district.
32. There is no significant interaction effect of Achievement motivation (High and Low), Personality traits (High and Low) and Social status (High and Low) on vocational aspirations of students of Pre-university College English medium students of Dharwad district.
33. There is no significant interaction effect of Achievement motivation (High and Low), Personality traits (High and Low) and Social status (High and Low) on vocational aspirations of students of government Pre-university Colleges of Dharwad district.
34. There is no significant interaction effect of Achievement motivation (High and Low), Personality traits (High and Low) and Social status (High and Low) on vocational aspirations of students of Aided Pre-university College students of Dharwad district.

35. There is no significant interaction effect of Achievement motivation (High and Low), Personality traits (High and Low) and Social status (High and Low) on vocational aspirations of students of Unaided Pre-university College students of Dharwad district.
36. There is no significant interaction effect of Achievement motivation (High and Low), Personality traits (High and Low) and Social status (High and Low) on vocational aspirations of Pre-university College students belong to GM of Dharwad district.
37. There is no significant interaction effect of Achievement motivation (High and Low), Personality traits (High and Low) and Social status (High and Low) on vocational aspirations of Pre-university College OBC students of Dharwad district.
38. There is no significant interaction effect of Achievement motivation (High and Low), Personality traits (High and Low) and Social status (High and Low) on vocational aspirations of Pre-university College SC/ST/Cat-I students of Dharwad district.
39. There is no significant interaction effect of Achievement motivation (High and Low), Personality traits (High and Low) and Social status (High and Low) on vocational aspirations of Pre-university College Rural students of Dharwad district.
40. There is no significant interaction effect of Achievement motivation (High and Low), Personality traits (High and Low) and Social status (High and Low) on vocational aspirations of Pre-university College Urban students of Dharwad district.
41. There is no significant relationship between Vocational aspirations of Pre-university College students and their Personality traits Achievement Motivation, Long term involvement, Unique accomplishment, Success in competition with standard of excellence, Desire to excel regardless of social reward, Social Status, Educational Status and Occupation Status as a whole.

42. There is no significant relationship between Vocational aspirations of Pre-university College male students and their Personality traits Achievement Motivation, Long term involvement, Unique accomplishment, Success in competition with standard of excellence, Desire to excel regardless of social reward, Social Status, Educational Status and Occupation Status.
43. There is no significant relationship between Vocational aspirations of Pre-university College female students and their Personality traits Achievement Motivation, Long term involvement, Unique accomplishment, Success in competition with standard of excellence, Desire to excel regardless of social reward, Social Status, Educational Status and Occupation Status.
44. There is no significant relationship between Vocational aspirations of Pre-university College Arts students and their Personality traits Achievement Motivation, Long term involvement, Unique accomplishment, Success in competition with standard of excellence, Desire to excel regardless of social reward, Social Status, Educational Status and Occupation Status.
45. There is no significant relationship between Vocational aspirations of Pre-university College Science students and their Personality traits Achievement Motivation, Long term involvement, Unique accomplishment, Success in competition with standard of excellence, Desire to excel regardless of social reward, Social Status, Educational Status and Occupation Status.
46. There is no significant relationship between Vocational aspirations of Pre-university College Commerce students and their Personality traits Achievement Motivation, Long term involvement, Unique accomplishment, Success in competition with standard of excellence, Desire to excel regardless of social reward, Social Status, Educational Status and Occupation Status.
47. There is no significant relationship between Vocational aspirations of Pre-university College Kannada medium students and their Personality traits, Achievement

Motivation, Long-term involvement, Unique accomplishment, Success in competition with standard of excellence, Desire to excel regardless of social reward, Social Status, Educational Status and Occupation Status.

48. There is no significant relationship between Vocational aspirations of Pre-university College English medium students and their Personality traits Achievement Motivation, Long-term involvement, Unique accomplishment, Success in competition with standard of excellence, Desire to excel regardless of social reward, Social Status, Educational Status and Occupation Status.

49. There is no significant relationship between Vocational aspirations of Pre-university Government College students and their Personality traits Achievement Motivation, Long-term involvement, Unique accomplishment, Success in competition with standard of excellence, Desire to excel regardless of social reward, Social Status, Educational Status and Occupation Status.

50. There is no significant relationship between Vocational aspirations of Pre-university Aided College students and their Personality traits Achievement Motivation, Long-term involvement, Unique accomplishment, Success in competition with standard of excellence, Desire to excel regardless of social reward, Social Status, Educational Status and Occupation Status.

51. There is no significant relationship between Vocational aspirations of Pre-university Unaided College students and their Personality traits Achievement Motivation, Long-term involvement, Unique accomplishment, Success in competition with standard of excellence, Desire to excel regardless of social reward, Social Status, Educational Status and Occupation Status.

52. There is no significant relationship between Vocational aspirations of Pre-university College GM students and their Personality traits Achievement Motivation, Long term involvement, Unique accomplishment, Success in competition with standard of excellence, Desire to excel

regardless of social reward, Social Status, Educational Status and Occupation Status.

53. There is no significant relationship between Vocational aspirations of Pre-university College OBC students and their Personality traits Achievement Motivation, Long term involvement, Unique accomplishment, Success in competition with standard of excellence, Desire to excel regardless of social reward, Social Status, Educational Status and Occupation Status.

54. There is no significant relationship between Vocational aspirations of Pre-university College SC/ST/Cat-I students and their Personality traits Achievement Motivation, Long-term involvement, Unique accomplishment, Success in competition with standard of excellence, Desire to excel regardless of social reward, Social Status, Educational Status and Occupation Status.

55. There is no significant relationship between Vocational aspirations of Pre-university College rural students and their Personality traits Achievement Motivation, Long term involvement, Unique accomplishment, Success in competition with standard of excellence, Desire to excel regardless of social reward, Social Status, Educational Status and Occupation Status.

56. There is no significant relationship between Vocational aspirations of Pre-university College urban students and their Personality traits Achievement Motivation, Long-term involvement, Unique accomplishment, Success in competition with standard of excellence, Desire to excel regardless of social reward, Social Status, Educational Status and Occupation Status.

57. There is no significant relationship between Vocational aspirations of Pre-university College total, male and female students and their Personality traits and its dimensions (A, B, C, D, E, F, G, H, I, J, O, Q2, Q3, Q4) as a whole

58. There is no significant relationship between Vocational aspirations of Pre-university College Arts, Science and commerce students and their Personality traits and its

dimensions (A, B, C, D, E, F, G, H, I, J, O, Q2, Q3, Q4) as a whole

59. There is no significant relationship between Vocational aspirations of Pre-University College Kannada and English medium students and their Personality traits and its dimensions (A, B, C, D, E, F, G, H, I, J, O, Q2, Q3, Q4) as a whole
60. There is no significant relationship between Vocational aspirations of Pre-University government, Aided and Unaided Students College and their Personality traits and its dimensions (A, B, C, D, E, F, G, H, I, J, O, Q2, Q3, Q4) as a whole
61. There is no significant relationship between Vocational aspirations of Pre-University College GM, OBC and SC/ ST/Cat-I students and their Personality traits and its dimensions (A, B, C, D, E, F, G, H, I, J, O, Q2, Q3, Q4) as a whole
62. There is no significant relationship between Vocational aspirations of Pre-University College Rural and Urban students and their Personality traits and its dimensions (A, B, C, D, E, F, G, H, I, J, O, Q2, Q3, Q4) as a whole
63. Achievement motivation, personality traits Social status, Educational status, and Vocational status are would not be a significant predictor of vocational aspirations of Pre-university College students as a total
64. Achievement motivation, personality traits Social status, Educational status, and Vocational status are would not be a significant predictor of vocational aspirations of Pre-university College male students
65. Achievement motivation, personality traits Social status, Educational status, and Vocational status are would not be a significant predictor of vocational aspirations of Pre-university College female students
66. Achievement motivation, personality traits Social status, Educational status, and Vocational status are would not be a significant predictor of vocational aspirations of Pre-university College arts students

67. Achievement motivation, personality traits Social status, Educational status, and Vocational status are would not be a significant predictor of vocational aspirations of Pre-university College science students
68. Achievement motivation, personality traits Social status, Educational status, and Vocational status are would not be a significant predictor of vocational aspirations of Pre-university College Commerce students
69. Achievement motivation, personality traits Social status, Educational status, and Vocational status are would not be a significant predictor of vocational aspirations of Pre-university College Kannada medium students
70. Achievement motivation, personality traits Social status, Educational status, and Vocational status are would not be a significant predictor of vocational aspirations of Pre-university College English medium students
71. Achievement motivation, personality traits Social status, Educational status, and Vocational status are would not be a significant predictor of vocational aspirations of Pre-university government College students
72. Achievement motivation, personality traits Social status, Educational status, and Vocational status are would not be a significant predictor of vocational aspirations of Pre-university Aided College students
73. Achievement motivation, personality traits Social status, Educational status, and Vocational status are would not be a significant predictor of vocational aspirations of Pre-university Unaided College students
74. Achievement motivation, personality traits Social status, Educational status, and Vocational status are would not be a significant predictor of vocational aspirations of Pre-university College GM students
75. Achievement motivation, personality traits Social status, Educational status, and Vocational status are would not be a significant predictor of vocational aspirations of Pre-university College OBC students

76. Achievement motivation, personality traits Social status, Educational status, and Vocational status are would not be a significant predictor of vocational aspirations of Pre-university College SC/ST/Cat-I students
77. Achievement motivation, personality traits Social status, Educational status, and Vocational status are would not be a significant predictor of vocational aspirations of Pre-university College rural students
78. Achievement motivation, personality traits Social status, Educational status, and Vocational status are would not be a significant predictor of vocational aspirations of Pre-university College urban students.

Population and Sample

Population: All the students those who are studying Pre-university colleges comprises the population of the study.

Nature and size of the sample : The required sample for the study was drawn from first year Pre-university students using stratified random sampling technique. This technique was necessitated because of the representation to be given to various types of colleges and other independent variables. In Dharwad urban district, out of 43 colleges, 4 Government colleges, 20 Aided colleges and 19 Unaided colleges were selected. In Dharwad rural district out of 20 colleges, 7 Government colleges, 11 Aided colleges and 2 Unaided colleges existed the following tables show the total number of colleges in Dharwad district.

Table 3.1: Total Number of Government, Aided and Unaided Colleges in Dharwad District

District	*No. of Govt. Colleges*	*No. of Aided Colleges*	*No. of Unaided*	*Grand Total Colleges*
Dharwad (Urban)	4	20	19	43
Dharwad (Rural)	7	11	2	20
Total	11	31	21	63

Selection of Colleges: In order to study the vocational aspirations of Pre-university colleges, the investigator selected 30 colleges out of 63 colleges in Dharwad district.

Table 3.2. Composition of the Sample - Location-wise

Location	*No. of colleges selected*			*Total No. of students selected*
	Govt.	*Aided*	*Unaided*	
Urban	4	8	10	22
Rural	2	4	2	08
Total	6	12	12	30

From Dharwad urban district four Government colleges, eight Aided colleges and 10 Unaided colleges were selected through stratified random technique from which 500 students were drawn through simple random technique of which 250 are female and 250 are male. From Dharwad rural district, 2 Government colleges, 4 Aided colleges and 2 Unaided colleges were selected through stratified random technique from which 500 students were drawn through simple random technique of which 250 are female and 250 are male. The total ratio of the colleges (Government colleges, Aided colleges and Unaided colleges) is 1 : 2 : 2.

Total sample consisted of 1000 students (500 female and 500 male).

The distribution of the students is shown in the tables 3.3 to 3.5 :

Table 3.3. Students with different medium of instruction (Kannada and English) and locality (Rural and urban)

Rural						*Urban*					
Kannada			*English*			*Kannada*			*English*		
Male	*Female*	*Total*	*Male*	*Female*	*Total*	*Male*	*Female*	*Total*	*Male*	*Female*	*Total*
249	247	496	1	3	4	74	100	174	176	150	326
Grand total – 496 +4 = 500						174+326= 500					

Table 3.3 shows that the sample consisted 670 students from Kannada medium and 330 students from English medium. It also reveals that students selected from rural areas are 500 and students from urban areas are 500.

Table 3.4. Aided/Unaided/Government colleges belong to different Type of management along with Locality

Aided											
Rural						*Urban*					
Kannada			*English*			*Kannada*			*English*		
Male	*Female*	*Total*	*Male*	*Female*	*Total*	*Male*	*Female*	*Total*	*Male*	*Female*	*Total*
149	162	311	1	1	2	71	22	93	52	8	60
total 313						total 153					
Grand total 466											

Unaided											
Rural						*Urban*					
Kannada			*English*			*Kannada*			*English*		
Male	*Female*	*Total*	*Male*	*Female*	*Total*	*Male*	*Female*	*Total*	*Male*	*Female*	*Total*
33	36	69	—	—	—	1	53	54	90	134	224
total 69						total 278					
Grand total 237											

Unaided											
Rural						*Urban*					
Kannada			*English*			*Kannada*			*English*		
Male	*Female*	*Total*	*Male*	*Female*	*Total*	*Male*	*Female*	*Total*	*Male*	*Female*	*Total*
67	49	116	—	2	2	2	25	27	34	08	42
total 118						total 69					
Grand total 187											

Table 3.4 shows that Government Aided colleges in rural place consists 313 students as sample and in urban place it is 153 in total it is 466 students whereas sample in Unaided rural colleges is 69 and urban colleges is 278, in total it is 347. From Government colleges, 118 students were drawn from rural colleges and 69 students from urban, in total it is 187 students.

Table 3.5. Students belong to different categories and locality

	Rural							Urban						
	Kannada			English			Grand Total	Kannada			English			Grand Total
	Male	*Female*	*Total*	*Male*	*Female*	*Total*		*Male*	*Female*	*Total*	*Male*	*Female*	*Total*	
GM	35	33	68	0	1	1	69	22	27	49	94	60	154	203
OBC	168	193	361	1	-	-	361	43	60	103	61	69	130	233
SC	16	08	24	01	-	1	25	05	05	10	13	10	23	33
ST	16	09	25	-	-	-	25	02	05	07	01	04	05	12
Cat-I	14	04	18	-	2	2	20	02	03	05	07	07	14	19

Table 3.5 reveals that number of students belong to each categories (GM, OBC, SC/ST/Cat-I).

Tools Used for Collecting Data

1. Vocational Aspiration Scale – Grewal (1973)
2. High School Students Personality Questionnaire – Cattell (1965)
3. Achievement Motivation Inventory constructed and Standardized by the researcher
4. Social Status Scale constructed by the researcher to collect data on education and occupation of parents

Description of the Tools

Vocational Aspiration Scale

Data relating to vocational aspiration wear collected using Vocational Aspiration Scale (OAS). This tool developed by Grewal (1973) which was adopted by getting the prestige rating of 150 vocational titles, identical with the list prepared by the National Opinion Research Centre (NORC, 1974) of the U.S.A. These titles were taken from the *Dictionary of Vocational Titles of India*. This number was reduced to 108 by a panel of judges who were employed in different occupations. The final list was administered on 200 persons and they were asked to rate each occupation on a five point scale ranging from an occupation of 'excellent' to 'poor' standing. Social standing of each occupation was calculated out of a rank of 100 by multiplying frequency ratings in each of the five categories by 1.0, 0.8, 0.6, 0.4, 0.2 respectively. Thus, all '0' at '9' depending upon their ranks ranged from '20' to '95' and above. Eighty out of 108 occupations with different prestige values were arranged in mixed order in eight multiple choice items in the format given below :

- Primary school teachers.
- Diplomat in foreign service.
- Barber.
- Psychologist.
- Motor mechanic.
- Traveling salesman.
- Postman.

It should be emphasized to the respondents that there are no "right" or "wrong" answers and that they are not bound by a time limit.

It is reported by Haller and Miller (1967) and also by Grewal (1973) that some of the respondents feel that they need more information. But the semi-projective nature of the Vocational Aspiration Scale requires that the tester gives no information beyond that which is specified leaving the testing situation as unstructured as possible. The test booklets are usable but separate answer sheet can also be provided. Like other tests and scales, the Vocational Aspiration Scale is also favourable. This limitation, however, can be overcome by giving specific instructions to the respondents. A proper rapport with the respondents is also necessary before the scale is administered.

Scoring Instructions

All the eight items are scored in the same way. There are ten alternatives for each question. Only one alternative may be checked. The scores for each alternative are as follows:

Alternative	*Score*
1	7
2	4
3	8
4	2
Alternative	*Score*
5	9
6	0
7	6
8	3
9	6
10	1

The total score is the sum of the scores for each of the eight questions.

The raw scores may be converted into standard or 't' scores depending upon the purpose of the study.

Norms

Norms have been determined by administering the scale to 1375 higher secondary students belonging to different sex, age, grade, residence and cultural groups.

Reliability

Co-efficient of stability as determined by the test-retest method was found to be 0.84. The test was further divided into two parallel halves (A and B) for assessing the internal consistency.

The co-efficient of internal consistency between the two halves, A and B, was found to be 0.54.

Validity

The OAS has been validated against Haller and Miller 'Vocational Aspiration' Scale (1973). The co-efficient of validity was found to be 0.75.

High School Personality Questionnaire (HSPQ)

The overwhelming verdict of research findings as well as clinical evidence shows that to predict almost anything effectively, at least a dozen unitary traits generally need to be taken in to account (Cattelle 1969).

For the general assessment of personality, High School Personality Questionnaire (HSPQ) is a standardized test which measures fourteen distinct dimensions or traits of personality thereby it nearly covers total personality. These fourteen factors are Reserved vs Warmhearted, Less Intelligent vs More Intelligent, Affected by feelings vs Emotionally Stable, Undemonstrative vs Excitable, Obedient vs Assertive, Sober vs Enthusiastic, Disregards Rules vs Conscientious, Shy vs Adventurous, Tough-minded vs Tender-minded, Zestful vs Circumspect Individualism, Self assured vs Apprehensive, Sociably Group-dependent vs Self-sufficient, Uncontrolled vs Controlled and Relaxed vs Tense. These traits are also designated alphabetically as A, B, C, D, E, F, G, H, I, J, O, Q2, Q3 and Q4 respectively. The description of these fourteen personality factors is given in Table 3.6.

Keeping this in mind the personality of the children was assessed in the present study, using Cattell's junior- senior High School Personality Questionnaire (HSPQ). The HSPQ covers all the major dimensions of personality which are factor analytically demonstrable in any attempt to describe individual differences comprehensively. It deals with psychologically meaningful and predicatively important traits having demonstrable functional unity, such as are central to any discussion in general psychological theory.

The HSPQ handles the multiplicity of predictions from one test, but not from one score. It helps to obtain scores on fourteen

Table 3.6. Brief Description of the Fourteen Personality Traits

Factors	*Low Score Description*	Alphabetic Designation	High Score Description
A	Reserved, Detached, Critical, Cool (Sizothymia)	A	Outgoing, Warm Hearted, Easy Going, Participating (Affectothymia, Formerly Cyclothymia)
B	Less Intelligent, Concrete Thinking (Lower Scholastic Mental Capacity)	B	More Intelligent, Abstract Thinking, Bright (Higher Scholastic Mental Capacity)
C	Affected By Feelings, Emotionally Less Stable, Easily Upset, Changeable (Lower Ego Strength)	C	Emotionally Stable, Faces Reality, Calm (Higher Ego Strength)
D	Phlegmatic, Deliberate, Inactive, Stodgy (Phlegmatic Temperament)	D	Excitable, Impatient, Demanding, Overactive (Excitability)
E	Obedient, Mild, Conforming(submissiveness)	E	Assertive, Independent Aggressive, Stubborn (Dominance)
F	Sober, Prudent, Serious, Taciturn(desurgency)	F	Happy-go-lucky, Impulsively Lively, Gay Enthusiastic (Surgency)
G	Expedient, Evades Rules, Feels Few Obligations (Weaker Superego Strength)	G	Conscientious, Persevering, Staid, Rule-bound (Stronger Superego Strength)
H	Shy, Restrained, Diffident, Timid (Threctia)	H	Venturesome, Socially Bold Uninhibited, Spontaneous (Parmia)
I	Tough-minded, Self-Reliant, Realistic, No-nonsense (Harrla)	I	Tender-minded, Dependent over Protected, Sensitive (Premsia)
J	Vigorous, Goes, Readily With Group Zestful, Given To Action (Zeppla)	J	Doubting, Obstructive, Individualistic, Internally Restrained, Reflective, Unwilling to Act (Coasthenia)
O	Placid, Self-assured, Confident, Serene (Untroubled Adequacy)	O	Apprehensive, Worrying Depressive, Troubled (Guilt Proneness)
Q2	Group-dependent, A "Joiner" And Sound Follower (group Adherence)	Q2	Self-sufficient, Prefers Own Dicisions, Resourceful (Self Sufficiency)
Q3	Undisciplined Self-Conflict, Follows Own Urges, Careless of Protocol (Low Integration)	Q3	Controlled, Socially, Precise Self-disciplined, Compulsive (High Self-concept Control)
Q4	Relaxed, Tranquil, Torpid, Unfrustrated (Low Ergic Tension)	Q4	Tense, Frustrated, Driven Overwrought(high Ergic Tension)

dimensions of personality. These future dimensions which have been confirmed to various experiments cover relatively independent aspects of personality. They represent basic concepts which are understood by psychology, so that insightful understanding of the individual and his development as well as statistical prediction is possible. The above points weighed in favour of selecting the HSPQ for assessing the personality traits of the children.

Having decided to use the HSPQ the questionnaire was translated into Kannada. The regional language of the subjects on whom it had to be used. The translation was checked by three judges who were well versed with psychological testing. Terms which were ambiguous were discussed and resolved. The Kannada version thus prepared was administered to a small group of 10 children of X class. They were asked to answer the items and also check those words which they could not understand such of those terms which the children marked were modified or substituted with simpler words.

Administration

The purpose of the tool and procedure were explained to the students in advance. This HSPQ consisted of 142 questions per booklet. The investigator then readout the instructions and the students were required to put tick mark for one of the statements in answer sheet. Answer sheet is given with the question booklet. 45 minutes of time should be taken for the questionnaire.

Scoring

The completed answer sheet is the usual record for obtaining the score. In special cases, e.g., an unusually young student, who has been allowed to answer directly on the questionnaire booklet, it will save total scoring time to transfer the responses to an answer sheet before scoring.

The answer sheet is scored by a streamlined hand stencil key. An experienced clerk can obtain the fourteen scores on an answer sheet in little more than a minute. Conveniently, the same key is applicable to all four forms. The scoring instructions are as follows:

1. Check to see that each question has been given one and only one, answer. At the same time, note whether there are gross oddities of response which could upset the key. Principally, which for the occasional child who

marks all positions, or who proceeds mechanically to mark all right hand responses, etc., reject such answer sheets.

2. Place cardboard stencil key number 1 on the left hand side of the answer sheet, adjusting it as described right on the key. All necessary instructions for applying the hand stencil key to get "raw scores" for seven of the factors are also printed on the key itself. Same thing is done with cardboard stencil key number 2 to get the other seven raw scores.

Standardization: Norms in STENS and CENTILES

Although there are a few purposes for which the raw scores suffice, most uses require the raw scores, listed on the right of the answer sheet, to be converted to standard scores. The main standard scores are stens, in which a person can score from 1 to 10; but, additionally, scores can be converted to centiles, which show what rank the examinee would have in a group of a hundred people. The average score on the sten scale would be 5.5. (not 5, since there is no 0 in the ten-point range). The average or middle range scores are actually considered as the values 4,5,6 and 7. The more extreme sten scores represent a person in the lower (1,2,3) or upper (8,9,10) ten or fifteen percent of the population (of this age group) on the characteristic indicated. To obtain the sten score or centile rank, simply take the raw score to get from applying the scoring key and enter in the appropriate table in the Tabular Supplement with Norms published separately for this test.

Reliability: The HSPQ was found highly reliable. Its reliability was examined at varying interval of time. The test-retest reliability factor-wise is as follows (Table 3.7) :

Table 3.7. Reliability Co-efficient for HSPQ

Interval Retest	*HSPQ FACTORS*													
	A	*B*	*C*	*D*	*E*	*F*	*G*	*H*	*I*	*J*	*Q1*	*Q2*	*Q3*	*Q4*
Immediate	.86	.85	.79	.81	.76	.82	.74	.81	.90	.82	.84	.85	.80	.91
After one day	.85	.78	.77	.80	.74	.76	.72	.81	.88	.81	.83	.82	.78	.84
After six months	.62	.60	.58	.65	.57	.53	.62	.69	.65	.58	.56	.55	.60	.58
After one year	.55	.38	.50	.55	.47	.52	.44	.48	.69	.49	.56	.39	.41	.39

Validity: The estimation of validity based on the multiple correlations between the items in each test scale and the corresponding pure factor are shown in the table appended below.

HSPQ FACTORS

A	B	C	D	E	F	G	H	I	J	Q1	Q2	Q3	Q4
.80	.81	.84	.77	.79	.81	.81	.84	.82	.72	.86	.74	.72	.85

Consistency: The term consistency is used to describe the content to which the individual scales of the test show inter and intra form agreement. This is conceptually broader than what is generally implied by test reliability and subsumes reliability as well as other indices of scale agreement.

Reliability is the agreement of a test with itself over time, when re-administered at brief intervals (dependability), or after longer periods (stability) where maturation, learning or fluctuation – real changes in the trait itself tend to lower the reliability values.

Conclusion: In order to enable the students studying in Kannada medium schools to understand the meaning of the statement better and also to know clearly what is expected from them, the HSPQ was translated into Kannada. The Kannada version of the test was administered on a sample of students to ascertain the clarity of expression.

Achievement Motivation Inventory

The large incidence of failure in the pre-university examination has been of great concern not only to the parents but also to the educators. With the constitutional provision aimed at making the elementary education free and compulsory throughout the country, the scope and responsibility of the educators have added new dimensions. One of the concerns of the educators has been how to maximize the achievement of all children with due recognition to individual difference in ability. Although there are many studies pertaining to achievement and abilities of adults, there are very few studies related to the motivational component of pupils achievement behaviour.

Reviews on Achievement Motivation Inventories

The first major report of the experimental work on measurement of human motivation, particularly the achievement motive, appeared in 1953. McCelland (1958) adapted Murry's TAT technique (1938) for the measurement of achievement motive. In this technique, certain pictures are used to obtain stories from the subjects on the basis of which, achievement motivation scores were derived.

The review of related literature reveals that it is only after 1966, that efforts were made to develop some techniques for the measurement of achievement motivation in our country. Researchers developed a sentence completion test with three alternatives for measuring the achievement motivation of adult males. It is developed a short scale consisting of six items for measuring the achievement motivation of farmers. Aaron *et al.* (1969) developed a projective technique consisting of five pictures for measuring the n-achievement of Secondary school male from South India. Mehta (1960) adapted McCelland (1958) TAT technique for assessing the level of need achievement of students.

A review on Indian test materials indicates that practically less number of inventories was developed on Achievement Motivation. It was therefore decided to construct a new instrument in English and Kannada on n-achievement with the statements for the population of pre-university college students.

Pooling the Statement

The items were constructed on the basis of description of the concept in the psychological literature, discussion with psychologists and the existing scales. As the purpose was to develop the achievement motivation inventory, only such of the statements pertaining to achievement motivation of the subjects were written.

As a result, 40 statements were written with four distractors. In each statement one statement was designed to have reference to achievement imagery and the other designed to have reference to doubtful achievement imagery. All the statements of the first category (achievement imagery) possessed one of the following criteria as enunciated by McClelland (1958, 1961).

1. Success in competition with a standard of excellence,
2. Unique accomplishment,
3. Long term involvement and
4. The desire to excel regardless of social rewards.

The second category of statements designated to contain doubtful achievement imagery had reference to either a common lace task or solving a routine problem or a social reward. All the statements were relevant to the situations close to the subjects. While preparing the statements, the age, academic level and mental ability of the subjects were kept in mind. The statements were direct, simple and unambiguous and directly related to the achievement motivation.

The 40 pairs of statements were edited and scrutinized again and again with the help of experts in that field and according to their suggestions. Thirty six statements were retained in the final list of the inventory.

Pre-study

The final list of inventory consists of 36 statements. These statements of 36 were administered to 20 male and 20 female of Ist year Pre-university randomly selected. These students were able to understand these statements easily and responded to them without any difficulty. Therefore these 36 statements were retained without any modification in the inventory and the pilot study was undertaken. Clear instructions were given on the top of the inventory as to what the respondents have to do. The pilot form of the achievement motivation inventory is given in the Appendix-

Pilot Study

The printed inventory was administered on a random sample of 100 students of Pre-university from four different colleges for a pilot study. In each college the inventory was administered to 25 students at a time. The investigator read out statements of each item together. The students had to listen to them carefully and they had to make a choice between the four distractors and tick out only one statement in the brackets provided against it.

Scoring

The scoring key was prepared along with the inventory. The right statements in the items with score one and the wrong items with zero. In other words a score was given to a statement pertaining to achievement imagery (AI) and no score was given to statement pertaining to the doubtful achievement imagery (DAI).

Item Selection

Numerous methods of expressing the discriminatory power of an item have been proposed in measurement literature. As far back as 1935, Long and Sandiford described 23 different methods of expressing item discrimination, Guilford (1967) listed 19 methods for calculating item discrimination. However the methods most commonly used by test constructors for assessing item discrimination are the correlation between each item and a criterion. If the co-efficient correlation is high one would expect correspondence between the trait as measured by the test and the item score. The most commonly used co-efficient correlations with dichotomously scored items are the point biserial and the biserial correlation co-efficient. Both were developed from the Pearson product moment correlation. The point biserial co-efficient is recommended when one of the variables being correlated represents a true dichotomy and the other variable (criterion or total test score) is continuous and normally distributed. Guilford (1967) has argued in favour of point biserial correlation on the basis that items selected using this method contribute more towards internal consistency and test variability, their items selected using biserial correlation co-efficient.

The discriminating index of the item was worked out through point biserial correlation between the top and bottom 27 per cent of total scores.

Final Form of Inventory

Thirty-two items were retained in the final inventory. The final achievement motivation inventory is given in the Appendix.

In the field of achievement motivation, a number of tools are available for the measurement of achievement motivation. To mention a few, some of them are the following. Mehta's (1960) achievement motivation test, a sentence completion test developed by Mukherjee, Mehta's adopted version of McClelland's Thematic Appreciation test, Thematic Appreciation test instrument to measure achievement by Aaron, Marihal and Malatesha, Achievement motivation Inventory.

For the measurement of achievement motivation in the present study, an inventory developed by the investigator was used.

The achievement motivation inventory consisted of thirty two items with four alternatives for each item, and the respondents were required to check one of the four alternatives. Among four alternatives, one is related to achievement motivation and remaining three is unrelated. For responding to all the statements of the inventory, the time stipulated was thirty minutes.

Administration

Before the administration of the tool, a psychological rapport was built up with the students. The students were taken into confidence and were requested to cooperate and help the researcher in carrying the investigation. They were informed that whatever the information they give would be kept confidential and used for the purpose of research only. Each student was given a copy of the inventory and explained how to respond to the statements in the test.

The students were told to read each item and its responses carefully and to put a tick mark against the response which they thought most appropriate. An example was also given.

Scoring Procedure

This inventory consists of 32 items and each item is followed by 4 alternatives. The students were asked to mark one of the alternatives among 4 alternatives. A score of +1 is given when the student has marked an achievement related alternative. Zero for the unrelated. The total score on the inventory is calculated by adding the total number of items marked as related one.

Reliability

The reliability of achievement motivation inventory developed by the investigator was established by using the split-Half technique. The reliability coefficient is found to be 0.63. The coefficient indicates that it is a reliable test to measure achievement motivation as given by investigator.

Validity

The items for the test were selected in terms of the degree to which they differentiated between the upper and lower percent of individuals in a distribution of scores. The validity of the inventory is found to be 0.79.

Social Status Scale

Among the social factors social status is an important one. The social status influences values, norms of behaviour, achievement motivation and social participation. It is worth studying here whether the social status has got any bearing on the vocational aspirations of the students in Pre-university colleges.

Different SES scales have been developed by Kuppuswamy (1962) and others. But some of these scales (e.g., Kuppuswamy) are constructed to be used on urban samples, while some others were developed to be used exclusively on rural children. this difficulty is overcome in a scale developed by Aaron, *et al.* (1970) since it was constructed to be used on urban as well as rural children.

It contains all relevant items related to the social status of the family, educational level of the father, educational level of the mother, occupational level of father and occupational level of mother. Thus the scale can be reasonably well assumed to have construct validity.

Therefore, in the present study "A Common Social status Scale for rural and Urban Areas" constructed by the researcher which is based on the scale Aaron, *et al.* (1970) was used. This tool is suitable for rural and urban areas. Following is the brief description of the social status scale.

The scale has four categories; each category consists of seven items. The subject has to put a cross mark in the brocket given against the suitable answer.

The investigator emphasized the following two ideas which influenced the construction of the scale.

1. The information elicited should be simple and reliable.
2. The ultimate aim of the scale is to identify and isolate groups of rural and urban people of similar social status.

Variables of the Scal

The variables used in this scale have been tested by other researchers and the combinations of these and other indicators are correlated well with measures of attitude and behaviour of the seven variables. First one refers to fathers' education; second one to mothers' education and third one to father's occupation and fourth one to mother's occupation. Regarding the weightages given to various items under seven categories, the investigator followed trail and error method of revising the weightages in a systematic way in order to obtain a normal distribution of the social status scores of rural and urban distributions.

Validity and Reliability

The validity and reliability for the entire social status scale were established. The concurrent validity of the scale was obtained by finding to what extent the scores obtained by pupils on the social status scale correspond to an outside criterion i.e., the social status scale score assigned by the teacher of the class where the pupils were studying. The Pearson's Product Moment correlation co-efficient was computed. The test-retest reliability was obtained by retesting after one month. The validity and reliability co-efficient were as follows:

Concurrent validity (N = 28) = 0.61 significant beyond 0.01

Test-retest (N= 23) = 0.77 significant beyond 0.01

Scoring procedure

There are seven categories viz., Education of father, Education of mother, occupation of father and occupation of mother. The subject was given a score under each of these categories so that the final social status index was the total of these scores. Only the maximum possible score was considered under each category. The scores of course, depended upon the weightage of the item. For instance, under category III (father's occupation) the subject may mark the first one i.e., 'unemployed' which has a weightage of 1 and for 'High school teacher/technician' a weightage 6 to be given. Eventually the scores of all seven categories were added and this represents the social status index.

The social status index was divided into two different levels higher and lower.

A copy of the social status scale used for collecting the data in this study is given in Appendix.

Statistical Techniques used for Analysis of the Data

The following techniques were used for analyzing the data as per the objectives of the study stated earlier

(*i*) Descriptive analysis.
(*ii*) Differential analysis.
(*iii*) Correlational analysis.
(*iv*) Regression analysis.

The analyses and interpretation of results is presented in succeeding pages that is Chapter-4.

4

Data Analyses and Results

Introduction

However valid, reliable and adequate the data may be, it does not serve any useful purpose unless it is carefully processed, systematically classified and tabulated, scientifically analyzed, intelligently interpreted and rationally concluded.

After the data had been collected, it was processed and tabulated using Microsoft Excel - 2000 Software. The data collected on Vocational aspiration, Personality traits and its factors (A, B, C, D, E, F, G, H, I, J, O, Q2, Q3, Q4), Achievement Motivation and its dimensions (Long term involvement, Unique accomplishment, Success in competition with standard of excellence, Desire to excel regardless of social reward) and Social status and its dimensions (Education and Occupation) of Pre-university college students of Dharwad district. Then the data were analyzed with reference to the objectives and hypotheses and then analyzed by using descriptive statistics, differential analysis including unpaired t-test, One way ANOVA, Two way analysis of variance with interaction, Pearson's correlation coefficient and step wise multiple linear regression analysis by using SPSS 11.0 statistical software and the results obtained there by have been interpreted.

It is also the intention of the investigator to find the out whether differences in the independent variables namely Sex, medium of Institution (Kannada and English), Type of managements (Government, Aided and unaided), Birth order (1-2, 3-4 and 5+), Caste (GM, OBC, SC, ST, Cat-I), Locality (Rural and urban), Personality traits (High and Low), and Social status

(High and Low) of Pre-university college students and consequently others.

The purpose of the convenience, the different sections of chapter IV of the study has been organized under the following sections:

1. Descriptive statistics and Differential statistics.
2. Differential statistics in the independent variables on Vocational aspirations of Pre-university college students i.e. Interaction effects of independent variable on Vocational aspiration of Pre-university college students of Dharwad district.
3. Correlation analysis using Karl's Pearson's coefficient correlation independent variables and on Vocational aspirations of Pre-university college students of Dharwad district
4. Regression analysis of independent variables and on Vocational aspirations of Pre-university college students of Dharwad district

Descriptive Analysis

In this section mean and standard values of vocational aspirations were calculated according to independent variables namely Sex, subjects, medium of instruction, Type of managements, Birth order, Category, Location, Achievement motivation (High and Low), Social status (High and Low) and Personality traits (High and Low) of Pre-university college students and presented in the following section.

Table 4.1. Mean and SD Scores of Vocational Aspirations by Sex

Summary	*Male*	*Female*	*Total*
Means	47.9020	48.0480	47.9750
SD	10.3190	8.5919	9.4903

Table 4.1 reveals the Mean and SD values of vocational aspirations of Pre-university College students by Sex.

The total mean of vocational aspirations of Pre-university college students is 47.9750 ± 9.4903 in which the female students have little higher vocational aspirations (48.0480 ± 8.5919) than the male students (47.9020 ± 10.3190) of Pre-university colleges of Dharwad district.

The Mean and SD values of vocational aspirations by Sex are also presented in Fig. 4.1.

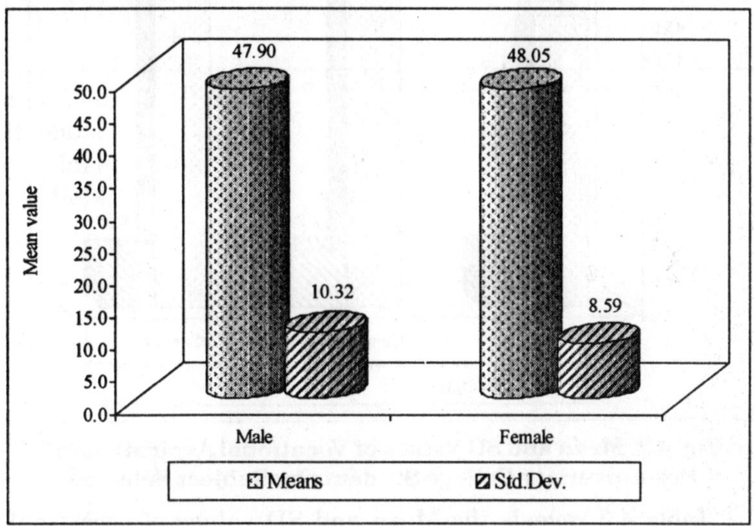

Fig. 4.1. Mean and SD Values of Vocational Aspirations of Pre-University College Students by Gender

Table 4.2 reveals the Mean and SD values of vocational aspirations of Pre-university College students by subjects selected (Arts, Science and Commerce).

Table 4.2. Mean and SD Scores of Vocational Aspirations of Students Based on their Subjects (Arts, Science and Commerce)

Summary	*Arts*	*Science*	*Commerce*	*Total*
Means	45.3207	52.7517	48.3129	47.9750
Std.Dev.	9.0577	8.6573	8.8904	9.4903

The total mean of vocational aspirations of Pre-university college students is 47.9750±9.4903 in which the (students studying) science subject have higher vocational aspirations (52.7517±8.6573) followed by students studying Commerce (48.3129±8.8904) and students studying Arts(45.32079.0577) of Pre-university colleges.

The Mean and SD values of vocational aspirations by subjects selected (Arts, Science and Commerce) are also presented in the following figure.

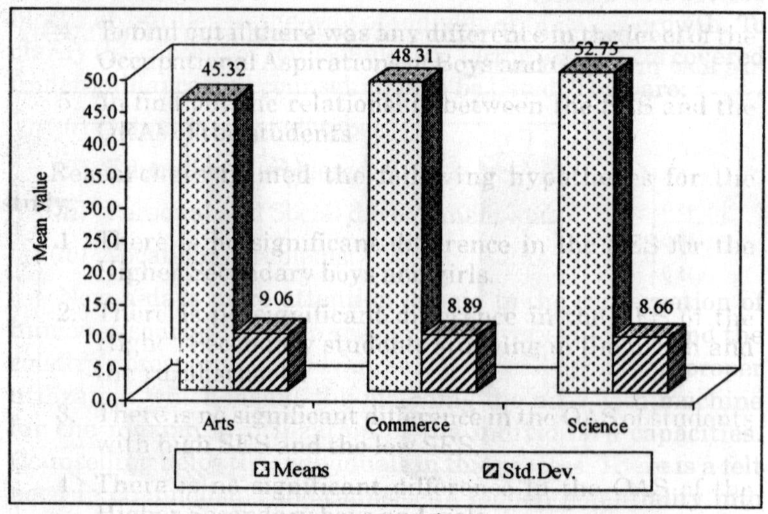

Fig. 4.2. Mean and SD Values of Vocational Aspirations of Pre-university College Students by Subject Selected

Table 4.3 reveals the Mean and SD values of vocational aspirations of Pre-university College students by medium of instruction (Kannada and English).

Table 4.3. Mean and SD Scores of Vocational Aspirations by Medium of Instruction

Summary	*Kannada*	*English*	*Total*
Means	45.7851	52.4212	47.9750
SD	9.1419	8.5992	9.4903

The total mean of vocational aspirations of Pre-university college students is 47.9750±9.4903 in which the English medium students have higher vocational aspirations (52.4212±8.5992) than the Kannada medium students (45.7851±9.1419) of Pre-university colleges.

The Mean and SD values of vocational aspirations by medium of instruction (Kannada and English) are also presented in Fig. 4.3.

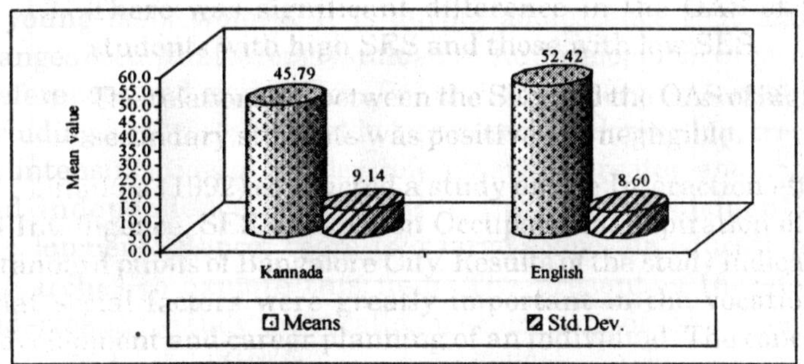

Fig. 4.3. Mean and SD Values of Vocational Aspiration of Pre-University College Students by Medium of Instruction

Table 4.4 reveals the Mean and SD values of vocational aspirations of Pre-university College students by Type of management (Government, Aided and Unaided).

Table 4.4. Mean and SD Scores of Vocational Aspirations by Type of Management (Government, Aided and Unaided)

Summary	*Government*	*Aided*	*Unaided*	*Total*
Means	45.4706	46.5258	51.2709	47.9750
SD	9.2657	9.7507	8.3071	9.4903

The total mean of vocational aspirations of Pre-university college students is 47.9750±9.4903 in which the unaided college students have higher vocational aspirations (51.2709±8.3071) followed by aided college students (46.5258±9.7507) and government college students (45.4706±9.2657) of Pre-university colleges.

The Mean and SD values of vocational aspirations by type of management (Government, Aided and Unaided) are also presented in Fig. 4.4.

Table 4.5 reveals the Mean and SD values of vocational aspirations of Pre-university College stu1dents by birth order (1-3, 3-4, and 5 and more than 5) in the family.

The total mean vocational aspirations of Pre-university college students is 47.9750±9.4903 in which the students belong to 1-2 order of birth in the family have higher vocational aspirations (48.1659±9.4984) followed by students belong to 5 and more than 5 order of birth (47.6250±8.3903) and students belong to 3-4 order of birth (47.5934±9.7286) of Pre-university colleges.

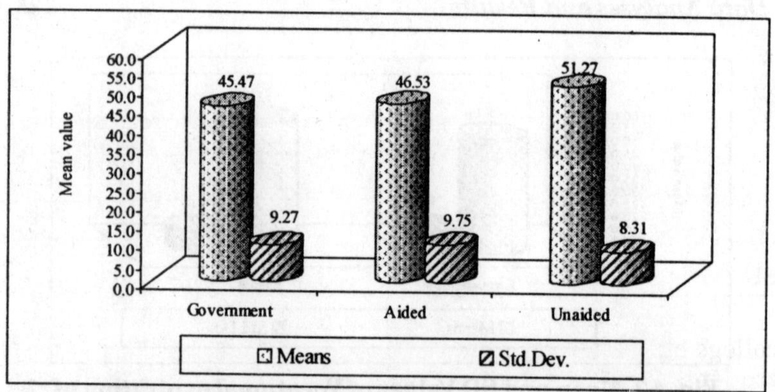

Fig. 4.4. Mean and SD Values of Vocational Aspirations of Pre-university College Students by Types of Management

Table 4.5. Mean and SD Scores of Vocational Aspirations by Birth Order in the Family (1-3, 3-4, and 5 and more than 5)

Summary	*1-2*	*3-4*	*5 and more than 5*	*Total*
Means	48.1659	47.5934	47.6250	47.9750
SD	9.4984	9.7286	8.3903	9.4903

The Mean and SD values of vocational aspirations by birth orders (1-3, 3-4, and 5 and more than 5) are also presented in Fig. 4.5.

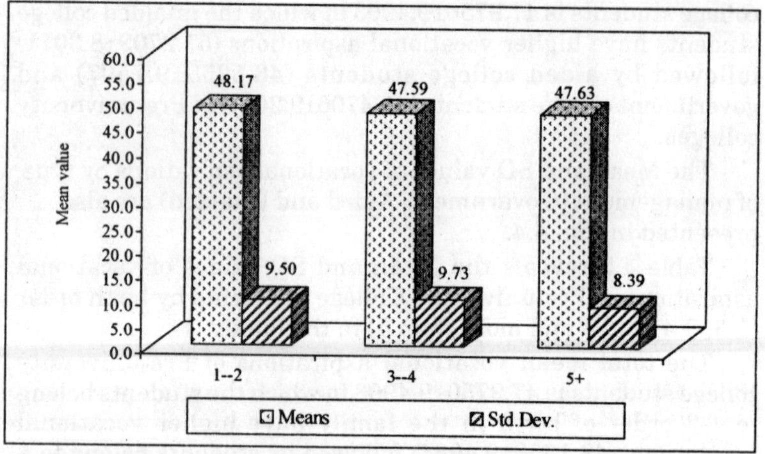

Fig. 4.5. Mean and SD Values of Vocational Aspirations of Pre-University College Students byBirth Order

Table 4.6 reveals the Mean and SD values of vocational aspirations of Pre-university College students by category (GM, OBC, SC/ST/Cat-I).

Table 4.6. Mean and SD Scores of Vocational Aspirations by Category (GM, OBC, SC/ST/Cat-I)

Summary	*GM*	*OBC*	*SC/ST/Cat-I*	*Total*
Means	50.5478	47.1684	46.3284	47.9750
SD	9.1336	9.3328	9.9501	9.4903

The total mean of vocational aspirations of Pre-university college students is 47.9750±9.4903 in which the GM category students have higher vocational aspirations (50.5478±9.1336) followed by OBC category students (47.1684±9.3328) and SC/ST/Cat-I category students (46.3284±9.9501) of Pre-university colleges.

The Mean and SD values of vocational aspirations by category (GM, OBC, SC/ST/Cat-I) are also presented in Fig. 4.6.

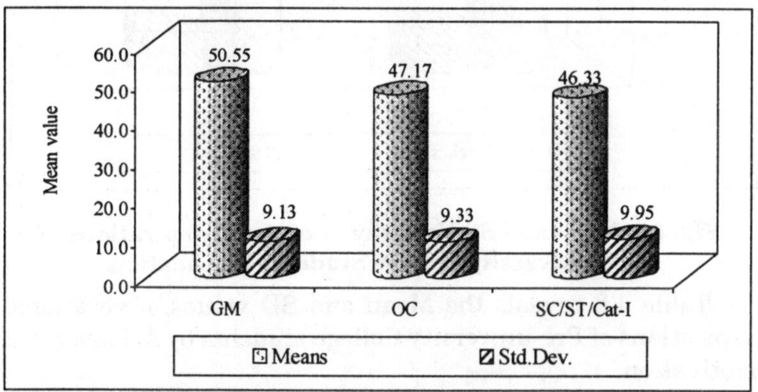

Fig. 4.6. Mean and SD Values of Vocational Aspirations of Pre-University College Students by Category

Table 4.7 reveals the Mean and SD values of vocational aspirations of Pre-university College students by Location (Rural and Urban).

Table 4.7 Mean and SD Scores of Vocational Aspirationsby Location

Summary	*Rural*	*Urban*	*Total*
Means	45.1760	50.7740	47.9750
Std.Dev.	9.2021	8.9406	9.4903

The total mean of vocational aspirations of Pre-university college students is 47.9750±9.4903 in which the urban students have higher vocational aspirations (50.7740±8.9406) than the rural students (45.1760±9.2021) of Pre-university colleges.

The Mean and SD values of vocational aspirations by location are also presented in the Fig. 4.7.

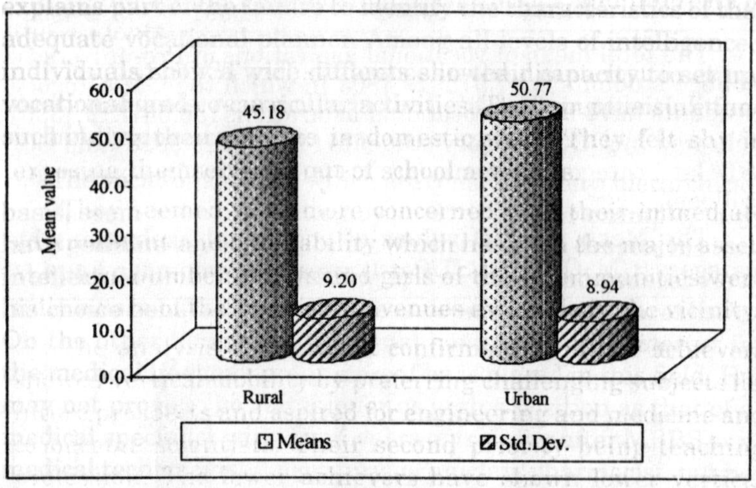

Fig. 4.7. Mean and SD Values of Vocational Aspirations of Pre-University College Students by Location

Table 4.8 reveals the Mean and SD values of vocational aspirations of Pre-university College students by Achievement motivation.

Table 4.8. Mean and SD Scores of Vocational Aspirations by Achievement Motivation

Summary	*Low achievement motivation*	*High achievement motivation*	*Total*
Means	46.7687	49.5228	47.9750
SD	9.8419	8.7906	9.4903

The total mean of vocational aspirations of Pre-university college students is 47.9750±9.4903 in which the students with high achievement motivation have higher vocational aspirations

(49.5228±8.7906) than the students with low achievement motivation (46.7687±9.8419) of Pre-university colleges.

The Mean and SD values of vocational aspirations by achievement motivation are also presented in Fig. 4.8.

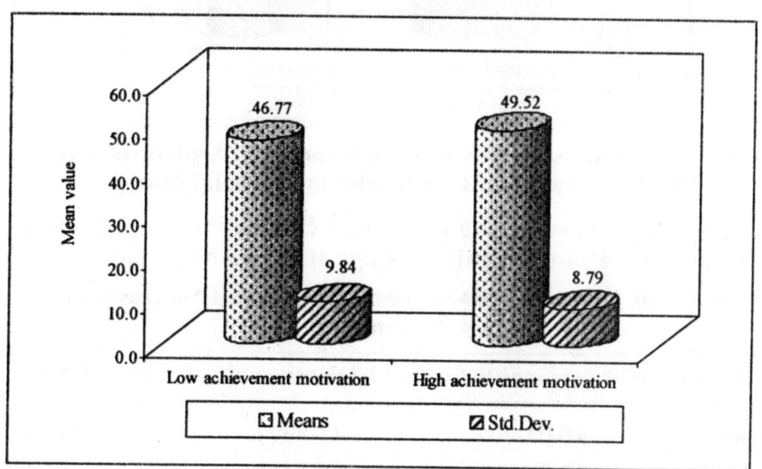

Fig. 4.8. Mean and SD Values of Vocational Aspirations of Pre-University College Students by Achievement Motivation

Table 4.9 the Mean and SD values of vocational aspirations of Pre-university college students by social status.

Table 4.9. Mean and SD Scores of Vocational Aspirations by Social Status

Summary	*Low social status*	*High social status*	*Total*
Means	46.2932	50.2319	47.9750
Std.Dev.	9.4029	9.1426	9.4903

The total mean of vocational aspirations of Pre-university college students is 47.9750±9.4903 in which the students with High social status have higher vocational aspirations (50.2319±9.1426) than the students with low social status (46.2932±9.4029) of Pre-university colleges.

The Mean and SD values of vocational aspirations by social status are also presented in Fig. 4.9.

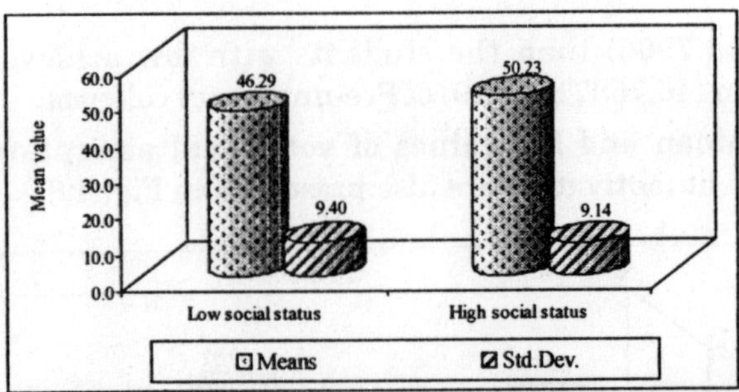

Fig. 4.9. Meant and SD Values of Vocational Aspirations of Pre-University College Students by Social Status

Table 4.10 reveals the Mean and SD values of vocational aspirations of Pre-university College students by personality.

Tabl 4.10. Mean and SD Scores of Vocational Aspirations by Personality

Summary	*Low personality traits s*	*High personality traits s*	*Total*
Means	48.0130	47.9307	47.9750
Std.Dev.	10.0200	8.8443	9.4903

The total mean of vocational aspirations of Pre-university college students is 47.9750±9.4903 in which the students with low personality have higher vocational aspirations (48.0130±10.0200) than the students with high personality (47.9307±8.8443) of Pre-university colleges.

The Mean and SD values of vocational aspirations by personality are also presented in Fig. 4.10.

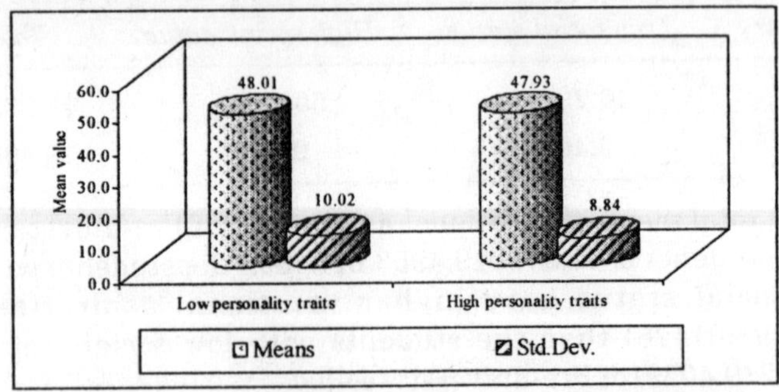

Fig. 4.10. Meant and SD Values of Vocational Aspirations of Pre-University College Students by Personality

Differential Analysis

Hypothesis: Male and female students of Pre-university college students do not differ significantly with respect to their vocational aspirations.

To test this hypothesis, the t-test was applied and the results are presented in Table 4.11.

Table 4.11. Results of t-test between Male and Female Students of Pre-University College Students with Respect to Vocational aspirations

Sex	*n*	*Mean*	*SD*	*t-value*	*p-value*	*Signi.*
Male	500	47.9020	10.3190	-0.2431	>0.05	NS
Female	500	48.0480	8.5919			

The above table clearly indicates that the male and female students of Pre-university college students do not differ significantly with respect to their vocational aspirations (t=-0.2431, >0.05) at 0.05% level of significance. Hence, the null hypothesis is accepted and alternative hypothesis is rejected. It can be concluded that the male and female students of Pre-university College students have same vocational aspirations.

Hypothesis: There is no significant difference between the students studying different subjects (Arts, Science, and Commerce) of Pre-University College with respect to their vocational aspirations.

To test this hypothesis, the one-way Analysis of variance (ANOVA) test was applied and the results are presented in Table 4.12.

Table 4.12. Results of Analysis of Variance (ANOVA) test between Students Studying Different Subjects (Arts, Science, and Commerce) with Respect to Vocational Aspirations

SV	*DF*	*SS*	*MSS*	*F-value*	*P-value*	*Signi.*
Between subjects	2	10726.23	5363.1168	67.4703	<0.01	S
Within subjects	997	79250.14	79.4886			
Total	999	89976.38				

The above table reveals that the Arts, Science and Commerce students of Pre-university college differ significantly with respect to their vocational aspirations (F=67.4703, <0.01) at 0.01% level of significance. Hence, the null hypothesis is rejected and alternative hypothesis is accepted. It can be concluded that Arts, Science and Commerce students of Pre-university College students have different vocational aspirations.

As F is significant, to know the pairs of Arts, Science and Commerce students of Pre-university College t-test was applied and the results are presented in Table 4.13.

Table 4.13. Results of t-test between Students Studying Arts, Science and Commerce Subjects with Respect to Vocational Aspirations

Subjects	*n*	*Mean*	*SD*	*t-value*	*p-value*	*Signi.*
Arts	555	45.3207	9.0577	-11.6001	<0.01	S
Science	298	52.7517	8.6573			
Arts	555	45.3207	9.0577	-3.5750	<0.01	S
Commerce	147	48.3129	8.8904			
Science	298	52.7517	8.6573	5.0419	<0.01	S
Commerce	147	48.3129	8.8904			

The above table reveals that:

1. The Arts and Science students of Pre-University College differ significantly with respect to their vocational aspirations (t=-11.6001, <0.01) at 0.01% level of significance. Hence, the null hypothesis is rejected and alternative hypothesis is accepted. Therefore, it can be concluded that the Pre-university college students belong to Arts subject has low vocational aspirations than Science students.
2. The Arts and Commerce students of Pre-university college differ significantly with respect to their vocational aspirations (t=-3.5750, <0.01) at 0.01% level of significance. Hence the null hypothesis is rejected and alternative hypothesis is accepted. It can be concluded that the Pre-university College students belong to Arts subject has low vocational aspirations than Commerce students.

3. The Science and Commerce students of Pre-university College differ significantly with respect to their vocational aspirations (t=5.0419, <0.01) at 0.01% level of significance. Hence, the null hypothesis is rejected and alternative hypothesis is accepted. It can be concluded that the pre-university college students belong to Commerce subject has low vocational aspirations than science students.

Hypothesis: Students studying in Kannada and English medium of instruction of pre-university colleges do not differ significantly with respect to their vocational aspirations.

To test this hypothesis, the t-test was applied and the results are presented in Table 4.14.

Table 4.14. Results of t-test between Kannada and English Medium Students of Pre-university College Students with Respect to Vocational Aspirations

Medium	*n*	*Mean*	*SD*	*t-value*	*p-value*	*Signi.*
Kannada	670	45.7851	9.1419	-11.0048	<0.01	S
English	330	52.4212	8.5992			

The above table clearly indicates that the Kannada and English medium of pre-university college differ significantly with respect to their vocational aspirations (t=-11.0048, <0.01) at 0.01% level of significance. Hence, the null hypothesis is rejected and alternative hypothesis is accepted. It can be concluded that the Kannada medium students of Pre-university College have low vocational aspirations when comparing to the students studying in English medium of instruction.

Hypothesis: There is no significant difference between type of management (Government, Aided and Unaided) of Pre-university College students do not differ significantly with respect to their vocational aspiration.

To test this hypothesis, the one-way Analysis of variance (ANOVA) test was applied and the results are presented in Table 4.15.

Table 4.15. Results of Analysis of Variance (ANOVA) test between Type of Managements (Government, Aided and Unaided) of Pre-University College Students with Respect to Vocational Aspirations

SV	*DF*	*SS*	*MSS*	*F-value*	*P-value*	*Signi.*
Between managements	2	5921.06	2960.5299	35.1155	<0.01	S
Within managements	997	84055.32	84.3082			
Total	999	89976.38				

From the above table it is seen that the government, aided and unaided type of management pre-university college students differ significantly with respect to their vocational aspirations (F=35.1155, <0.01) at 0.01% level of significance. Hence, the null hypothesis is rejected and alternative hypothesis is accepted. It can be concluded that government, aided and unaided type of management pre-university college students have different vocational aspirations.

As F is significant, to know the significance between type of management (Government, aided and unaided) t-test was applied and the results are presented in Table 4.16.

Table 4.16. Results of t-test between the Students Belong to Different Type of Managements (Government, Aided and Unaided) with Respect to their Vocational Aspirations

Management	*n*	*Mean*	*SD*	*t-value*	*p-value*	*Signi.*
Government	187	45.4706	9.2657	-1.2678	>0.05	NS
Aided	466	46.5258	9.7507			
Government	187	45.4706	9.2657	-7.3881	<0.01	S
Unaided	347	51.2709	8.3071			
Aided	466	46.5258	9.7507	-7.3037	<0.01	S
Unaided	347	51.2709	8.3071			

From the above table, it is seen that:

1. The students belong to government and aided type of managements Pre-university college do not differ

significantly with respect to their vocational aspirations (t=-1.2678, >0.05) at 0.05% level of significance. Hence the null hypothesis is accepted and alternative hypothesis is rejected. It can be concluded that students belong to government colleges have low vocational aspirations than the aided pre-university college students.

2. The students belong to government and unaided type of management's pre-university colleges differ significantly with respect to their vocational aspirations (t=-7.3881, <0.01) at 0.01% level of significance. Hence, the null hypothesis is rejected and alternative hypothesis is accepted. It can be concluded that students belong to unaided colleges have higher vocational aspirations than the students of government pre-university colleges.
3. The students belong to aided and unaided type of management pre-university college differ significantly with respect to their vocational aspirations (t=-7.3037, <0.01) at 0.01% level of significance. Hence, the null hypothesis is rejected and alternative hypothesis is accepted. It can be concluded that students belong to unaided colleges have higher vocational aspirations than the students of colleges aided.

Hypothesis: There is no significant difference between different birth order (1-2, 3-4 and 5 and more than 5) of Pre-university College students with respect to vocational aspirations.

To test this hypothesis, the one-way Analysis of variance (ANOVA) test was applied and the results are presented in Table 4.17.

Table 4.17. Results of Analysis of Variance (ANOVA) test between Different Birth Order (1-2, 3-4 and 5 and more than 5) of Pre-University College Students with Respect to Vocational Aspirations

SV	*DF*	*SS*	*MSS*	*F-value*	*P-value*	*Signi.*
Between orders	2	71.76	35.8786	0.3979	>0.05	NS
Within orders	997	89904.62	90.1751			
Total	999	89976.38				

The above table reveals that different birth order (1-2, 3-4 and 5 and more than 5) of Pre-university college students do not differ significantly with respect to their vocational aspirations (F=0.3979, >0.05) at 0.05% level of significance. Hence, the null hypothesis is accepted and alternative hypothesis is rejected. It can be concluded that the different birth order (1-2, 3-4 and 5 and more than 5) of students of Pre-university colleges have similar vocational aspirations.

Hypothesis: There is no significant difference between students belong to different categories (GM, OBC, SC/ST/Cat-I) with respect to vocational aspirations.

To test this hypothesis, the one-way Analysis of variance (ANOVA) test was applied and the results are presented in Table 4.18.

Table 4.18. Results of Analysis of Variance (ANOVA) test between Categories (GM, OBC, SC/ST/Cat-I) with Respect to Vocational Aspirations

SV	*DF*	*SS*	*MSS*	*F-value*	*P-value*	*Signi.*
Between categories	2	2550.2791	1275.1396	14.5416	<0.01	S
Within categories	997	87426.0959	87.6892			
Total	999	89976.3750				

The above table reveals the pre-university college students belong to different categories (GM, OBC, SC/ST/Cat-I) differ significantly with respect to their vocational aspirations (F=14.5416, <0.01) at 0.01% level of significance. Hence, the null hypothesis is rejected and alternative hypothesis is accepted. It can be concluded that students of Pre-university colleges belong to different categories (GM, OBC, SC/ST/Cat-I) have different vocational aspirations.

Because F is significant, to know the pairs of different categories (GM, OBC, SC/ST/Cat-I) by applying the t-test and the results are presented in Table 4.19.

Table 4.19. Results of t-test between Students Belong to Different Categories (GM, OBC, SC/ST/Cat-I) with Respect to Vocational Aspirations

Categories	*n*	*Mean*	*SD*	*t-value*	*p-value*	*Signi.*
GM	272	50.5478	9.1336	4.9791	<0.01	S
OBC	594	47.1684	9.3328			
GM	272	50.5478	9.1336	4.2484	<0.01	S
SC/ST/Cat-I	134	46.3284	9.9501			
OBC	594	47.1684	9.3328	0.9296	>0.05	NS
SC/ST/Cat-I	134	46.3284	9.9501			

From the above table, it is observe that,

1. The students belong to GM and OBC categories of Pre-university college students differ significantly with respect to their vocational aspirations (t=4.9791, <0.01) at 0.01% level of significance. Hence, the null hypothesis is rejected and alternative hypothesis is accepted. It can be concluded that students belong to GM have higher vocational aspirations than the students belong to OBC category of Pre-university colleges.
2. The students belong to GM and SC/ST/Cat-I categories of students belong to Pre-university colleges differ significantly with respect to their vocational aspirations (t=4.2484, <0.01) at 0.01% level of significance. Hence, the null hypothesis is rejected and alternative hypothesis is accepted. It can be concluded that students belong to GM have higher vocational aspirations than the students belong to SC/ST/Cat-I category of Pre-university colleges.
3. The students belong to OBC and SC/ST/Cat-I categories of Pre-university college students do not differ significantly with respect to vocational aspirations (t=0.9296, >0.05) at 0.05% level of significance. Hence, the null hypothesis is accepted and alternative hypothesis is rejected. It can be concluded that students belong to OBC and SC/ST/Cat-I have similar vocational aspirations

Hypothesis: Students belong to Rural and Urban Pre-university Colleges do not differ significantly with respect to vocational aspiration.

To test this hypothesis, the t-test was applied and the results are presented in Table 4.20.

Table 4.20. Results of t-test between Rural and Urban Pre-university College Students with Respect to Vocational Aspirations

Location	*n*	*Mean*	*SD*	*t-value*	*p-value*	*Signi.*
Rural	500	45.1760	9.2021	-9.7563	<0.01	S
Urban	500	50.7740	8.9406			

The above table reveals that students belong to Rural and Urban of pre-university colleges differ significantly with respect to their vocational aspirations (t=-9.7563, <0.01) at 0.01% level of significance. Hence, the null hypothesis is rejected and alternative hypothesis is accepted. It can be concluded that the students belong to urban pre-university colleges have higher vocational aspirations than the student belong to rural Pre-university Colleges.

Hypothesis: There is no significant difference between the students belong to High and low achievement motivation of Pre-university college students with respect to vocational aspiration.

To test this hypothesis, the t-test was applied and the results are presented in Table 4.21.

Table 4.21. Results of t-test between Students with High and Low Achievement Motivation of Pre-university College Students with respect to Vocational Aspirations

Achievement motivation	*n*	*Mean*	*SD*	*t-value*	*p-value*	*Signi.*
Low	562	46.7687	9.8419	-4.5988	<0.01	S
High	438	49.5228	8.7906			

The above table reveals that the students belong to Pre-university Colleges with high and low achievement motivation differ significantly with respect to their vocational aspirations (t=-4.5988, <0.01) at 0.01% level of significance. Hence, the null hypothesis is rejected and alternative hypothesis is accepted. It can be concluded that students with high achievement motivation have higher vocational aspirations than the students with low achievement motivation.

Hypothesis: There is no significant difference between students belong to High and low social status of Dharwad district with respect to vocational aspirations.

To test this hypothesis, the t-test was applied and the results are presented in Table 4.22.

Table 4.22. Results of t-test between Students belong to High and Low Social Status of Pre-university College with Respect to their Vocational Aspirations

Social status	*n*	*Mean*	*SD*	*t-value*	*p-value*	*Signi.*
Low	573	46.2932	9.4029	-6.6298	<0.01	S
High	427	50.2319	9.1426			

The above table reveals that the Pre-university Colleges with high and low social status differ significantly with respect to their vocational aspirations (t=-6.6298, <0.01) at 0.01% level of significance. Hence, the null hypothesis is rejected and alternative hypothesis is accepted. It can be concluded that students with high social status have higher vocational aspirations than the students of low social status.

Hypothesis: There is no significance difference between students with High and Low Personality traits of Pre-university Colleges of Dharwad district do not differ significantly with respect to vocational aspiration.

To test this hypothesis, the t-test was applied and the results are presented in Table 4.23.

Table 4.23. Results of t-test between Students with High and Low Personality Traits of Pre-university College with Respect to Vocational Aspirations

Personality traits s	*n*	*Mean*	*SD*	*t-value*	*p-value*	*Signi.*
Low	538	48.0130	10.0200	0.1366	>0.05	NS
High	462	47.9307	8.8443			

The above table reveals that the students of Pre-university Colleges with high and low personality traits do not differ significantly with respect to vocational aspirations (t=0.1366, >0.05) at 0.05% level of significance. Hence the null hypothesis is accepted and alternative hypothesis is rejected. It can be concluded that students with low and high Personality traits have similar vocational aspirations.

Hypothesis: Reserved, average and out-going students of Pre-university Colleges of Dharwad district do not differ significantly with respect to vocational aspirations.

To test this hypothesis, the one-way ANOVA test was applied and the results are presented in Table 4.24.

Table 4.24. kesults of ANOVA between Reserved, Average and Warm-hearted Nature of Factor A with Respect to Vocational Aspirations

SV	*DF*	*SS*	*MSS*	*F-value*	*P-value*	*Signi.*
Between groups	2	132.7497	66.3749	0.7366	>0.05	NS
Within groups	997	89843.6253	90.1140			
Total	999	89976.3750				

The above table shows that the Reserved, average and warm-hearted natured students of Pre-university Colleges do not differ significantly with respect to their vocational aspirations (F=0.7366, >0.05) at 0.05% level of significance. Hence the null hypothesis is accepted and alternative hypothesis is rejected. It can be concluded that the Reserved, average and warm-hearted students of Pre-university Colleges students have similar vocational aspirations.

Hypothesis: Less intelligence, Average intelligence and more intelligence students of Pre-university Colleges do not differ significantly with respect to vocational aspirations.

To test this hypothesis, the one-way ANOVA was applied and the results are presented in Table 4.25.

Table 4.25. Results of ANOVA between Factor B with Respect to Vocational Aspirations

SV	*DF*	*SS*	*MSS*	*F-value*	*P-value*	*Signi.*
Between groups	2	152.8434	76.4217	0.8482	>0.05	NS
Within groups	997	89823.5316	90.0938			
Total	999	89976.3750				

The above table reveals that the students with less intelligence, average intelligence and more intelligence of Pre-university College differ significantly with respect to their vocational aspirations (F=0.8482, >0.05) at 0.05% level of significance. Hence, the null hypothesis is accepted and alternative hypothesis is rejected. It can be concluded that less intelligence of the students of Pre-university colleges have similar vocational aspirations.

Hypothesis: Affected by feeling, Average and Emotionally stable students of Pre-university Colleges do not differ significantly with respect to vocational aspirations.

To test this hypothesis, the one-way ANOVA was applied and the results are presented Table 4.26.

Table 4.26. Results of ANOVA between Affected by Feeling, Average and Emotionally Stable Students of Factor C with Respect to Vocational Aspirations

SV	*DF*	*SS*	*MSS*	*F-value*	*P-value*	*Signi.*
Between groups	3	430.8830	143.6277	1.5975	>0.05	NS
Within groups	996	89545.4920	89.9051			
Total	999	89976.3750				

The above table reveals that the students Affected by feeling, average and Emotionally stable of Pre-university College do not differ significantly with respect to their vocational aspirations (F=1.5975, >0.05) at 0.05% level of significance. Hence, the null hypothesis is accepted and alternative hypothesis is rejected. It can be concluded that the students Affected by feeling, Normal, Emotionally stable of Pre-university Colleges have similar vocational aspirations.

Hypothesis: Phlegmatic, average and Excitable students of Pre-university Colleges of Dharwad district do not differ significantly with respect to vocational aspirations.

To test this hypothesis the one-way ANOVA was applied and the results are presented in the following table.

Table 4.27. Results of ANOVA between Phlegmatic, Average and Excitable Students of Factor D with Respect to Vocational Aspirations

SV	*DF*	*SS*	*MSS*	*F-value*	*P-value*	*Signi.*
Between groups	2	206.8171	103.4085	1.1485	>0.05	NS
Within groups	997	89769.5579	90.0397			
Total	999	89976.3750				

The above table clearly shows that the Phlegmatic, average and Excitable students of Pre-university Colleges do not differ significantly with respect to their vocational aspirations (F=1.1485, >0.05) at 0.05% level of significance. Hence the null hypothesis is accepted and alternative hypothesis is rejected. It can be concluded that the Phlegmatic, Average, Excitable students of Pre-university College students have similar vocational aspirations.

Hypothesis: Obedient, Average and Assertive students of Pre-university Colleges do not differ significantly with respect to vocational aspirations.

To test this hypothesis, the one-way ANOVA was applied and the results are presented in Table 4.28.

Table 4.28. Results of ANOVA between Obedient, Average and Assertive Students of Factor E with Respect to Vocational Aspirations

SV	*DF*	*SS*	*MSS*	*F-value*	*P-value*	*Signi.*
Between groups	2	418.9140	209.4570	2.3318	>0.05	NS
Within groups	997	89557.4610	89.8269			
Total	999	89976.3750				

The above table shows that the Obedient, Average and Assertive students of Pre-university Colleges do not differ significantly with respect to their vocational aspirations (F=2.3318, >0.05) at 0.05% level of significance. Hence the null hypothesis is accepted and alternative hypothesis is rejected. It can be concluded that the Obedient, Average and Assertive students of Pre-university Colleges have similar vocational aspirations.

Hypothesis: Sober, Average and Happy go lucky students of Pre-university Colleges do not differ significantly with respect to vocational aspirations.

To test this hypothesis, the one-way ANOVA was applied and the results are presented in Table 4.29.

Table 4.29. Results of ANOVA between Sober, Average and Happy Go Lucky Students of Factor F with Respect to Vocational Aspirations

SV	*DF*	*SS*	*MSS*	*F-value*	*P-value*	*Signi.*
Between groups	2	297.1070	148.5535	1.6515	>0.05	NS
Within groups	997	89679.2680	89.9491			
Total	999	89976.3750				

The above table reveals that the Sober, Average and Happy go lucky students of Pre-university Colleges do not differ significantly with respect to their vocational aspirations (F=1.6515, >0.05) at 0.05% level of significance. Hence the null hypothesis is accepted and alternative hypothesis is rejected. It can be concluded that the Sober, Average and Happy go lucky students of Pre-university Colleges have similar vocational aspirations.

Hypothesis: Expedient, Average and Conscientious students of Pre-university Colleges do not differ significantly with respect to vocational aspirations.

To test this hypothesis, the one-way ANOVA was applied and the results are presented in Table 4.30.

Table 4.30. Results of ANOVA between Expedient, Average and Conscientious Students of Factor G with Respect to Vocational Aspirations

SV	*DF*	*SS*	*MSS*	*F-value*	*P-value*	*Signi.*
Between groups	2	370.5774	185.2887	2.0616	>0.05	NS
Within groups	997	89605.7976	89.8754			
Total	999	89976.3750				

The above table reveals that the Expedient, Average and Conscientious students of Pre-university Colleges do not differ significantly with respect to their vocational aspirations (F=2.0616, >0.05) at 0.05% level of significance. Hence, the null hypothesis is accepted and alternative hypothesis is rejected. It can be concluded that the Expedient, Average and Conscientious students of Pre-university Colleges have similar vocational aspirations.

Hypothesis: Shy, Average and Venturesome students of Pre-university Colleges of Dharwad district do not differ significantly with respect to vocational aspirations.

To test this hypothesis, the one-way ANOVA was applied and the results are presented in Table 4.3.

Table 4.31. Results of ANOVA test between Shy, Average and Venturesome Students of Factor H with Respect to Vocational Aspirations

SV	*DF*	*SS*	*MSS*	*F-value*	*P-value*	*Signi.*
Between groups	2	112.5703	56.2852	0.6245	>0.05	NS
Within groups	997	89863.8047	90.1342			
Total	999	89976.3750				

The above table reveals that the Shy, Average and Venturesome students of Pre-university Colleges do not differ significantly with respect to their vocational aspirations (F=0.6245, >0.05) at 0.05% level of significance. Hence the null hypothesis is accepted and alternative hypothesis is rejected. It can be concluded that the Shy, Average and Venturesome students of Pre-university Colleges have similar vocational aspirations.

Hypothesis: Tough minded, Average minded and Tended minded students of Pre-university Colleges of Dharwad district do not differ significantly with respect to vocational aspirations.

To test this hypothesis, the one-way ANOVA was applied and the results are presented in Table 4.32.

Table 4.32. Results of ANOVA test between Tough Minded, Average Minded and Tended Minded Students of Factor I with Respect to Vocational Aspiration

SV	*DF*	*SS*	*MSS*	*F-value*	*P-value*	*Signi.*
Between groups	2	355.2590	177.6295	1.9761	>0.05	NS
Within groups	997	89621.1160	89.8908			
Total	999	89976.3750				

The above table reveals that the Tough minded, Average minded and Tended minded students of Pre-university Colleges do not differ significantly with respect to their vocational aspirations (F=1.9761, >0.05) at 0.05% level of significance. Hence the null hypothesis is accepted and alternative hypothesis is rejected. It can be concluded that the Tough minded, Average minded and Tended minded students of Pre-university Colleges have similar vocational aspirations.

Hypothesis: Vigorous, Average and doubting students of Pre-university Colleges of Dharwad district do not differ significantly with respect to vocational aspirations.

To test this hypothesis, the one-way ANOVA was applied and the results are presented in Table 4.33.

Table 4.33. Results of ANOVA between Vigorous, Average and Doubting Students of Factor J with Respect to Vocational Aspirations

SV	*DF*	*SS*	*MSS*	*F-value*	*P-value*	*Signi.*
Between groups	2	101.8179	50.9089	0.5647	>0.05	NS
Within groups	997	89874.5571	90.1450			
Total	999	89976.3750				

The above table reveals that the Vigorous, Average and doubting students of Pre-university Colleges do not differ significantly with respect to their vocational aspirations (F=0.5647, >0.05) at 0.05% level of significance. Hence, the null hypothesis is accepted and alternative hypothesis is rejected. It can be concluded that the Vigorous, Average and doubting students of Pre-university Colleges have similar vocational aspirations.

Hypothesis: Placid, Average and Apprehensive students of Pre-university Colleges of Dharwad district do not differ significantly with respect to vocational aspirations

To test this hypothesis, the one-way ANOVA was applied and the results are presented in Table 4.34.

Table 4.34. Results of ANOVA between Placid, Average and Apprehensive Students of Factor O with Respect to Vocational Aspirations

SV	*DF*	*SS*	*MSS*	*F-value*	*P-value*	*Signi.*
Between groups	2	382.5889	191.2944	2.1287	>0.05	NS
Within groups	997	89593.7861	89.8634			
Total	999	89976.3750				

The above table reveals that the Placid, Average and Apprehensive students of Pre-university Colleges do not differ significantly with respect to their vocational aspirations (F=2.1287, >0.05) at 0.05% level of significance. Hence, the null hypothesis is accepted and alternative hypothesis is rejected. It can be concluded that the Placid, Average and Apprehensive students of Pre-university Colleges have similar vocational aspirations.

Hypothesis: Group dependent, Average and Self-sufficient students of Pre-university Colleges of Dharwad district do not differ significantly with respect to vocational aspirations

To test this hypothesis, the one-way ANOVA was applied and the results are presented in Table 4.35.

Table 4.35. Results of ANOVA between Group Dependent, Average and Self-Sufficient Students of Factor Q2 with Respect to Vocational Aspirations

SV	*DF*	*SS*	*MSS*	*F-value*	*P-value*	*Signi.*
Between groups	2	1248.5105	624.2553	7.0145	<0.01	S
Within groups	997	88727.8645	88.9948			
Total	999	89976.3750				

The above table reveals that the Group dependent, Average and Self-sufficient students of Pre-university Colleges differ significantly with respect to their vocational aspirations (F=7.0145, <0.01) at 0.01% level of significance. Hence the null hypothesis is rejected and alternative hypothesis is accepted. It can be concluded that the Group dependent, Average and Self-sufficient students of Pre-university Colleges have different vocational aspirations.

Because f is significant, to know the significant difference between pairs of Group dependent, Average and Self-sufficient by applying the t-test and the results are presented in Table 4.30.

Table 4.36. Results of t-test between Group Dependent, Average and Self-sufficient of Factor Q2 with Respect to Vocational Aspirations

Factor Q2	*n*	*Mean*	*SD*	*t-value*	*P-value*	*Signi.*
Group dependent	399	49.2231	9.6636	3.7232	<0.01	S
Normal	310	46.5677	9.0960			
Group dependent	399	49.2231	9.6636	1.9769	<0.05	S
Self-sufficient	291	47.7629	9.4677			
Normal	310	46.5677	9.0960	-1.5782	>0.05	NS
Self-sufficient	291	47.7629	9.4677			

The above table reveals that:

1. Group dependent and Average students of Pre-university Colleges differ significantly with respect to their vocational aspirations (t=3.7232, <0.01) at 0.01% level of significance. Hence the null hypothesis is rejected and alternative hypothesis is accepted. It can be concluded that the Group dependent students are higher in vocational aspiration than Average students of Pre-university Colleges.
2. Group dependent and Self-sufficient students of Pre-university Colleges differ significantly with respect to their vocational aspirations (t=1.9769, <0.05) at 0.05% level of significance. Hence the null hypothesis is rejected and alternative hypothesis is accepted. It can be concluded that the Group dependent are higher in vocational aspiration than Self-sufficient students of Pre-university Colleges.

3. Average and Self-sufficient students of Pre-university Colleges do not differ significantly with respect to their vocational aspirations (t=-1.5782, >0.05) at 0.05% level of significance. Hence the null hypothesis is accepted and alternative hypothesis is rejected. It can be concluded that the Average and Self-sufficient students of Pre-university Colleges have similar vocational aspirations.

Hypothesis: Undisciplined self-conflict, Average and controlled students of Dharwad district Pre-university Colleges do not differ significantly with respect to vocational aspirations

To test this hypothesis, the one-way ANOVA was applied and the results are presented in Table 4.37.

Table 4.37. Results of ANOVA between Undisciplined Self-conflict, Average and Controlled Students of Factor Q3 with Respect to Vocational Aspirations

SV	*DF*	*SS*	*MSS*	*F-value*	*P-value*	*Signi.*
Between groups	2	196.0221	98.0110	1.0884	>0.05	NS
Within groups	997	89780.3529	90.0505			
Total	999	89976.3750				

The above table reveals that the undisciplined self-conflict, Average and controlled students of Pre-university Colleges do not differ significantly with respect to their vocational aspirations (F=1.0884, >0.05) at 0.05% level of significance. Hence, the null hypothesis is accepted and alternative hypothesis is rejected. It can be concluded that the undisciplined self-conflict, Average and controlled students of Pre-university Colleges have similar vocational aspirations.

Hypothesis: Relaxed, Average and Tense students of Pre-university College of Dharwad district do not differ significantly with respect to vocational aspirations

To test this hypothesis, the one-way ANOVA was applied and the results are presented in Table 4.38.

Table 4.38. Results of ANOVA between Relaxed, Average and Tense Students of Factor Q4 with Respect to Vocational Aspirations

SV	*DF*	*SS*	*MSS*	*F-value*	*P-value*	*Signi.*
Between groups	2	358.0470	179.0235	1.9916	>0.05	NS
Within groups	997	89618.3280	89.8880			
Total	999	89976.3750				

The above table reveals that the Relaxed, Average and Tense students of Pre-university Colleges do not differ significantly with respect to their vocational aspirations (F=1.9916, >0.05) at 0.05% level of significance. Hence the null hypothesis is accepted and alternative hypothesis is rejected. It can be concluded that the Relaxed, Average and Tense students of Pre-university Colleges have similar vocational aspirations.

Differential statistics in the independent variables on vocational aspirations i.e. Interaction effects of independent variables on vocational aspirations of students of Pre-university College (Analysis of variance with 3-way Interactions)

Hypothesis: There is no significant interaction effect of Achievement motivation (High and Low), Personality traits (High and Low) and Social status (High and Low) on vocational aspirations of students of Pre-university Colleges of Dharwad district.

To test this hypothesis, the Three-way ANOVA with interaction effect design was applied and the results are presented in the Table 4.39.

Table 4.39 reveals that

- The main effect of achievement motivation (High and Low) on vocational aspirations of Pre-university Colleges is found to be significant at 0.01% level of significance. Since the obtained F value 21.2033 is greater than the F table value 3.8400 the null hypothesis is rejected and alternative hypothesis is accepted. It can be concluded that the students with high and low achievement motivation of Pre-university College students differs in their vocational aspirations.

Table 4.39. Results of ANOVA with 3-way Interaction between Achievement Motivation (High and Low), Personality traits (High and Low) and Social Status (High and Low) with Respect to Vocational Aspirations

SV	*DF*	*SS*	*MSS*	*F-value*	*P-value*	*Signi.*
Main effects						
Achievement motivation	1	1377.77	1377.77	21.2033	<0.01	S
Personality traits	1	15.31	15.31	0.2357	>0.05	NS
Social status	1	3256.55	3256.55	50.1171	<0.01	S
2-way interactions						
Achievement motivation × Personality traits s	1	624.44	624.44	9.6099	<0.01	S
Achievement motivation × Social status	1	6.82	6.82	0.1050	>0.05	NS
Personality traits × Social status	1	98.02	98.02	1.5084	>0.05	NS
3-way interactions						
Achievement motivation × Personality traits × Social status	1	10.05	10.05	0.1540	>0.05	NS
Error	992	64459.07	64.98			
Total	999	69847.99				

- The main effect of personality traits (High and Low) on vocational aspirations of Pre-university Colleges is found to be not significant at 0.05% level of significance. Since the obtained F value 0.2357 is lesser than the F table value 3.8400 the null hypothesis is accepted and alternative hypothesis is rejected. It can be concluded that the vocational aspirations of students with high and low Personality traits of Pre-university College students differs significantly.
- The main effect of social status (High and Low) on vocational aspirations of Pre-university Colleges is found to be significant at 0.01% level of significance. Since the

obtained F value 50.1171 is greater than the F table value 3.8400 the null hypothesis is rejected and alternative hypothesis is accepted. It can be concluded that the vocational aspiration of students with high and low social status of Pre-university College differs significantly.

- The interaction effect of achievement motivation (High and Low) and Personality traits (High and Low) on vocational aspirations of Pre-university Colleges is found to be significant at 0.01% level of significance. Since the obtained F value 9.6099 is greater than the F table value 3.8400 the null hypothesis is rejected and alternative hypothesis is accepted. It can be concluded that the vocational aspirations of the students is influenced by interaction effect of achievement motivation and personality.
- The interaction effect of achievement motivation (High and Low) and social status (High and Low) on vocational aspirations of Pre-university Colleges is found to be not significant at 0.05% level of significance. Since the obtained F value 0.1050 is lesser than the F table value 3.8400 the null hypothesis is accepted and alternative hypothesis is rejected. It can be concluded that interaction effect of achievement motivation and social status do not affect occupation aspirations of students.
- The interaction effect of Personality traits (High and Low) and social status (High and Low) on vocational aspirations of Pre-university Colleges is found to be not significant at 0.05% level of significance. Since the obtained F value 1.5084 is lesser than the F table value 3.8400 the null hypothesis is accepted and alternative hypothesis is rejected. It can be concluded that interaction effect of Personality traits and social status do not affect vocational aspirations of students.
- The interaction effect of achievement motivation (High and Low), Personality traits (High and Low) and social status (High and Low) on vocational aspirations of Pre-university Colleges is found to be not significant at 0.05% level of significance. Since the obtained F value 0.1540 is lesser than the F table value 3.8400. Hence, the null

hypothesis is accepted and alternative hypothesis is rejected. It can be concluded that the interaction effect of achievement motivation, Personality traits and social status do not affect vocational aspirations of the students.

Because F is significant, to know the pairs of interaction effects of achievement motivation (High and Low) and Personality traits (High and Low) on vocational aspirations by applying the Scheffes post hoc multiple comparison tests and the results are presented in Table 4.40.

Table 4.40. Scheffes Post Hoc Test between Achievement Motivation × Personality Traits

Achievement motivation × Personality traits	*High × High*	*High × Low*	*Low × High*	*Low × Low*
Means	49.03741	50.15728	47.60330	46.78209
High × High	-			
High × Low	0.6572	-		
Low × High	0.4301	0.0255*	-	
Low × Low	0.0417*	0.0005**	0.7756	-

*Significant at 0.05% level of significance.

**significant at 0.05 level of significance.

The above table reveals that

- The interaction effect of students with high achievement motivation and high Personality traits and students with low achievement motivation and low Personality traits of Pre-university Colleges on vocational aspirations is found to be significant at 0.05 level of significance.
- The interaction effect of students with high achievement motivation and low Personality traits and students with low achievement motivation and high Personality traits of Pre-university Colleges on vocational aspirations is found to be significant at 0.05 level of significance.
- The interaction effect of students with high achievement motivation and low Personality traits and students with low achievement motivation and low Personality traits of Pre-university College students on vocational aspirations is found to be significant at 0.01level of significance.

Hypothesis: There is no significant interaction effect of Achievement motivation (High and Low), Personality traits (High and Low) and Social status (High and Low) on vocational aspirations of Pre-university College male students of Dharwad district.

To test this hypothesis, the Three-way ANOVA with interaction effect design was applied and the results are presented in Table 4.41.

Table 4.41. Results of ANOVA with 3-way Interaction between Achievement Motivation (High and Low), Personality traits (High and Low) and Social Status (High and Low) with Respect to Vocational Aspirations

SV	*DF*	*SS*	*MSS*	*F-value*	*P-value*	*Signi.*
Main effects						
Achievement motivation	1	149.15	149.15	1.4567	>0.05	NS
Personality traits s	1	30.72	30.72	0.3001	>0.05	NS
Social status	1	1841.57	1841.57	17.9864	<0.01	S
2-way interactions						
Achievement motivation × Personality traits s	1	197.83	197.83	1.9322	>0.05	NS
Achievement motivation × Social status	1	169.01	169.01	1.6507	>0.05	NS
Personality traits × Social status	1	34.49	34.49	0.3369	>0.05	NS
3-way interactions						
Achievement motivation × Personality traits × Social status	1	0.59	0.59	0.0058	>0.05	NS
Error	492	50374.33	102.39			
Total	499	52797.70				

The result of the above table clears that

- The main effect of achievement motivation (High and Low) on vocational aspirations of Pre-university Colleges male students is found to be not significant at 0.05% level of significance. Since the obtained F value 1.4567 is lesser than the F table value 3.8400, the null hypothesis is accepted and alternative hypothesis is rejected. It can be concluded that the vocational aspiration is similar among male students inspite of their high and low achievement motivation.

- The main effect of Personality traits (High and Low) on vocational aspirations of Pre-university College male students is found to be not significant at 0.05% level of significance. Since the obtained F value 0.3001 is lesser than the F table value 3.8400, the null hypothesis is accepted and alternative hypothesis is rejected. It can be concluded that the vocational aspiration is similar among male students inspite of their high and low personality traits.
- The main effect of social status (High and Low) on vocational aspirations of Pre-university College male students is found to be significant at 0.01% level of significance. Since the obtained F value 17.9864 is greater than the F table value 3.8400, the null hypothesis is rejected and alternative hypothesis is accepted. It can be concluded that the vocational aspiration is different among male students with high and low social status.
- The interaction effect of achievement motivation (High and Low) and Personality traits (High and Low) on vocational aspirations of Pre-university College male students is found to be not significant at 0.05% level of significance. Since the obtained F value 1.9322 is lesser than the F table value 3.8400, the null hypothesis is rejected and alternative hypothesis is accepted. It can be concluded that the vocational aspiration is similar among male students with interaction effect of achievement motivation and not personality traits s.
- The interaction effect of achievement motivation (High and Low) and social status (High and Low) on vocational

aspirations of Pre-university College male students is found to be not significant at 0.05% level of significance. Since the obtained F value 1.6507 is lesser than the F table value 3.8400 the null hypothesis is accepted and alternative hypothesis is rejected. It can be concluded that vocational aspiration is similar among male students with interaction effect of achievement motivation and social status.

- The interaction effect of Personality traits (High and Low) and social status (High and Low) on vocational aspirations of Pre-university College male students is found to be not significant at 0.05% level of significance. Since the obtained F value 0.3369 is lesser than the F table value 3.8400 the null hypothesis is accepted and alternative hypothesis is rejected. It can be concluded that the vocational aspiration is similar among male students with interaction effect of Personality traits and social status.
- The interaction effect of achievement motivation (High and Low), Personality traits (High and Low) and social status (High and Low) on vocational aspirations of Pre-university College male students is found to be not significant at 0.05% level of significance. Since the obtained F value 0.0058 is lesser than the F table value 3.8400 the null hypothesis is accepted and alternative hypothesis is rejected. It can be concluded that the vocational aspirations is similar among male students with interaction effect of achievement motivation, Personality traits and social status.

Hypothesis: There is no significant interaction effect of Achievement motivation (High and Low), Personality traits (High and Low) and Social status (High and Low) on vocational aspirations of Pre-university College female students of Dharwad district.

To test this hypothesis, the Three-way ANOVA with interaction effect design was applied and the results are presented in Table 4.42.

Table 4.42. Results of ANOVA with 3-way Interaction between Achievement Motivation (High and Low), Personality traits (High and Low) and Social status (High and Low) with respect to vocational aspirations

SV	*DF*	*SS*	*MSS*	*F-value*	*P-value*	*Signi.*
Main effects						
Achievement motivation	1	1492.21	1492.21	22.2833	<0.01	S
Personality traits s	1	4.02	4.02	0.0600	>0.05	NS
Social status	1	1540.14	1540.14	22.9992	<0.05	S
2-way interactions						
Achievement motivation × Personality traits s	1	63.68	63.68	0.9509	>0.05	NS
Achievement motivation × Social status	1	280.12	280.12	4.1831	<0.05	S
Personality traits × Social status	1	61.03	61.03	0.9113	>0.05	NS
3-way interactions						
Achievement motivation × Personality traits × Social status	1	6.86	6.86	0.1025	>0.05	NS
Error	492	32946.82	66.97			
Total	499	36394.88				

The above table reveals that

(*a*) The main effect of achievement motivation (High and Low) on vocational aspirations of Pre-university College female students is found to be significant at 0.01% level of significance. Since the obtained F value 22.2833 is greater than the F table value 3.8400 the null hypothesis is rejected and alternative hypothesis is accepted. It can be concluded that the vocational aspiration is different in female students with high and low achievement motivation.

(*b*) The main effect of Personality traits (High and Low) on vocational aspirations of Pre-university College female students is found to be not significant at 0.05% level of significance. Since the obtained F value 0.0600 is lesser than the F table value 3.8400, the null hypothesis is accepted and alternative hypothesis is rejected. It can be concluded that the vocational aspiration is similar among female students with high and low personality traits s.

(*c*) The main effect of social status (High and Low) on vocational aspirations of Pre-university College female students is found to be significant at 0.05% level of significance. Since the obtained F value 22.9992 is greater than the F table value 3.8400 the null hypothesis is rejected and alternative hypothesis is accepted. It can be concluded that the vocational aspiration is influenced by high and low social status of Pre-university College female students.

(*d*) The interaction effect of achievement motivation (High and Low) and Personality traits (High and Low) on vocational aspirations of Pre-university College female students is found to be not significant at 0.05% level of significance. Since the obtained F value 0.9509 is lesser than the F table value 3.8400, the null hypothesis is accepted and alternative hypothesis is rejected. It can be concluded that the vocational aspiration of female students do not influenced by the interaction effect of achievement motivation and personality traits s.

(*e*) The interaction effect of achievement motivation (High and Low) and social status (High and Low) on vocational aspirations of Pre-university College female students is found to be significant at 0.05% level of significance. Since the obtained F value 4.1831 is greater than the F table value 3.8400, the null hypothesis is rejected and alternative hypothesis is accepted. It can be concluded that vocational aspiration of female students influenced by the interaction effect of achievement motivation and social status.

(*f*) The interaction effect of Personality traits (High and Low) and social status (High and Low) on vocational aspirations of Pre-university College female students is found to be not significant at 0.05% level of significance. Since the obtained F value 0.9113 is lesser than the F table value 3.8400, the null hypothesis is accepted and alternative hypothesis is rejected. It can be concluded that vocational aspiration of female students do not influenced by Personality traits and social status.

(*g*) The interaction effect of achievement motivation (High and Low), Personality traits (High and Low) and social status (High and Low) on vocational aspirations of Pre-university College female students is found to be not significant at 0.05% level of significance. Since the obtained F value 0.1025 is lesser than the F table value 3.8400, the null hypothesis is accepted and alternative hypothesis is rejected. It can be concluded that vocational aspiration of female students do not influenced by achievement motivation, Personality traits and social status.

Because F is significant, to know the pairs of interaction effects of achievement motivation (High and Low) and Social status (High and Low) on vocational aspirations by applying the Scheffes post hoc multiple comparison tests and the results are presented in Table 4.43.

Table 4.43. Scheffes post hoc test between Achievement motivation × Social status

Achievement motivation × Social status	*High × High*	*High × Low*	*Low × High*	*Low × Low*
Means	51.01633	48.96429	49.02041	43.91657
High × High	-			
High × Low	0.2430	-		
Low × High	0.3710	0.9987	-	
Low × Low	0.0000**	0.0000**	0.0001**	-

*Significant at 5% level of significance.
**significant at 1% level of significance.

The above table reveals that :

- The interaction effect of female students with high achievement motivation and high social status and female students with low achievement motivation and low social status of Pre-university Colleges on vocational aspirations is found to be significant at 0.05% level of significance. It can be concluded that the vocational aspirations of female students influenced by the interaction effect of achievement motivation and social status.
- The interaction effect of female students with high achievement motivation and low social status and female students with low achievement motivation and low social status of Pre-university Colleges on vocational aspirations is found to be significant at 0.05% level of significance. It can be concluded vocational aspirations of female students influenced by high achievement motivation and low social status.
- The interaction effect of female students with low achievement motivation and high social status and female students with low achievement motivation and low social status of Pre-university Colleges on vocational aspirations is found to be significant at 0.05% level of significance. It can be concluded that the vocational aspiration of female students is influenced by interaction effect of low achievement motivation and social status.

Hypothesis: There is no significant interaction effect of Achievement motivation (High and Low), Personality traits (High and Low) and Social status (High and Low) on vocational aspirations of students of Pre-university College with arts subject of Dharwad district.

To test this hypothesis, the Three-way ANOVA with interaction effect design was applied and the results are presented in Table 4.44.

Table 4.44. Results of ANOVA with 3-way interaction between Achievement motivation (High and Low), Personality traits (High and Low) and Social status (High and Low) with respect to vocational aspirations of Students with arts subject

SV	*DF*	*SS*	*MSS*	*F-value*	*P-value*	*Signi.*
Main effects						
Achievement motivation	1	562.51	562.51	7.0310	<0.05	S
Personality traits s	1	296.79	296.79	3.7096	>0.05	NS
Social status	1	32.19	32.19	0.4024	>0.05	NS
2-way interactions						
Achievement motivation × Personality traits s	1	93.70	93.70	1.1712	>0.05	NS
Achievement motivation × **Social status**	1	15.43	15.43	0.1928	>0.05	NS
Personality traits × Social status	1	20.97	20.97	0.2621	>0.05	NS
3-way interactions						
Achievement motivation × Personality traits × Social status	1	24.61	24.61	0.3076	>0.05	NS
Error	547	43762.25	80.00			
Total	554	44808.43				

The above table reveals that :

➢ The main effect of achievement motivation (High and Low) on vocational aspirations of Pre-university Colleges students with arts subject is found to be significant at 0.05% level of significance. Since the obtained F value 7.0310 is greater than the F table value 3.8400, the null hypothesis is rejected and alternative hypothesis is accepted. It can be concluded that the vocational aspiration of students with arts subject is influenced by high and low achievement motivation of Pre-university College.

- The main effect of personality traits (High and Low) on vocational aspirations of Pre-university College arts subject students is found to be not significant at 0.05% level of significance. Since the obtained F value 3.7096 is lesser than the F table value 3.8400, the null hypothesis is accepted and alternative hypothesis is rejected. It can be concluded that the vocational aspiration of students with arts subject is similar in high and low personality traits of Pre-university College.
- The main effect of social status (High and Low) on vocational aspirations of Pre-university College students with arts subject is found to be not significant at 0.05% level of significance. Since the obtained F value 0.4024 is lesser than the F table value 3.8400, the null hypothesis is accepted and alternative hypothesis is rejected. It can be concluded that the vocational aspiration of students with arts subject is similar with high and low social status.
- The interaction effect of achievement motivation (High and Low) and Personality traits (High and Low) on vocational aspirations of Pre-university College students with arts subject is found to be not significant at 0.05% level of significance. Since the obtained F value 1.1712 is lesser than the F table value 3.8400, the null hypothesis is accepted and alternative hypothesis is rejected. It can be concluded that the vocational aspirations of students with arts subject do not influenced by interaction of achievement motivation and personality traits s.
- The interaction effect of achievement motivation (High and Low) and social status (High and Low) on vocational aspirations of Pre-university College students with arts subject is found to be not significant at 0.05% level of significance. Since the obtained F value 0.1928 is lesser

than the F table value 3.840, the null hypothesis is accepted and alternative hypothesis is rejected. It can be concluded that the vocational aspirations of students with arts subject do not influenced by the interaction effect of achievement motivation and social status.

- The interaction effect of Personality traits (High and Low) and social status (High and Low) on vocational aspirations of Pre-university College students with arts subject is found to be not significant at 0.05% level of significance. Since the obtained F value 0.2621 is lesser than the F table value 3.8400, the null hypothesis is accepted and alternative hypothesis is rejected. It can be concluded that the vocational aspirations of the students with arts subject do not influenced by the interaction effect of Personality traits and social status.
- The interaction effect of achievement motivation (High and Low), Personality traits (High and Low) and social status (High and Low) on vocational aspirations of Pre-university College students with arts subject is found to be not significant at 0.05% level of significance. Since the obtained F value 0.3076 is lesser than the F table value 3.8400, the null hypothesis is accepted and alternative hypothesis is rejected. Therefore it can be concluded that vocational aspirations of students with arts subject do not influenced by the interaction effect of achievement motivation and personality traits s.

Hypothesis: There is no significant interaction effect of Achievement motivation (High and Low), Personality traits (High and Low) and Social status (High and Low) on vocational aspirations of Pre-university Colleges students with science subject of Dharwad district.

To test this hypothesis, the Three-way ANOVA with interaction effect design was applied and the results are presented in Table 4.45.

Table 4.45. Results of ANOVA with 3-way interaction between Achievement motivation (High and Low), Personality traits (High and Low) and Social status (High and Low) with respect to vocational aspirations

SV	*DF*	*SS*	*MSS*	*F-value*	*P-value*	*Signi.*
Main effects						
Achievement motivation	1	5.71	5.71	0.0771	>0.05	NS
Personality traits s	1	118.13	118.13	1.5968	>0.05	NS
Social status	1	467.70	467.70	6.3218	<0.05	S
2-way interactions						
Achievement motivation × Personality traits s	1	36.63	36.63	0.4952	>0.05	NS
Achievement motivation × Social status	1	20.60	20.60	0.2784	>0.05	NS
Personality traits × Social status	1	14.66	14.66	0.1982	>0.05	NS
3-way interactions						
Achievement motivation × Personality traits × Social status	1	21.82	21.82	0.2950	>0.05	NS
Error	290	21454.89	73.98			
Total	297	22140.15				

The above table reveals that

- The main effect of achievement motivation (High and Low) on vocational aspirations of Pre-university College students with science subject is found to be not significant at 0.05% level of significance. Since the obtained F value 0.0771 is lesser than the F table value 3.8400, the null hypothesis is accepted and alternative hypothesis is rejected. It can be concluded that the vocational aspirations of students with science subject is similar in high and low achievement motivation.

- The main effect of personality traits (High and Low) on vocational aspirations of Pre-university College students with science subject is found to be not significant at 0.05% level of significance. Since the obtained F value 1.5968 is lesser than the F table value 3.8400, the null hypothesis is accepted and alternative hypothesis is rejected. It can be concluded that the vocational aspiration of students with science subject is similar in high and low personality traits.
- The main effect of social status (High and Low) on vocational aspirations of Pre-university College students with science subject is found to be significant at 0.05% level of significance. Since the obtained F value 6.3218 is greater than the F table value 3.8400, the null hypothesis is rejected and alternative hypothesis is accepted. It can be concluded that the vocational aspiration of students with science subject is influenced in high and low social status.
- The interaction effect of achievement motivation (High and Low) and Personality traits (High and Low) on vocational aspirations of Pre-university College students with science subject is found to be not significant at 0.05% level of significance. Since the obtained F value 0.4952 is lesser than the F table value 3.8400, the null hypothesis is accepted and alternative hypothesis is rejected. It can be concluded that the vocational aspiration of students with science subject is not influenced by the interaction effect of achievement motivation and personality traits.
- The interaction effect of achievement motivation (High and Low) and social status (High and Low) on vocational aspirations of Pre-university College students with science subject is found to be not significant at 0.05%

level of significance. Since the obtained F value 0.2784 is lesser than the F table value 3.8400, the null hypothesis is accepted and alternative hypothesis is rejected. It can be concluded that the vocational aspiration of students with science subject is not influenced by the interaction effect of achievement motivation and social status.

- The interaction effect of Personality traits (High and Low) and social status (High and Low) on vocational aspirations of Pre-university College students with science subject is found to be not significant at 0.05% level of significance. Since the obtained F value 0.1982 is lesser than the F table value 3.8400, the null hypothesis is accepted and alternative hypothesis is rejected. It can be concluded that the vocational aspirations of students with science subject is not influenced by the interaction effect of personality.
- The interaction effect of achievement motivation (High and Low), Personality traits (High and Low) and social status (High and Low) on vocational aspirations of Pre-university College students with science subject is found to be not significant at 0.05% level of significance. Since the obtained F value 0.2950 is lesser than the F table value 3.8400, the null hypothesis is accepted and alternative hypothesis is rejected. It can be concluded that the vocational aspiration of students with science subject is not influenced by achievement motivation, personality traits and social status.

Hypothesis: There is no significant interaction effect of Achievement motivation (High and Low), Personality traits (High and Low) and Social status (High and Low) on vocational aspirations of students of Pre-university College students with Commerce subject of Dharwad district.

To test this hypothesis, the Three-way ANOVA with interaction effect design was applied and the results are presented in Table 4.46.

Table 4.46. Results of ANOVA with 3-way interaction between Achievement motivation (High and Low), Personality traits (High and Low) and Social status (High and Low) with respect to vocational aspirations

SV	*DF*	*SS*	*MSS*	*F-value*	*P-value*	*Signi.*
Main effects						
Achievement motivation	1	1.43	1.43	0.0580	>0.05	NS
Personality traits s	1	70.19	70.19	0.8807	>0.05	NS
Social status	1	105.89	105.89	1.3287	>0.05	NS
2-way interactions						
Achievement motivation × Personality traits s	1	36.48	36.48	0.4577	>0.05	NS
Achievement motivation × Social status	1	170.80	170.80	2.1432	>0.05	NS
Personality traits × Social status	1	10.18	10.18	0.1277	>0.05	NS
3-way interactions						
Achievement motivation × Personality traits × Social status	1	5.55	5.55	0.0696	>0.05	NS
Error	139	11077.73	79.70			
Total	146	11478.25				

The above table reveals that

1. The main effect of achievement motivation (High and Low) on vocational aspirations of Pre-university College students with commerce subject is found to be not significant at 0.05% level of significance. Since the obtained F value 0.0580 is lesser than the F table value 3.8400. Hence the null hypothesis is accepted and alternative hypothesis is rejected. It can be concluded that the vocational aspiration of students with commerce subjects is similar in high and low achievement motivation.

2. The main effect of personality traits (High and Low) on vocational aspirations of Pre-university College students with commerce subject is found to be not significant at 0.05% level of significance. Since the obtained F value 0.8807 is lesser than the F table value 3.8400, the null hypothesis is accepted and alternative hypothesis is rejected. It can be concluded that the vocational aspiration is similar in high and low personality traits.
3. The main effect of social status (High and Low) on vocational aspirations of Pre-university College students with commerce subject is found to be not significant at 0.05% level of significance. Since the obtained F value 1.3287 is lesser than the F table value 3.8400, the null hypothesis is accepted and alternative hypothesis is rejected. It can be concluded that the vocational aspiration is similar in high and low social status of Pre-university College students with commerce subject.
4. The interaction effect of achievement motivation (High and Low) and Personality traits (High and Low) on vocational aspirations of Pre-university College students with commerce subject is found to be not significant at 0.05% level of significance. Since the obtained F value 0.4577 is lesser than the F table value 3.8400, the null hypothesis is accepted and alternative hypothesis is rejected. It can be concluded that the vocational aspiration of students of commerce with achievement motivation and personality traits is similar.
5. The interaction effect of achievement motivation (High and Low) and social status (High and Low) on vocational aspirations of Pre-university College students with commerce subject is found to be not significant at 0.05% level of significance. Since the obtained F value 2.1432 is lesser than the F table value 3.8400, the null hypothesis is accepted and alternative hypothesis is rejected. It can be concluded that the vocational aspiration of students of commerce is not influenced by the interaction effect of achievement motivation and social status.

6. The interaction effect of Personality traits (High and Low) and social status (High and Low) on vocational aspirations of Pre-university College students with commerce subject is found to be not significant at 0.05% level of significance. Since the obtained F value 0.1277 is lesser than the F table value 3.8400, the null hypothesis is accepted and alternative hypothesis is rejected. It can be concluded that vocational aspiration of students of commerce do not influence by the interaction effect of personality traits and social status.
7. The interaction effect of achievement motivation (High and Low), Personality traits (High and Low) and social status (High and Low) on vocational aspirations of Pre-university College students with commerce subject is found to be not significant at 0.05% level of significance. Since the obtained F value 0.0696 is lesser than the F table value 3.8400, the null hypothesis is accepted and alternative hypothesis is rejected. It can be concluded that vocational aspiration of students of commerce do not influenced by the interaction effect of achievement motivation and personality traits.

Hypothesis: There is no significant interaction effect of Achievement motivation (High and Low), Personality traits (High and Low) and Social status (High and Low) on vocational aspirations of students of Pre-university College Kannada medium students of Dharwad district.

To test this hypothesis, the Three-way ANOVA with interaction effect design was applied and the results are presented in Table 4.47.

The table reveals that

- The main effect of achievement motivation (High and Low) on vocational aspirations of Pre-university College Kannada medium students is found to be significant at 0.05% level of significance. Since the obtained F value 6.8434 is greater than the F table value 3.8400, the null hypothesis is rejected and alternative hypothesis is accepted. It can be concluded that the vocational aspiration is different in high and low achievement motivation of Pre-university College Kannada medium students.

Table 4.47. Results of ANOVA with 3-way interaction between Achievement motivation (High and Low), Personality traits (High and Low) and Social status (High and Low) with respect to vocational aspirations

SV	*DF*	*SS*	*MSS*	*F-value*	*P-value*	*Signi.*
Main effects						
Achievement motivation	1	560.02	560.02	6.8434	<0.05	S
Personality traits s	1	252.54	252.54	3.0860	>0.05	NS
Social status	1	141.94	141.94	1.7346	>0.05	NS
2-way interactions						
Achievement motivation × Personality traits s	1	71.93	71.93	0.8790	>0.05	NS
Achievement motivation × Social status	1	91.00	91.00	1.1120	>0.05	NS
Personality traits × Social status	1	3.03	3.03	0.0370	>0.05	NS
3-way interactions						
Achievement motivation × Personality traits × Social status	1	17.42	17.42	0.2129	>0.05	NS
Error	662	54173.09	81.83			
Total	669	55310.97				

- The main effect of personality traits (High and Low) on vocational aspirations of Pre-university College Kannada medium students is found to be not significant at 0.05% level of significance. Since the obtained F value 3.0860 is lesser than the F table value 3.8400, the null hypothesis is accepted and alternative hypothesis is rejected. It can be concluded that the vocational aspiration is similar in high and low personality traits of Pre-university College Kannada medium students.
- The main effect of social status (High and Low) on vocational aspirations of Pre-university College Kannada

medium students is found to be not significant at 0.05% level of significance. Since the obtained F value 1.7346 is lesser than the F table value 3.8400, the null hypothesis is accepted and alternative hypothesis is rejected. It can be concluded that the vocational aspiration is similar in high and low social status of Pre-university College Kannada medium students.

- The interaction effect of achievement motivation (High and Low) and Personality traits (High and Low) on vocational aspirations of Pre-university College Kannada medium students is found to be not significant at 0.05% level of significance. Since the obtained F value 0.8790 is lesser than the F table value 3.8400, the null hypothesis is accepted and alternative hypothesis is rejected. It can be concluded that the vocational aspiration is similar with interaction effect of achievement motivation and personality traits.
- The interaction effect of achievement motivation (High and Low) and social status (High and Low) on vocational aspirations of Pre-university College Kannada medium students is found to be not significant at 0.05% level of significance. Since the obtained F value 1.1120 is lesser than the F table value 3.8400, the null hypothesis is accepted and alternative hypothesis is rejected. It can be concluded that vocational aspiration is similar with interaction effect of achievement motivation and social status.
- The interaction effect of Personality traits (High and Low) and social status (High and Low) on vocational aspirations of Pre-university College Kannada medium students is found to be not significant at 0.05% level of significance. Since the obtained F value 0.0370 is lesser than the F table value 3.8400 the null hypothesis is accepted and alternative hypothesis is rejected. It can be concluded that the vocational aspiration is similar with interaction effect of personality traits and social status.

- The interaction effect of achievement motivation (High and Low), Personality traits (High and Low) and social status (High and Low) on vocational aspirations of Pre-university College Kannada medium students is found to be not significant at 0.05% level of significance. Since the obtained F value 0.2129 is lesser than the F table value 3.8400, the null hypothesis is accepted and alternative hypothesis is rejected. It can be concluded that the vocational aspiration is similar with interaction effect of achievement motivation, personality traits and social status.

Hypothesis: There is no significant interaction effect of Achievement motivation (High and Low), Personality traits (High and Low) and Social status (High and Low) on vocational aspirations of students of Pre-university College English medium students of Dharwad district.

To test this hypothesis, the Three-way ANOVA with interaction effect design was applied and the results are presented in Table 4.48.

Table 4.48 reveals that

1. The main effect of achievement motivation (High and Low) on vocational aspirations of Pre-university College English medium students is found to be not significant at 0.05% level of significance. Since the obtained F value 0.2209 is lesser than the F table value 3.8400, the null hypothesis is rejected and alternative hypothesis is accepted. It can be concluded that the vocational aspiration is similar in high and low achievement motivation of Pre-university College English medium students.
2. The main effect of personality traits (High and Low) on vocational aspirations of Pre-university College English medium students is found to be not significant at 0.05% level of significance. Since the obtained F value 1.4258 is lesser than the F table value 3.8400 the null hypothesis is accepted and alternative hypothesis is rejected. It can be concluded that the vocational aspiration is similar in high and low personality traits of Pre-university College English medium students.

Table 4.48. Results of ANOVA with 3-way interaction between Achievement motivation (High and Low), Personality traits (High and Low) and Social status (High and Low) with respect to vocational aspirations

SV	*DF*	*SS*	*MSS*	*F-value*	*P-value*	*Signi.*
Main effects						
Achievement motivation	1	16.00	16.00	0.2209	>0.05	NS
Personality traits s	1	103.29	103.29	1.4258	>0.05	NS
Social status	1	601.73	601.73	8.3063	<0.05	S
2-way interactions						
Achievement motivation × Personality traits s	1	77.80	77.80	1.0739	>0.05	NS
Achievement motivation × Social status	1	2.22	2.22	0.0307	>0.05	NS
Personality traits × Social status	1	0.07	0.07	0.0010	>0.05	NS
3-way interactions						
Achievement motivation × Personality traits × Social status	1	5.74	5.74	0.0792	>0.05	NS
Error	322	23326.69	72.44			
Total	329	24133.55				

3. The main effect of social status (High and Low) on vocational aspirations of Pre-university College English medium students is found to be significant at 0.05% level of significance. Since the obtained F value 8.3063 is greater than the F table value 3.8400, the null hypothesis is rejected and alternative hypothesis is accepted. It can be concluded that the vocational aspiration is different in high and low social status of Pre-university College English medium students.
4. The interaction effect of achievement motivation (High and Low) and Personality traits (High and Low) on

vocational aspirations of Pre-university College English medium students is found to be not significant at 0.05% level of significance. Since the obtained F value 1.0739 is lesser than the F table value 3.8400, the null hypothesis is accepted and alternative hypothesis is rejected. It can be concluded that the vocational aspiration is similar with the interaction effect of achievement motivation and personality traits.

5. The interaction effect of achievement motivation (High and Low) and social status (High and Low) on vocational aspirations of Pre-university College English medium students is found to be not significant at 0.05% level of significance. Since the obtained F value 0.0307 is lesser than the F table value 3.8400, the null hypothesis is accepted and alternative hypothesis is rejected. It can be concluded that the vocational aspiration is similar with the interaction effect of achievement motivation and social status.
6. The interaction effect of Personality traits (High and Low) and social status (High and Low) on vocational aspirations of Pre-university College English medium students is found to be not significant at 0.05% level of significance. Since the obtained F value 0.0010 is lesser than the F table value 3.8400, the null hypothesis is accepted and alternative hypothesis is rejected. It can be concluded that the vocational aspiration is similar with the interaction effect of personality and social status.
7. The interaction effect of achievement motivation (High and Low), Personality traits (High and Low) and social status (High and Low) on vocational aspirations of Pre-university College English medium students is found to be not significant at 0.05% level of significance. Since the obtained F value 0.0792 is lesser than the F table value 3.8400, the null hypothesis is accepted and alternative hypothesis is rejected. It can be concluded that the vocational aspiration is similar with the interaction effect of achievement motivation, personality traits and social status.

Hypothesis: There is no significant interaction effect of Achievement motivation (High and Low), Personality traits (High and Low) and Social status (High and Low) on vocational aspirations of students of government Pre-university Colleges of Dharwad district.

To test this hypothesis, the Three-way ANOVA with interaction effect design was applied and the results are presented in Table 4.49.

Table 4.49. Results of ANOVA with 3-way interaction between Achievement motivation (High and Low), Personality traits (High and Low) and Social status (High and Low) with respect to vocational aspirations

SV	*DF*	*SS*	*MSS*	*F-value*	*P-value*	*Signi.*
Main effects						
Achievement motivation	1	266.23	266.23	3.0801	>0.05	NS
Personality traits s	1	15.69	15.69	0.1815	>0.05	NS
Social status	1	70.87	70.87	0.8199	>0.05	NS
2-way interactions						
Achievement motivation × Personality traits s	1	30.80	30.80	0.3563	>0.05	NS
Achievement motivation × Social status	1	8.55	8.55	0.0989	>0.05	NS
Personality traits × Social status	1	56.88	56.88	0.6580	>0.05	NS
3-way interactions						
Achievement motivation × Personality traits × Social status	1	117.32	117.32	1.3572	>0.05	NS
Error	179	15472.25	86.44			
Total	186	16038.58				

The above table reveals that

- The main effect of achievement motivation (High and Low) on vocational aspirations of government Pre-

University College students is found to be not significant at 0.05% level of significance. Since the obtained F value 3.0801 is lesser than the F table value 3.8400, the null hypothesis is accepted and alternative hypothesis is rejected. It can be concluded that the vocational aspiration is similar in high and low achievement motivation of government Pre-University College students.

- The main effect of personality traits (High and Low) on vocational aspirations of government Pre-University College students is found to be not significant at 0.05% level of significance. Since the obtained F value 0.1815 is lesser than the F table value 3.8400, the null hypothesis is accepted and alternative hypothesis is rejected. It can be concluded that the vocational aspiration is similar in high and low personality traits of government Pre-University College students.
- The main effect of social status (High and Low) on vocational aspirations of government Pre-University College students is found to be not significant at 0.05% level of significance. Since the obtained F value 0.8199 is lesser than the F table value 3.8400, the null hypothesis is accepted and alternative hypothesis is rejected. It can be concluded that the vocational aspiration is similar in high and low social status of government Pre-University College students.
- The interaction effect of achievement motivation (High and Low) and Personality traits (High and Low) on vocational aspirations of Government Pre-University College students is found to be not significant at 0.05% level of significance. Since the obtained F value 0.3563 is lesser than the F table value 3.8400, the null hypothesis is accepted and alternative hypothesis is rejected. It can be concluded that the vocational aspiration of Government college students is similar with the interaction effect of achievement motivation and personality traits.
- The interaction effect of achievement motivation (High and Low) and social status (High and Low) on vocational

aspirations of Government Pre-University College students is found to be not significant at 0.05% level of significance. Since the obtained F value 0.0989 is lesser than the F table value 3.8400, the null hypothesis is accepted and alternative hypothesis is rejected. It can be concluded that the vocational aspiration of Government college students is similar with the interaction effect of achievement motivation and social status.

- The interaction effect of Personality traits (High and Low) and social status (High and Low) on vocational aspirations of Government Pre-University College students is found to be not significant at 0.05% level of significance. Since the obtained F value 0.6580 is lesser than the F table value 3.8400 the null hypothesis is accepted and alternative hypothesis is rejected. It can be concluded that the vocational aspiration of Government college students is similar with the interaction effect of personality traits and social status.
- The interaction effect of achievement motivation (High and Low), Personality traits (High and Low) and social status (High and Low) on vocational aspirations of government Pre-University College students is found to be not significant at 0.05% level of significance. Since the obtained F value 1.3572 is lesser than the F table value 3.8400, the null hypothesis is accepted and alternative hypothesis is rejected. It can be concluded that the vocational aspiration of the Government college students is similar with the interaction effect of achievement motivation and personality traits.

Hypothesis: There is no significant interaction effect of Achievement motivation (High and Low), Personality traits (High and Low) and Social status (High and Low) on vocational aspirations of students of aided Pre-university College students of Dharwad district.

To test this hypothesis, the Three-way ANOVA with interaction effect design was applied and the results are presented in the following Table:

Table 4.50. Results of ANOVA with 3-way interaction between Achievement motivation (High and Low), Personality traits (High and Low) and Social status (High and Low) with respect to vocational aspirations

SV	*DF*	*SS*	*MSS*	*F-value*	*P-value*	*Signi.*
Main effects						
Achievement motivation	1	736.49	736.49	7.9955	<0.01	S
Personality traits s	1	9.47	9.47	0.1028	>0.05	NS
Social status	1	217.89	217.89	2.3654	>0.05	NS
2-way interactions						
Achievement motivation × Personality traits s	1	315.54	315.54	3.4256	>0.05	NS
Achievement motivation × Social status	1	20.95	20.95	0.2275	>0.05	NS
Personality traits x Social status	1	187.97	187.97	2.0406	>0.05	NS
3-way interactions						
Achievement motivation × Personality traits × Social status	1	18.49	18.49	0.2008	>0.05	NS
Error	458	42187.45	92.11			
Total	465	43694.24				

The above table reveals that

1. The main effect of achievement motivation (High and Low) on vocational aspirations of aided Pre-University College students is found to be significant at 0.01% level of significance. Since the obtained F value 7.9955 is greater than the F table value 3.8400, the null hypothesis is rejected and alternative hypothesis is accepted. It can be concluded that the vocational aspiration is different in high and low achievement motivation of aided Pre-University College students.

2. The main effect of personality traits (High and Low) on vocational aspirations of aided Pre-University College students is found to be not significant at 0.05% level of significance. Since the obtained F value 0.1028 is lesser than the F table value 3.8400, the null hypothesis is accepted and alternative hypothesis is rejected. It can be concluded that the vocational aspiration is similar in high and low personality traits of aided Pre-University College students.
3. The main effect of social status (High and Low) on vocational aspirations of aided Pre-University College students is found to be not significant at 0.05% level of significance. Since the obtained F value 2.3654 is lesser than the F table value 3.8400, the null hypothesis is accepted and alternative hypothesis is rejected. It can be concluded that the vocational aspiration is similar in high and low social status of aided Pre-University College students.
4. The interaction effect of achievement motivation (High and Low) and Personality traits (High and Low) on vocational aspirations of aided Pre-University College students is found to be not significant at 0.05% level of significance. Since the obtained F value 3.4256 is lesser than the F table value 3.8400, the null hypothesis is accepted and alternative hypothesis is rejected. It can be concluded that the vocational aspiration is similar with the interaction effect of achievement motivation and personality traits.
5. The interaction effect of achievement motivation (High and Low) and social status (High and Low) on vocational aspirations of aided Pre-University College students is found to be not significant at 0.05% level of significance. Since the obtained F value 0.2275 is lesser than the F table value 3.8400 the null hypothesis is accepted and alternative hypothesis is rejected. It can be concluded that the vocational aspiration is similar with the interaction effect of achievement motivation and social status.

6. The interaction effect of Personality traits (High and Low) and social status (High and Low) on vocational aspirations of aided Pre-University College students is found to be not significant at 0.05% level of significance. Since the obtained F value 2.0406 is lesser than the F table value 3.8400, the null hypothesis is accepted and alternative hypothesis is rejected. It can be concluded that the vocational aspiration is similar with the interaction effect of personality traits and social status.
7. The interaction effect of achievement motivation (High and Low), Personality traits (High and Low) and social status (High and Low) on vocational aspirations of aided Pre-University College students is found to be not significant at 0.05% level of significance. Since the obtained F value 0.2008 is lesser than the F table value 3.8400, the null hypothesis is accepted and alternative hypothesis is rejected. It can be concluded that the vocational aspiration of aided college students is similar with the interaction effect of achievement motivation, personality traits and social status.

Hypothesis: There is no significant interaction effect of Achievement motivation (High and Low), Personality traits (High and Low) and Social status (High and Low) on vocational aspirations of students of unaided Pre-university College students of Dharwad district.

To test this hypothesis, the Three-way ANOVA with interaction effect design was applied and the results are presented in the following Table:

The above table reveals that

- The main effect of achievement motivation (High and Low) on vocational aspirations of unaided Pre-University College students is found to be not significant at 0.05% level of significance. Since the obtained F value 0.7041 is lesser than the F table value 3.8400, the null hypothesis is accepted and alternative hypothesis is rejected. It can be concluded that the vocational aspiration of unaided college students is similar in high and low achievement motivation of unaided Pre-University College students.

Table 4.51. Results of ANOVA with 3-way interaction between Achievement motivation (High and Low), Personality traits (High and Low) and Social status (High and Low) with respect to vocational aspirations

SV	*DF*	*SS*	*MSS*	*F-value*	*P-value*	*Signi.*
Main effects						
Achievement motivation	1	30.96	30.96	0.7041	>0.05	NS
Personality traits s	1	17.78	17.78	0.4044	>0.05	NS
Social status	1	1942.30	1942.30	44.1654	<0.01	S
2-way interactions						
Achievement motivation × Personality traits s	1	614.79	614.79	13.9797	<0.01	S
Achievement motivation × Social status	1	57.33	57.33	1.3035	>0.05	NS
Personality traits × Social status	1	13.57	13.57	0.3085	>0.05	NS
3-way interactions						
Achievement motivation × Personality traits × Social status	1	12.92	12.92	0.2938	>0.05	NS
Error	339	14908.47	43.98			
Total	346	17598.13				

- The main effect of personality traits (High and Low) on vocational aspirations of unaided Pre-University College students is found to be not significant at 0.05% level of significance. Since the obtained F value 0.4044 is lesser than the F table value 3.8400, the null hypothesis is accepted and alternative hypothesis is rejected. It can be concluded that the vocational aspiration of unaided college students is similar in high and low personality traits of unaided Pre-University College students.
- The main effect of social status (High and Low) on vocational aspirations of unaided Pre-University College students is found to be significant at 0.05% level of

significance. Since the obtained F value 44.1654 is greater than the F table value 3.8400, the null hypothesis is rejected and alternative hypothesis is accepted. It can be concluded that the vocational aspiration of unaided college students influenced by is high and low social status of unaided Pre-University College students.

- ➢ The interaction effect of achievement motivation (High and Low) and Personality traits (High and Low) on vocational aspirations of unaided Pre-University College students is found to be significant at 0.01% level of significance. Since the obtained F value 13.9797 is greater than the F table value 3.8400, the null hypothesis is rejected and alternative hypothesis is accepted. It can be concluded that the vocational aspiration of unaided college students influenced by the interaction effect of achievement motivation and personality traits.
- ➢ The interaction effect of achievement motivation (High and Low) and social status (High and Low) on vocational aspirations of unaided Pre-University College students is found to be not significant at 0.05% level of significance. Since the obtained F value 1.3035 is lesser than the F table value 3.8400, the null hypothesis is accepted and alternative hypothesis is rejected. It can be concluded that the vocational aspiration of unaided college students is similar with the interaction effect of achievement motivation and social status.
- ➢ The interaction effect of Personality traits (High and Low) and social status (High and Low) on vocational aspirations of unaided Pre-University College students is found to be not significant at 0.05% level of significance. Since the obtained F value 0.3085 is lesser than the F table value 3.8400, the null hypothesis is accepted and alternative hypothesis is rejected. Therefore it can be concluded that the vocational aspiration of unaided college students are similar with the interaction effect of personality traits and social status.

➢ The interaction effect of achievement motivation (High and Low), Personality traits (High and Low) and social status (High and Low) on vocational aspirations of unaided Pre-University College students is found to be not significant at 0.05% level of significance. Since the obtained F value 0.2938 is lesser than the F table value 3.8400, the null hypothesis is accepted and alternative hypothesis is rejected. It can be concluded that the vocational aspiration of unaided college students is similar with the interaction effect of achievement motivation personality traits and social status.

If F is significant, to know the pairs of interaction effects of achievement motivation (High and Low) and Personality traits (High and Low) on vocational aspirations by applying the Scheffes post hoc multiple comparison tests and the results are presented in Table 4.52.

Table 4.52. Scheffes post hoc test between Achievement motivation x Personality traits

Achievement motivation × Personality traits	*High ×High*	*High × Low*	*Low × High*	*Low × Low*
Means	49.63016	51.33333	51.48704	50.74591
High × High	-			
High × Low	0.0487*	-		
Low × High	0.0319*	0.9995	-	
Low × Low	0.8315	0.9702	0.9521	-

* Significant at 5% level of significance.

The above table reveals that:

➢ The interaction effect of high achievement motivation and high personality traits students with high achievement motivation and low Personality traits of unaided Pre-University College students on vocational aspirations is found to be significant at 0.05% level of significance. It can be concluded that vocational aspiration of unaided college students influenced by the interaction effect of high achievement motivation and high personality traits and high achievement motivation with low personality traits.

- ➢ The interaction effect of high achievement motivation and high personality traits students with low achievement motivation and high Personality traits of unaided Pre-University College students on vocational aspirations is found to be significant at 0.05% level of significance. It can be concluded that the vocational aspiration of unaided college students is influenced with interaction effect of high achievement motivation and low personality traits.

Hypothesis: There is no significant interaction effect of Achievement motivation (High and Low), Personality traits (High and Low) and Social status (High and Low) on vocational aspirations of Pre-university College students belong to GM of Dharwad district.

To test this hypothesis, the Three-way ANOVA with interaction effect design was applied and the results are presented in Table 4.53:

Table 4.53 reveals that

1. The main effect of achievement motivation (High and Low) on vocational aspirations of Pre-University College general merit (GM) students is found to be significant at 0.05% level of significance. Since the obtained F value 4.7307 is greater than the F table value 3.8400, the null hypothesis is rejected and alternative hypothesis is accepted. It can be concluded that the vocational aspiration of students belong to GM is influenced in high and low achievement motivation.
2. The main effect of personality traits (High and Low) on vocational aspirations of Pre-University College general merit (GM) students is found to be not significant at 0.05% level of significance. Since the obtained F value 0.9875 is lesser than the F table value 3.8400, the null hypothesis is accepted and alternative hypothesis is rejected. It can be concluded that the vocational aspiration is similar in high and low personality traits of Pre-University College general merit (GM) students.

Table 4.53. Results of ANOVA with 3-way interaction between Achievement motivation (High and Low), Personality traits (High and Low) and Social status (High and Low) with respect to vocational aspirations

SV	*DF*	*SS*	*MSS*	*F-value*	*P-value*	*Signi.*
Main effects						
Achievement motivation	1	364.89	364.89	4.7307	<0.05	S
Personality traits s	1	76.16	76.16	0.9875	>0.05	NS
Social status	1	1068.86	1068.86	13.8575	<0.01	S
2-way interactions						
Achievement motivation × Personality traits s	1	27.46	27.46	0.3560	>0.05	NS
Achievement motivation × Social status	1	46.86	46.86	0.6076	>0.05	NS
Personality traits × Social status	1	59.31	59.31	0.7690	>0.05	NS
3-way interactions						
Achievement motivation × Personality traits × Social status	1	92.20	92.20	1.1953	>0.05	NS
Error	264	20362.77	77.13			
Total	271	22098.51				

3. The main effect of social status (High and Low) on vocational aspirations of Pre-University College general merit (GM) students is found to be significant at 0.01% level of significance. Since the obtained F value 13.8575 is greater than the F table value 3.8400, the null hypothesis is rejected and alternative hypothesis is accepted. It can be concluded that the vocational aspiration of students with General merit is influenced by social status of Pre-University Colleges.
4. The interaction effect of achievement motivation (High and Low) and Personality traits (High and Low) on

vocational aspirations of Pre-University College general merit (GM) students is found to be not significant at 0.05% level of significance. Since the obtained F value 0.3560 is lesser than the F table value 3.8400, the null hypothesis is accepted and alternative hypothesis is rejected. It can be concluded that the vocational aspiration is similar with the interaction effect of achievement motivation and personality traits.

5. The interaction effect of achievement motivation (High and Low) and social status (High and Low) on vocational aspirations of Pre-University College general merit (GM) students is found to be not significant at 0.05% level of significance. Since the obtained F value 0.6076 is lesser than the F table value 3.8400, the null hypothesis is accepted and alternative hypothesis is rejected. It can be concluded that the vocational aspiration is similar with the interaction effect of achievement motivation and social status.
6. The interaction effect of Personality traits (High and Low) and social status (High and Low) on vocational aspirations of Pre-University College general merit (GM) students is found to be not significant at 0.05% level of significance. Since the obtained F value 0.7690 is lesser than the F table value 3.8400, the null hypothesis is accepted and alternative hypothesis is rejected. It can be concluded that the vocational aspiration is similar with the interaction effect of personality traits and social status.
7. The interaction effect of achievement motivation (High and Low), Personality traits (High and Low) and social status (High and Low) on vocational aspirations of Pre-University College general merit (GM) students is found to be not significant at 0.05% level of significance. Since the obtained F value 1.1953 is lesser than the F table value 3.8400, the null hypothesis is accepted and alternative hypothesis is rejected. It can be concluded that the vocational aspiration is similar with the interaction effect of achievement motivation, personality traits and social status.

Hypothesis: There is no significant interaction effect of Achievement motivation (High and Low), Personality traits (High and Low) and Social status (High and Low) on vocational aspirations of Pre-university College OBC students of Dharwad district.

To test this hypothesis, the Three-way ANOVA with interaction effect design was applied and the results are presented in Table 4.54.

Table 4.54. Results of ANOVA with 3-way interaction between Achievement motivation (High and Low), Personality traits (High and Low) and Social status (High and Low) with respect to vocational aspirations

SV	*DF*	*SS*	*MSS*	*F-value*	*P-value*	*Signi.*
Main effects						
Achievement motivation	1	445.99	445.99	5.2676	<0.05	S
Personality traits s	1	57.45	57.45	0.6786	>0.05	NS
Social status	1	848.88	848.88	10.0262	<0.01	S
2-way interactions						
Achievement motivation × Personality traits s	1	16.00	16.00	0.1890	>0.05	NS
Achievement motivation × Social status	1	60.30	60.30	0.7122	>0.05	NS
Personality traits × Social status	1	47.06	47.06	0.5558	>0.05	NS
3-way interactions						
Achievement motivation × Personality traits × Social status	1	36.25	36.25	0.4282	>0.05	NS
Error	586	49614.59	84.67			
Total	593	51126.53				

The above table reveals that

- The main effect of achievement motivation (High and Low) on vocational aspirations of Pre-University College other backward community (OBC) students is found to be significant at 0.05% level of significance. Since the obtained F value 5.2676 is greater than the F table value 3.8400, the null hypothesis is rejected and alternative hypothesis is accepted. It can be concluded that the vocational aspiration influenced by achievement motivation of Pre-University College other backward community (OBC) students.

- The main effect of personality traits (High and Low) on vocational aspirations of Pre-University College other backward community (OBC) students is found to be not significant at 0.05% level of significance. Since the obtained F value 0.6786 is lesser than the F table value 3.8400, the null hypothesis is accepted and alternative hypothesis is rejected. It can be concluded that the vocational aspiration is similar in high and low personality traits of Pre-University College other backward community (OBC) students.
- The main effect of social status (High and Low) on vocational aspirations of Pre-University College other backward community (OBC) students is found to be significant at 0.01% level of significance. Since the obtained F value 10.0262 is greater than the F table value 3.8400, the null hypothesis is rejected and alternative hypothesis is accepted. It can be concluded that the vocational aspiration if students belong to OBC influenced by social status of Pre-University College other backward community (OBC) students.
- The interaction effect of achievement motivation (High and Low) and Personality traits (High and Low) on vocational aspirations of Pre-University College other backward community (OBC) students is found to be not significant at 0.05% level of significance. Since the obtained F value 0.1890 is lesser than the F table value 3.8400, the null hypothesis is accepted and alternative hypothesis is rejected. It can be concluded that the vocational aspiration of students is similar with the interaction effect of achievement motivation and personality traits.

- The interaction effect of achievement motivation (High and Low) and social status (High and Low) on vocational aspirations of Pre-University College other backward community (OBC) students is found to be not significant at 0.05% level of significance. Since the obtained F value 0.7122 is lesser than the F table value 3.8400, the null hypothesis is accepted and alternative hypothesis is rejected. It can be concluded that the vocational aspiration of OBC students is similar with the interaction effect of achievement motivation and social status.
- The interaction effect of Personality traits (High and Low) and social status (High and Low) on vocational aspirations of Pre-University College other backward community (OBC) students is found to be not significant at 0.05% level of significance. Since the obtained F value 0.5558 is lesser than the F table value 3.8400, the null hypothesis is accepted and alternative hypothesis is rejected. It can be concluded that the vocational aspiration of OBC students is similar with the interaction effect of personality traits and social status.
- The interaction effect of achievement motivation (High and Low), Personality traits (High and Low) and social status (High and Low) on vocational aspirations of Pre-University College other backward community (OBC) students is found to be not significant at 0.05% level of significance. Since the obtained F value 0.4282 is lesser than the F table value 3.8400, the null hypothesis is accepted and alternative hypothesis is rejected. It can be concluded that the vocational aspiration of OBC students is similar with the interaction effect of achievement motivation, personality traits and social status.

Hypothesis: There is no significant interaction effect of Achievement motivation (High and Low), Personality traits (High and Low) and Social status (High and Low) on vocational aspirations of Pre-university College SC/ST/Cat-I students of Dharwad district.

To test this hypothesis, the Three-way ANOVA with interaction effect design was applied and the results are presented in Table 4.55.

Table 4.55. Results of ANOVA with 3-way interaction between Achievement motivation (High and Low), Personality traits (High and Low) and Social status (High and Low) with respect to vocational aspirations

SV	*DF*	*SS*	*MSS*	*F-value*	*P-value*	*Signi.*
Main effects						
Achievement motivation	1	438.84	438.84	4.5727	<0.05	S
Personality traits s	1	84.40	84.40	0.8794	>0.05	NS
Social status	1	400.29	400.29	4.1710	<0.05	S
2-way interactions						
Achievement motivation × Personality traits s	1	96.75	96.75	1.0082	>0.05	NS
Achievement motivation × Social status	1	30.13	30.13	0.3140	>0.05	NS
Personality traits × Social status	1	82.57	82.57	0.8603	>0.05	NS
3-way interactions						
Achievement motivation × Personality traits × Social status	1	29.99	29.99	0.3125	>0.05	NS
Error	126	12092.14	95.97			
Total	133	13255.11				

Table 4.55 reveals that

1. The main effect of achievement motivation (High and Low) on vocational aspirations of Pre-University College SC/ST/Cat-I students is found to be significant at 0.05% level of significance. Since the obtained F value 4.5727 is greater than the F table value 3.8400, the null hypothesis is rejected and alternative hypothesis is

accepted. It can be concluded that the vocational aspiration of SC/ST/Cat-I students is influenced by achievement motivation.

2. The main effect of personality traits (High and Low) on vocational aspirations of Pre-University College SC/ST/Cat-I students is found to be not significant at 0.05% level of significance. Since the obtained F value 0.8794 is lesser than the F table value 3.8400, the null hypothesis is accepted and alternative hypothesis is rejected. It can be concluded that the vocational aspiration is similar in high and low personality traits of Pre-University College SC/ST/Cat-I students.
3. The main effect of social status (High and Low) on vocational aspirations of Pre-University College SC/ST/Cat-I students is found to be significant at 0.05% level of significance. Since the obtained F value 4.1710 is greater than the F table value 3.8400, the null hypothesis is rejected and alternative hypothesis is accepted. It can be concluded that the vocational aspiration of SC/ST/Cat-I students is influenced social status.
4. The interaction effect of achievement motivation (High and Low) and Personality traits (High and Low) on vocational aspirations of Pre-University College SC/ST/Cat-I students is found to be not significant at 0.05% level of significance. Since the obtained F value 1.0082 is lesser than the F table value 3.8400, the null hypothesis is accepted and alternative hypothesis is rejected. It can be concluded that the vocational aspiration is similar with the interaction effect of achievement motivation and personality traits.
5. The interaction effect of achievement motivation (High and Low) and social status (High and Low) on vocational aspirations of Pre-University College SC/ST/Cat-I students is found to be not significant at 0.05% level of significance. Since the obtained F value 0.3140 is lesser than the F table value 3.8400, the null hypothesis is accepted and alternative hypothesis is rejected. It can

be concluded that the vocational aspiration of SC/ST/ Cat-I students is similar with the interaction effect of achievement motivation and social status.

6. The interaction effect of Personality traits (High and Low) and social status (High and Low) on vocational aspirations of Pre-University College SC/ST/Cat-I students is found to be not significant at 0.05% level of significance. Since the obtained F value 0.8603 is lesser than the F table value 3.8400, the null hypothesis is accepted and alternative hypothesis is rejected. It can be concluded that the vocational aspiration of SC/ST/ Cat-I students is similar with the interaction effect of personality traits and social status.
7. The interaction effect of achievement motivation (High and Low), Personality traits (High and Low) and social status (High and Low) on vocational aspirations of Pre-University College SC/ST/Cat-I students is found to be not significant at 0.05% level of significance. Since the obtained F value 0.3125 is lesser than the F table value 3.8400, the null hypothesis is accepted and alternative hypothesis is rejected. It can be concluded that the vocational aspiration of SC/ST/Cat-I students is similar with the interaction effect of achievement motivation, personality traits and social status.

Hypothesis: There is no significant interaction effect of Achievement motivation (High and Low), Personality traits (High and Low) and Social status (High and Low) on vocational aspirations of Pre-university College Rural students of Dharwad district.

To test this hypothesis, the Three-way ANOVA with interaction effect design was applied and the results are presented in Table 4.56:

Table 4.56 reveals that

- The main effect of achievement motivation (High and Low) on vocational aspirations of Pre-University College Rural students is found to be significant at 0.05% level of significance. Since the obtained F value 5.0716 is greater than the F table value 3.8400, the null hypothesis is rejected and alternative hypothesis is accepted. It can be concluded that the vocational aspiration of students of rural colleges is influenced by achievement motivation.

Table 4.56. Results of ANOVA with 3-way interaction between Achievement motivation (High and Low), Personality traits (High and Low) and Social status (High and Low) with respect to vocational aspirations

SV	*DF*	*SS*	*MSS*	*F-value*	*P-value*	*Signi.*
Main effects						
Achievement motivation	1	417.09	417.09	5.0716	<0.05	S
Personality traits s	1	147.53	147.53	1.7938	>0.05	NS
Social status	1	21.03	21.03	0.2558	>0.05	NS
2-way interactions						
Achievement motivation × Personality traits s	1	36.69	36.69	0.4461	>0.05	NS
Achievement motivation × Social status	1	442.26	442.26	5.3776	<0.05	S
Personality traits × Social status	1	2.38	2.38	0.0290	>0.05	NS
3-way interactions						
Achievement motivation × Personality traits × Social status	1	77.89	77.89	0.9471	>0.05	NS
Error	492	40462.59	82.24			
Total	499	41607.48				

- The main effect of personality traits (High and Low) on vocational aspirations of Pre-University College Rural students is found to be not significant at 0.05% level of significance. Since the obtained F value 1.7938 is lesser than the F table value 3.8400, the null hypothesis is accepted and alternative hypothesis is rejected. It can be concluded that the vocational aspiration is similar in high and low personality traits of Pre-University College Rural students.

- The main effect of social status (High and Low) on vocational aspirations of Pre-University College Rural students is found to be not significant at 0.05% level of significance. Since the obtained F value 0.2558 is lesser than the F table value 3.8400, the null hypothesis is rejected and alternative hypothesis is accepted. It can be concluded that the vocational aspiration is similar in high and low social status of Pre-University College Rural students.
- The interaction effect of achievement motivation (High and Low) and Personality traits (High and Low) on vocational aspirations of Pre-University College Rural students is found to be not significant at 0.05% level of significance. Since the obtained F value 0.4461 is lesser than the F table value 3.8400, the null hypothesis is accepted and alternative hypothesis is rejected. It can be concluded that the vocational aspiration of rural students is similar with the interaction effect of achievement motivation.
- The interaction effect of achievement motivation (High and Low) and social status (High and Low) on vocational aspirations of Pre-University College Rural students is found to be significant at 0.05% level of significance. Since the obtained F value 5.3776 is greater than the F table value 3.8400, the null hypothesis is rejected and alternative hypothesis is accepted. It can be concluded that the vocational aspiration of rural students is influenced by the interaction effect of achievement motivation.
- The interaction effect of Personality traits (High and Low) and social status (High and Low) on vocational aspirations of Pre-University College Rural students is found to be not significant at 0.05% level of significance. Since the obtained F value 0.0290 is lesser than the F table value 3.8400, the null hypothesis is accepted and alternative hypothesis is rejected. It can be concluded

that the vocational aspiration of rural students is similar with the interaction effect of personality traits and social status.

- The interaction effect of achievement motivation (High and Low), Personality traits (High and Low) and social status (High and Low) on vocational aspirations of Pre-University College Rural students is found to be not significant at 0.05% level of significance. Since the obtained F value 0.9471 is lesser than the F table value 3.8400, the null hypothesis is accepted and alternative hypothesis is rejected. It can be concluded that the vocational aspiration of rural students is similar with the interaction effect of achievement motivation and social status.

If F is significant, to know the pairs of interaction effects of achievement motivation (High and Low) and social status (High and Low) on vocational aspirations by applying the Scheffes post hoc multiple comparison tests and the results are presented in Table 4.57.

Table 4.57. Scheffes post hoc test between Achievement motivation x Social status

Achievement motivation x Social status	*High x High*	*High x Low*	*Low x High*	*Low x Low*
Means	46.39538	47.21353	45.44857	43.60817
High × High	-			
High × Low	0.9686	-		
Low × High	0.9616	0.5585	-	
Low × Low	0.0492*	0.0027**	0.4698	-

* Significant at 5% level of significance.
** Significant at 1% level of significance.

The above table reveals that

1. The interaction effect of high achievement motivation and high Personality traits with low achievement motivation and low Personality traits of Pre-University College Rural students on vocational aspirations is found

to be significant at 0.05% level of significance. It can be concluded that vocational aspiration of rural students is influenced by the interaction effect of achievement motivation and personality traits.

2. The interaction effect of high achievement motivation and low Personality traits with low achievement motivation and low Personality traits of Pre-University College Rural students on vocational aspirations is found to be significant at 0.05% level of significance. It can be concluded that the vocational aspiration of rural students is influenced by the interaction effect of achievement motivation and personality traits.

Hypothesis: There is no significant interaction effect of Achievement motivation (High and Low), Personality traits (High and Low) and Social status (High and Low) on vocational aspirations of Pre-university College Urban students of Dharwad district.

To test this hypothesis, the Three-way ANOVA with interaction effect design was applied and the results are presented in Table 4.58:

Tabnle 4.58 reveals that

- The main effect of achievement motivation (High and Low) on vocational aspirations of Pre-University College Urban students is found to be not significant at 0.05% level of significance. Since the obtained F value 1.1466 is lesser than the F table value 3.8400, the null hypothesis is accepted and alternative hypothesis is rejected. It can be concluded that the vocational aspiration is similar in high and low achievement motivation of Pre-University College Urban students.
- The main effect of personality traits (High and Low) on vocational aspirations of Pre-University College Urban students is found to be not significant at 0.05% level of significance. Since the obtained F value 2.1001 is lesser than the F table value 3.8400, the null hypothesis is accepted and alternative hypothesis is rejected. It can be concluded that the vocational aspiration is similar in high and low personality traits of Pre-University College Urban students.

Table 4.58. Results of ANOVA with 3-way interaction between Achievement motivation (High and Low), Personality traits (High and Low) and Social status (High and Low) with respect to vocational aspirations

SV	*DF*	*SS*	*MSS*	*F-value*	*P-value*	*Signi.*
Main effects						
Achievement motivation	1	88.51	88.51	1.1466	>0.05	NS
Personality traits s	1	162.13	162.13	2.1001	>0.05	NS
Social status	1	1205.18	1205.18	15.6113	<0.01	S
2-way interactions						
Achievement motivation × Personality traits s	1	7.18	7.18	0.0930	>0.05	NS
Achievement motivation × Social status	1	10.12	10.12	0.1310	>0.05	NS
Personality traits × Social status	1	31.48	31.48	0.4078	>0.05	NS
3-way interactions						
Achievement motivation × Personality traits × Social status	1	82.84	82.84	1.0730	>0.05	NS
Error	492	37981.87	77.20			
Total	499	39569.30				

- The main effect of social status (High and Low) on vocational aspirations of Pre-University College Urban students is found to be significant at 0.01% level of significance. Since the obtained F value 15.6113 is greater than the F table value 3.8400, the null hypothesis is rejected and alternative hypothesis is accepted. It can be concluded that the vocational aspiration of urban college students is influenced by social status.
- The interaction effect of achievement motivation (High and Low) and Personality traits (High and Low) on

vocational aspirations of Pre-University College Urban students is found to be not significant at 0.05% level of significance. Since the obtained F value 0.0930 is lesser than the F table value 3.8400, the null hypothesis is accepted and alternative hypothesis is rejected. It can be concluded that the vocational aspirations of urban college students is similar with the interaction effect of achievement motivation and personality traits.

- The interaction effect of achievement motivation (High and Low) and social status (High and Low) on vocational aspirations of Pre-University College Urban students is found to be not significant at 0.05% level of significance. Since the obtained F value 0.1310 is lesser than the F table value 3.8400, the null hypothesis is accepted and alternative hypothesis is rejected. It can be concluded that the vocational aspirations of urban college students is similar with the interaction effect of achievement motivation.
- The interaction effect of Personality traits (High and Low) and social status (High and Low) on vocational aspirations of Pre-University College Urban students is found to be not significant at 0.05% level of significance. Since the obtained F value 0.4078 is lesser than the F table value 3.8400, the null hypothesis is accepted and alternative hypothesis is rejected. Therefore it can be concluded that vocational aspiration of urban college students is similar with the interaction effect of personality traits and social status.
- The interaction effect of achievement motivation (High and Low), Personality traits (High and Low) and social status (High and Low) on vocational aspirations of Pre-University College Urban students is found to be not significant at 0.05% level of significance. Since the obtained F value 1.0730 is lesser than the F table value 3.8400, the null hypothesis is accepted and alternative hypothesis is rejected. Therefore, it can be concluded that the vocational aspiration of urban college students is similar with the interaction effect of achievement motivation, personality traits and social status.

Correlation Analysis

Correlation analysis deals with the association between two or more variables. It attempts to determine the degree of relationship between variables. The measure of correlation is called the correlation coefficient summarizes in one figure the direction and degree of correlation. Once we know that two variables are closely related, we can estimate the value of one variable given the value of another. This is done with the help of regression analysis.

The problems of analyzing the relation between different series are broken down into the following three steps :

1. Determining whether a relaxation exists and if it does, measuring it.
2. Testing whether it is significant and
3. Establishing the cause and effect relation if any

In this section, 1 and 2 are discussed thoroughly,

Different notations/symbols used in the analysis for convenience

Vocational aspirations is the criterion/dependent variable Y1

Independent variables are denoted by

1. Personality traits X1
2. Achievement Motivation X2
   - I. Long term involvement X3
   - II. Unique accomplishment X4
   - III. Success in competition with standard of excellence X5
   - IV. Desire to excel regardless of social reward X6
3. Social Status X7
4. Educational Status X8
5. Occupational Status X9

Also in this section, the relationship of each of the nine independent variables X1, X2, X3, X4, X5, X6, X7, X8, X9 with the dependent variable Y1 was studied by computing correlation coefficients. This section describes the relationship between certain selected factors with vocational aspirations were calculated.

Relationship between Certain selected factors with vocational aspirations

Hypothesis: There is no significant relationship between Vocational aspirations of Pre-University College students and their Personality traits s, Achievement Motivation, Long term involvement, Unique accomplishment, Success in competition with standard of excellence, Desire to excel regardless of social reward, Social Status, Educational Status and Occupation Status as a whole.

To test the hypothesis, the Karl-Pearson's correlation coefficient technique was applied between dependent variable i.e. vocational aspirations and independent variables (Table 4.59).

Table 4.59. Results of correlation coefficient between vocational aspirations and independent variables of Pre-University College students as a whole

Variables	*Vocational asperiations*	*Person-ality traits s*	*Long term involve-ment*	*Unique accomp-lishment*	*Succ-ess in compe-tition with stand-ard of excee-lence*	*Desire-to excel regard-less of social reward*	*Educ-ational status*	*Occu-pational status*
Vocational aspirations	1.000							
Personality traits	0.0905*	1.0000						
Long term involvement	0.0896*	0.0248	1.0000					
Unique accomplishment	0.0324	0.0703*	0.1976*	1.0000				
Success in competition with standard of excellence	0.0393	0.0916*	0.3161*	0.2861*	1.0000			
Desire to excel regardless of social reward	0.1570**	0.0283	0.2379*	0.1040*	0.2104*	1.0000		
Education status	0.2848**	-0.0544	0.0949*	-0.0069	0.0548	0.1647*	1.0000	
Occupation status	0.1216**	0.0562	-0.0581	0.0218	0.0554	0.0452	0.3466*	1.0000

* Significant at 0.05% level of significance.

** Significant at 0.01 level of significance

The Table 4.59 reveals that:

The significant positive relationship was found between vocational aspirations and Personality traits (r=0.0905), vocational aspirations and Long-term involvement (r=0.0896), vocational aspirations and Desire to excel regardless of social reward (r=0.1570), vocational aspirations and educational status (r=0.2848), vocational aspirations and occupational status (r=0.1216) at 0.05% level of significance. Hence, the null hypothesis is rejected and alternative hypothesis is accepted. It means that increase in the variables like personality traits, long term involvement, desire to excel regardless of social reward, educational status and occupational status these variables are significantly supporting to increase the vocational aspirations of Pre-university College students.

But the relationship between vocational aspirations and unique accomplishment (r=0.0324), Success in competition with standard of excellence (r=0.0393) were found to be not significant at same level of significance. Hence the null hypothesis is accepted and alternative hypothesis is rejected. It means that these variables are not significantly supports to increase the vocational aspirations of Pre-university College students.

Hypothesis: There is no significant relationship between Vocational aspirations of Pre-University College male students and their Personality traits s, Achievement Motivation, Long term involvement, Unique accomplishment, Success in competition with standard of excellence, Desire to excel regardless of social reward, Social Status, Educational Status and Occupation Status.

To test the hypothesis, the Karl-Pearson's correlation coefficient technique was applied between dependent variable i.e. vocational aspirations and independent variables (Table 4.60).

Table 4.60 reveals that:

The significant positive relationship was found between vocational aspirations and educational status (r=0.2538), vocational aspirations and occupational status (r=0.1085) at 0.05% level of significance. Hence, the null hypothesis is rejected and alternative hypothesis is accepted. It means that increase in the variables like educational status and occupational status increases the vocational aspirations of Pre-university College male students.

Table 4.60. Results of correlation coefficient between vocational aspirations and independent variables of Pre-University College male students of Dharwad district

Variables	*Vocational aspiriations*	*Personality traits s*	*Long term involvement*	*Unique accomplishment*	*Success in competition with standard of excellence*	*Desire to excel regardless of social reward*	*Educational status*	*Occupational status*
Vocational aspirations	1.0000							
Personality traits s	-0.1065*	1.0000						
Long term involvement	0.0326	-0.0512	1.0000					
Unique accomplishment	0.0597	0.0918*	0.1843*	1.0000				
Success in competition with standard of excellence	-0.0546	0.0999*	0.2674*	0.3345*	1.0000			
Desire to excel regardless of social reward	0.0601	-0.0053	0.2015*	0.1938*	0.1748*	1.0000		
Education status	0.2538**	-0.1538*	0.0581	0.0237	0.0274	0.0065	1.0000	
Occupation status	0.1085*	-0.0634	-0.1093*	0.0248	-0.0548	-0.0511	0.2709*	1.0000

* Significant at 0.05% level of significance.
** Significant at 0.01 level of significance.

The significant negative relationship was found between vocational aspirations and Personality traits (r=-0.1065) at 0.05% level of significance. Hence, the null hypothesis is rejected and alternative hypothesis is accepted. It means that the increase in personality traits decreases the vocational aspirations of Pre-university College male students.

But the relationship between vocational aspirations and long-term involvement (r=0.0326), unique accomplishment (r=0.0597), Success in competition with standard of excellence (r=-0.0546) and Desire to excel regardless of social reward (r=0.0601) were found to be not significant at same level of significance. Hence the null hypothesis is accepted and alternative hypothesis is rejected. It means that these variables are not significantly supporting the vocational aspirations of Pre-university College male students.

Hypothesis: There is no significant relationship between Vocational aspirations of Pre-University College female students and their Personality traits s, Achievement Motivation, Long term involvement, Unique accomplishment, Success in competition with standard of excellence, Desire to excel regardless of social reward, Social Status, Educational Status and Occupation Status,

To test the hypothesis, the Karl-Pearson's correlation coefficient technique was applied between dependent variable i.e. vocational aspirations and independent variables (Table 4.61).

Table 4.61. Results of correlation coefficient between vocational aspirations and independent variables of Pre-University College female students of Dharwad district

Variables	*Vocational asperiations*	*Personality traits s*	*Long term involvement*	*Unique accomplishment*	*Success in competition with standard of excellence*	*Desire to excel regardless of social reward*	*Educational status*	*Occupational status*
Vocational aspirations	1.0000							
Personality traits s	0.1256*	1.0000						
Long term involvement	0.1620*	0.0507	1.0000					
Unique accomplishment	0.0467	0.0565	0.1741*	1.0000				
Success in competition with standard of excellence	0.1114*	0.0249	0.3169*	0.1859*	1.0000			
Desire to excel regardless of social reward	0.2798**	0.0234	0.2416*	-0.0258	0.2036*	1.0000		
Education status	0.3256**	0.0885*	0.1083*	-0.0620	0.0500	0.3147*	1.0000	
Occupation status	0.1383*	0.0815*	-0.0510	0.0588	0.0472	0.0998*	0.4211*	1.0000

*Significant at 0.05% level of significance.
**Significant at 0.01% level of significance.

Table 4.61 reveals that:

The significant positive relationship was found between vocational aspirations and Personality traits (r=0.1256), vocational aspirations and Long-term involvement (r=0.1620), vocational aspirations and success in competition with standard of excellence (r=0.1114), vocational aspirations and desire to excel regardless of social reward (r=0.2798), vocational aspirations and educational status (r=0.3256), vocational aspirations and occupational status (r=0.1383) at 0.05% level of significance. Hence, the null hypothesis is rejected and alternative hypothesis is accepted. It means that increase the variables like personality traits, long-term investment, success in competition with standard of excellence, desire to excel regardless of social reward, educational status and occupational status increases the vocational aspirations of Pre-university College female students.

But the relationship between vocational aspiration and unique accomplishment (r=0.0597) was found to be not significant at same level of significance. Hence, the null hypothesis is accepted and alternative hypothesis is rejected. It means that this variable is not significantly supporting the vocational aspirations of Pre-university College female students.

Hypothesis: There is no significant relationship between Vocational aspirations of Pre-University College Arts students and their Personality traits s, Achievement Motivation, Long term involvement, Unique accomplishment, Success in competition with standard of excellence, Desire to excel regardless of social reward, Social Status, Educational Status and Occupation Status.

To test the hypothesis, the Karl-Pearson's correlation coefficient technique was applied between dependent variable i.e. vocational aspirations and independent variables (Table 4.62).

Table 4.62 reveals that:

The significant positive relationship was found between vocational aspirations and personality traits (r=0.0752), vocational aspirations and Long-term involvement (r=0.0789), vocational aspirations and desire to excel regardless of social reward (r =0.1022), and vocational aspirations and educational

status (r=0.1038) at 0.05% level of significance. Hence, the null hypothesis is rejected and alternative hypothesis is accepted. It means that increase in the variables personality traits, long-term involvement, desire to excel regardless of social reward and educational status increases the vocational aspirations of Pre-university College arts students.

Table 4.62. Results of correlation coefficient between vocational aspirations and independent variables of Pre-University College Arts students of Dharwad district

Variables	*Vocational asperiations*	*Personality traits s*	*Long term involvement*	*Unique accomplishment*	*Success in competition with standard of excellence*	*Desire to excel regardless of social reward*	*Educational status*	*Occupational status*
Vocational aspirations	1.0000							
Personality traits s	0.0752*	1.0000						
Long term involvement	0.0789*	-0.0701*	1.0000					
Unique accomplishment	0.0581	0.0487	0.1725*	1.0000				
Success in competition with standard of excellence	0.0274	0.0075	0.2683*	0.1770*	1.0000			
Desire to excel regardless of social reward	0.1022*	-0.0295	0.1688*	0.0281	0.0843*	1.0000		
Education status	0.1038*	-0.0528	0.0592	0.0394	-0.0452	0.0501	1.0000	
Occupation status	-0.0023	-0.0465	-0.1510*	0.0081	0.0014	-0.0607	0.1918*	1.0000

* Significant at 0.05% level of significance.

But, the relationship between vocational aspiration and success in competition with standard of excellence (r=0.0274), occupation status (r=-0.0023) was found to be not significant at 0.05% level of significance. Hence the null hypothesis is accepted and alternative hypothesis is rejected. It means that these variables are not significantly supporting the vocational aspirations of Pre-university College arts students.

Hypothesis: There is no significant relationship between Vocational aspirations of Pre-University College Science students and their Personality traits s, Achievement Motivation, Long term involvement, Unique accomplishment, Success in competition with standard of excellence, Desire to excel regardless of social reward, Social Status, Educational Status and Occupation Status.

To test the hypothesis, the Karl-Pearson's correlation coefficient technique was applied between dependent variable i.e. vocational aspirations and independent variables

Table 4.63. Results of correlation coefficient between vocational aspirations and independent variables of Pre-University College Science students of Dharwad district

Variables	*Vocational asperiations*	*Personality traits s*	*Long term involvement*	*Unique accomplishment*	*Success in competition with standard of excellence*	*Desire to excel regardless of social reward*	*Educational status*	*Occupational status*
Vocational aspirations	1.0000							
Personality traits s-	0.1205*	1.0000						
Long term involvement	0.0693	0.0889	1.0000					
Unique accomplishment	0.0460	0.1241*	0.2305*	1.0000				
Success in competition with standard of excellence	0.0769	0.1480*	0.3956*	0.4474*	1.0000			
Desire to excel regardless of social reward	0.0434	0.1109	0.3018*	0.2756*	0.3602*	1.0000		
Education status	0.2223**	0.0963	0.1439*	-0.0036	0.1820*	0.0542	1.0000	
Occupation status	0.1699**	0.1229*	-0.0270	0.0756	0.0548	0.0367	0.4382*	1.0000

* Significant at 0.05% level of significance.

** Significant at 0.01% level of significance

Table 4.63 reveals that:

The significant positive relationship was found between vocational aspirations and occupational status (r =0.2223), and vocational aspirations and educational status (r=0.1699) at 0.05% level of significance. Hence, the null hypothesis is rejected and alternative hypothesis is accepted. It means that increase in the variables like educational status and occupational status increases the vocational aspirations of Pre-university College science students.

However, the significant negative relationship was found between vocational aspirations and Personality traits (r =-0.1205) at 0.05% level of significance. Hence, the null hypothesis is rejected and alternative hypothesis is accepted. It means that increase in the variable like personality traits decreases the vocational aspirations of Pre-university College science students.

But, the relationship between vocational aspiration and long term involvement (r=0.0693), unique accomplishment (r=0.0460), success in competition with standard of excellence (r=0.0769) and desire to excel regardless of social reward (r=00.0434) was found to be not significant at 0.05% level of significance. Hence the null hypothesis is accepted and alternative hypothesis is rejected. It means that these variables are not significantly supporting the vocational aspirations of Pre-university College science students.

Hypothesis: There is no significant relationship between Vocational aspirations of Pre-University College Commerce students and their Personality traits s, Achievement Motivation, Long term involvement, Unique accomplishment, Success in competition with standard of excellence, Desire to excel regardless of social reward, Social Status, Educational Status and Occupation Status.

To test the hypothesis, the Karl-Pearson's correlation coefficient technique was applied between dependent variable i.e. vocational aspirations and independent variables Table 4.64.

Table 4.64 reveals that:

The non-significant positive relationship was found between vocational aspiration and long-term involvement (r=0.0006), vocational aspirations and success in competition with standard of excellence (r=0.0500), vocational aspirations and desire to excel regardless of social reward (r=0.1076), vocational aspirations and educational status (r=0.1053) and vocational aspirations and occupation status (r=0.0599) at 0.05% level of significance. Hence the null hypothesis is accepted and alternative hypothesis is rejected. It means that these variables are significantly not supporting the increase the vocational aspirations of Pre-university College commerce students.

Table 4.64. Results of correlation coefficient between vocational aspirations and independent variables of Pre-University College Commerce students of Dharwad district

Variables	*Vocational asperiations*	*Personality traits s*	*Long term involvement*	*Unique accomplishment*	*Success in competition with standard of excellence*	*Desire to excel regardless of social reward*	*Educational status*	*Occupational status*
Vocational aspirations	1.0000							
Personality traits s	-0.0388	1.0000						
Long term involvement	0.0006	0.2047*	1.0000					
Unique accomplishment	-0.0523	0.0244	0.2219*	1.0000				
Success in competition with standard of excellence	0.0500	0.1012	0.2747*	0.2909*	1.0000			
Desire to excel regardless of social reward	0.1076	0.1030	0.2084*	0.0227	0.1363	1.0000		
Education status	0.1053	0.0514	0.0430	-0.0647	0.0780	0.0246	1.0000	
Occupation status	0.0599	0.0901	0.0453	-0.0574	-0.0202	0.0831	0.3633*	1.0000

* Significant at 0.05% level of significance

But the non-significant negative relationship was found between vocational aspirations and Personality traits (r =-0.0388) and vocational aspiration and unique accomplishment (r=-0.0523) at 0.05% level of significance. Hence the null hypothesis is accepted and alternative hypothesis is rejected. It means that these variables are significantly not supporting to decrease the vocational aspirations of Pre-university College commerce students.

Hypothesis: There is no significant relationship between Vocational aspirations of Pre-University College Kannada medium students and their Personality traits s, Achievement Motivation, Long term involvement, Unique accomplishment, Success in competition with standard of excellence, Desire to excel regardless of social reward, Social Status, Educational Status and Occupation Status.

To test the hypothesis, the Karl-Pearson's correlation coefficient technique was applied between dependent variable i.e. vocational aspirations and independent variables (Table 4.65).

Table 4.65. Results of correlation coefficient between vocational aspirations and independent variables of Pre-University College Kannada medium students of Dharwad district

Variables	*Vocational asperiations*	*Personality traits s*	*Long term involvement*	*Unique accomplishment*	*Success in competition with standard of excellence*	*Desire to excel regardless of social reward*	*Educational status*	*Occupational status*
Vocational aspirations	1.0000							
Personality traits s	0.1407*	1.0000						
Long term involvement	0.0694	0.0961	1.0000					
Unique accomplishment	0.0470	0.1141*	0.2326*	1.0000				
Success in competition with standard of excellence	0.0548	0.1441*	0.3631*	0.4170*	1.0000			
Desire to excel regardless of social reward	0.0706	0.1134*	0.2547*	0.2553*	0.3271*	1.0000		
Education status	0.2086*	0.0928	0.1306*	-0.0344	0.1462*	0.0701	1.0000	
Occupation status	0.1643*	0.1195*	-0.0249	0.0837	0.0438	0.0838	0.4666*	1.0000

* Significant at 0.05% level of significance

Table 4.65 reveals that:

The significant positive relationship was found between vocational aspirations and Personality traits (r=0.1407), vocational aspirations and Educational Status (r=0.2086), and vocational aspirations and occupation status (r=0.1643) at 0.05% level of significance. Hence, the null hypothesis is rejected and alternative hypothesis is accepted. It means that increase in the personality traits, educational status and occupational status increases the vocational aspirations of Pre-university College Kannada medium students.

But the non-significant positive relationship was found between vocational aspirations and long term involvement (r =0.0694), vocational aspiration and unique accomplishment (r=0.0470), vocational aspiration and success in competition with standard of excellence (r=0.0548), vocational aspiration and desire to excel regardless of social reward (r=0.0706) at 0.05% level of significance. Hence the null hypothesis is accepted and alternative hypothesis is rejected. It means that these variables are not supporting to increase the vocational aspirations of Pre-university College Kannada medium students.

Hypothesis: There is no significant relationship between Vocational aspirations of Pre-University College English medium students and their Personality traits s, Achievement Motivation, Long-term involvement, Unique accomplishment, Success in competition with standard of excellence, Desire to excel regardless of social reward, Social Status, Educational Status and Occupation Status.

To test the hypothesis, the Karl-Pearson's correlation coefficient technique was applied between dependent variable i.e. vocational aspirations and independent variables Table 4.66.

Table 4.66 reveals that:

The significant positive relationship was found between vocational aspirations and Educational Status (r=0.2086) and vocational aspirations and occupation status (r=0.1643) at 0.05% level of significance. Hence, the null hypothesis is rejected and alternative hypothesis is accepted. It means that increase in the variable like educational status and occupational status increases the vocational aspirations of Pre-university College English medium students.

Table 4.66. Results of correlation coefficient between vocational aspirations and independent variables of Pre-University College English medium students of Dharwad district

Variables	*Vocation-al asperiations*	*Person-ality traits s*	*Long term involve-ment*	*Unique accomp-lishment*	*Succ-ess in compe-tition with stand-ard of exce-llence*	*Desire-to excel regar-dless of social reward*	*Educ-ational status*	*Occu-pational status*
Vocational aspirations	1.0000							
Personality traits s	-0.1398*	1.0000						
Long term involvement	0.0694	0.0961	1.0000					
Unique accomplishment	0.0470	0.1141*	0.2326*	1.0000				
Success in competition with standard of excellence	0.0548	0.1441*	0.3631*	0.4170*	1.0000			
Desire to excel regardless of social reward	0.0706	0.1134*	0.2547*	0.2553*	0.3271*	1.0000		
Education status	0.2086**	0.0928	0.1306*	-0.0344	0.1462*	0.0701	1.0000	
Occupation status	0.1643*	0.1195*	-0.0249	0.0837	0.0438	0.0838	0.4666*	1.0000

* Significant at 0.05% level of significance.

**Significant at 0.01% level of significance

However, the significant negative relationship was found between vocational aspirations and Personality traits (r=-0.1398) at 0.05% level of significance. Hence the null hypothesis is rejected and alternative hypothesis is accepted. It means that personality traits is decreases the vocational aspirations of Pre-university College English medium students.

But the non-significant positive relationship was found between vocational aspirations and long term involvement (r =0.0694), vocational aspiration and unique accomplishment (r=0.0470), vocational aspiration and success in competition with standard of excellence (r=0.0548), vocational aspiration and desire to excel regardless of social reward (r=0.0706) at 0.05%

level of significance. Hence, the null hypothesis is accepted and alternative hypothesis is rejected. It means that these variables are not supporting to increase the vocational aspirations of Pre-university College English medium students.

Hypothesis: There is no significant relationship between Vocational aspirations of Pre-University Government College students and their Personality traits s, Achievement Motivation, Long term involvement, Unique accomplishment, Success in competition with standard of excellence, Desire to excel regardless of social reward, Social Status, Educational Status and Occupation Status.

To test the hypothesis, the Karl-Pearson's correlation coefficient technique was applied between dependent variable i.e. vocational aspirations and independent variables (Table 4.67).

Table 4.67. Results of correlation coefficient between vocational aspirations and independent variables of Pre-University Government College students of Dharwad district

Variables	*Vocational asperiations*	*Personality traits s*	*Long term involvement*	*Unique accomplishment*	*Success in competition with standard of excellence*	*Desire to excel regardless of social reward*	*Educational status*	*Occupational status*
Vocational aspirations	1.0000							
Personality traits s	0.1743*	1.0000						
Long term involvement	0.0636	0.0935	1.0000					
Unique accomplishment	0.0904	-0.0608	0.1600*	1.0000				
Success in competition with standard of excellence	-0.0236	-0.0531	0.1422*	0.3123*	1.0000			
Desire to excel regardless of social reward	0.0466	-0.0719	0.1325	0.1288	0.1218	1.0000		
Education status	0.1454*	-0.0050	-0.0216	0.0267	-0.1242	0.0668	1.0000	
Occupation status	-0.0513	-0.0415	-0.0803	-0.0534	-0.1099	-0.0519	0.1196	1.0000

* Significant at 0.05% level of significance

Table 4.67 reveals that:

The significant positive relationship was found between vocational aspirations and Personality traits (r=0.1743) and vocational aspirations and Educational Status (r=0.1454) at 0.05% level of significance. Hence, the null hypothesis is rejected and alternative hypothesis is accepted. It means that increase in the variables like personality traits and educational status increases the vocational aspirations of Pre-university Government College students.

However, the significant negative relationship was found between vocational aspirations and success in competition with standard of excellence (r=-0.0236) and vocational aspirations and occupation status (r=-0.0513) at 0.05% level of significance. Hence the null hypothesis is rejected and alternative hypothesis is accepted. It means that this variable is significantly decreases the vocational aspirations of Pre-university Government College students.

But the non-significant positive relationship was found between vocational aspirations and long-term involvement (r =0.0636), vocational aspiration and unique accomplishment (r=0.0904), and vocational aspiration and desire to excel regardless of social reward (r=0.0466) at 0.05% level of significance. Hence the null hypothesis is accepted and alternative hypothesis is rejected. It means that these variables are not supporting to increase the vocational aspirations of Pre-university Government College students.

Hypothesis: There is no significant relationship between Vocational aspirations of Pre-University Aided College students and their Personality traits s, Achievement Motivation, Long term involvement, Unique accomplishment, Success in competition with standard of excellence, Desire to excel regardless of social reward, Social Status, Educational Status and Occupation Status.

To test the hypothesis, the Karl-Pearson's correlation coefficient technique was applied between dependent variable i.e. vocational aspirations and independent variables (Table 4.68).

Table 4.68. Results of correlation coefficient between vocational aspirations and independent variables of Pre-University Aided College students of Dharwad district

Variables	*Vocational asperiations*	*Personality traits s*	*Long term involvement*	*Unique accomplishment*	*Success in competition with standard of excellence*	*Desire to excel regardless of social reward*	*Educational status*	*Occupational status*
Vocational aspirations	1.0000							
Personality traits s	-0.0976*	1.0000						
Long term involvement	0.0788	-0.0560	1.0000					
Unique accomplishment	0.0597	0.1403*	0.1771*	1.0000				
Success in competition with standard of excellence	-0.0012	0.1729*	0.2954*	0.2497*	1.0000			
Desire to excel regardless of social reward	0.1956**	-0.0567	0.1574*	0.0226	0.1203*	1.0000		
Education status	0.1676*	-0.1034*	0.0012	0.0252	0.0019	0.0523	1.0000	
Occupation status	0.0007	-0.0559	-0.1929*	-0.0087	-0.0488	-0.1044*	0.2573*	1.0000

*Significant at 0.05% level of significance, significant at 0.01% level of significance

The above table reveals that:

The significant positive relationship was found between vocational aspirations and desire to excel regardless of social reward (r=0.1956) and vocational aspirations and Educational Status (r=0.1676) at 0.05% level of significance. Hence, the null hypothesis is rejected and alternative hypothesis is accepted. It means that the variables like desire to excel regardless of social reward and educational status increases the vocational aspirations of Pre-university Aided College students.

While, the significant negative relationship was found between vocational aspirations and Personality traits (r=-0.0976)

at 0.05% level of significance. Hence the null hypothesis is rejected and alternative hypothesis is accepted. It means that this variable is significantly decreases the vocational aspirations of Pre-university Aided College students.

However, the significant negative relationship was found between vocational aspirations and success in competition with standard of excellence (r=-0.0012) at 0.05% level of significance. Hence, the null hypothesis is rejected and alternative hypothesis is accepted. It means that this variable is significantly supporting to decrease the vocational aspirations of Pre-university Aided College students.

But the non-significant positive relationship was found between vocational aspiration and unique accomplishment (r=0.0597), and vocational aspiration and occupation status (r=0.0007) at 0.05% level of significance. Hence, the null hypothesis is accepted and alternative hypothesis is rejected. It means that these variables are not supporting to increase the vocational aspirations of Pre-university Aided College students.

Hypothesis: There is no significant relationship between Vocational aspirations of Pre-University Unaided College students and their Personality traits s, Achievement Motivation, Long term involvement, Unique accomplishment, Success in competition with standard of excellence, Desire to excel regardless of social reward, Social Status, Educational Status and Occupation Status.

To test the hypothesis, the Karl-Pearson's correlation coefficient technique was applied between dependent variable i.e. vocational aspirations and independent variables (Table 4.69).

Table 4.69 reveals that:

The significant positive relationship was found between vocational aspirations and Educational Status (r=0.3101) and vocational aspirations and Occupation status (r=0.2333) at 0.05% level of significance. Hence the null hypothesis is rejected and alternative hypothesis is accepted. It means that increase in variables like educational status and occupational status increases the vocational aspirations of Pre-university Unaided College students.

Table 4.69. Results of correlation coefficient between vocational aspirations and independent variables of Pre-University Unaided College students of Dharwad district

Variables	*Vocational asperiations*	*Personality traits s*	*Long term involvement*	*Unique accomplishment*	*Success in competition with standard of excellence*	*Desire to excel regardless of social reward*	*Educational status*	*Occupational status*
Vocational aspirations	1.0000							
Personality traits s	-0.0440	1.0000						
Long term involvement	0.0586	0.0965	1.0000					
Unique accomplishment	0.0596	0.0658	0.2675*	1.0000				
Success in competition with standard of excellence	0.0609	0.0901	0.3891*	0.3338*	1.0000			
Desire to excel regardless of social reward	-0.0034	0.1056*	0.3292*	0.2275*	0.2886*	1.0000		
Education status	0.3101**	0.0514	0.1905*	0.0563	0.1133*	0.1351*	1.0000	
Occupation status	0.2333*	0.0787	0.0475	0.1017	0.0866	0.0957	0.4583*	1.0000

* Significant at 0.05% level of significance.
** Significant at 0.01% level of significance

However, the non-significant negative relationship was found between vocational aspirations and Personality traits (r=-0.0440) and vocational aspirations and Desire to excel regardless of social reward (r=-0.0034) at 0.05% level of significance. Hence the null hypothesis is accepted and alternative hypothesis is rejected. It means that personality traits is significantly decreases the vocational aspirations of Pre-university Unaided College students.

But the non-significant positive relationship was found between vocational aspiration and long-term involvement (r=0.0586), vocational aspiration and unique accomplishment (r=0.0596) and vocational aspiration and success in competition with standard of excellence (r=0.0609) at 0.05% level of significance. Hence, the null hypothesis is accepted and alternative hypothesis is rejected. It means that these variables are not supporting to increase the vocational aspirations of Pre-university Unaided College students.

Hypothesis: There is no significant relationship between Vocational aspirations of Pre-University College GM students and their Personality traits s, Achievement Motivation, Long term involvement, Unique accomplishment, Success in competition with standard of excellence, Desire to excel regardless of social reward, Social Status, Educational Status and Occupation Status.

To test the hypothesis, the Karl-Pearson's correlation coefficient technique was applied between dependent variable i.e. vocational aspirations and independent variables (Table 4.70).

Table 4.70. Results of correlation coefficient between vocational aspirations and independent variables of Pre-University College GM students of Dharwad district

Variables	*Vocational asperiations*	*Personality traits s*	*Long term involvement*	*Unique accomplishment*	*Success in competition with standard of excellence*	*Desire to excel regardless of social reward*	*Educational status*	*Occupational status*
Vocational aspirations	1.0000							
Personality traits s	-0.1808*	1.0000						
Long term involvement	0.1072	0.0201	1.0000					
Unique accomplishment	0.1055	0.1538*	0.1091	1.0000				
Success in competition with standard of excellence	0.0705	0.0981	0.3806*	0.2530*	1.0000			
Desire to excel regardless of social reward	0.2170**	0.0534	0.3000*	0.1960*	0.3225*	1.0000		
Education status	0.3025**	-0.1143	0.1069	-0.0070	0.0736	0.1761*	1.0000	
Occupation status	0.2014**	-0.0793	-0.1145	0.0200	-0.0015	0.0264	0.3547*	1.0000

* Significant at 0.05% level of significance.
** Significant at 0.01% level of significance.

Table 4.70 reveals that:

The significant positive relationship was found between vocational aspirations and desire to excel regardless of social reward (r=0.2170), vocational aspirations and Educational Status (r=0.3025) and vocational aspirations and Occupation status (r=0.2014) at 0.05% level of significance. Hence, the null hypothesis is rejected and alternative hypothesis is accepted. It means that the variables like desire to excel regardless of social reward, educational status and occupational status increases the vocational aspirations of Pre-university General merit students.

The significant negative relationship was found between vocational aspirations and Personality traits (r=-0.1808) at 0.05% level of significance. Hence, the null hypothesis is rejected and alternative hypothesis is accepted. It means that personality traits are significantly supporting to increases the vocational aspirations of Pre-university General merit students.

However, the non-significant positive relationship was found between vocational aspiration and long-term involvement (r=0.1072), vocational aspiration and unique accomplishment (r=0.1055) and vocational aspiration and success in competition with standard of excellence (r=0.0705) at 0.05% level of significance. Hence, the null hypothesis is accepted and alternative hypothesis is rejected. It means that these variables are not supporting to increase the vocational aspirations of Pre-university General merit students.

Hypothesis: There is no significant relationship between Vocational aspirations of Pre-University College OBC students and their Personality traits s, Achievement Motivation, Long term involvement, Unique accomplishment, Success in competition with standard of excellence, Desire to excel regardless of social reward, Social Status, Educational Status and Occupation Status.

To test the hypothesis, the Karl-Pearson's correlation coefficient technique was applied between dependent variable i.e. vocational aspirations and independent variables (Table 4.71).

Table 4.71. Results of correlation coefficient between vocational aspirations and independent variables of Pre-University College OBC students of Dharwad district

Variables	*Vocational asperiations*	*Personality traits s*	*Long term involvement*	*Unique accomplishment*	*Success in competition with standard of excellence*	*Desire to excel regardless of social reward*	*Educational status*	*Occupational status*
Vocational aspirations	1.0000							
Personality traits s	0.0517	1.0000						
Long term involvement	0.0813	0.0279	1.0000					
Unique accomplishment	-0.0094	0.0480	0.2587*	1.0000				
Success in competition with standard of excellence	0.0574	0.0664	0.2769*	0.3064*	1.0000			
Desire to excel regardless of social reward	0.1483*	0.0276	0.2027*	0.0472	0.1380*	1.0000		
Education status	0.2181*	0.0459	0.0824	-0.0097	0.0505	0.1435*	1.0000	
Occupation status	0.0557	0.0384	-0.0731	0.0521	-0.0003	0.0257	0.2542*	1.0000

*Significant at 0.05% level of significance

Table 4.71 reveals that:

The significant positive relationship was found between vocational aspirations and desire to excel regardless of social reward (r=0.1483), and vocational aspirations and educational status (r=0.2181) at 0.05% level of significance. Hence the null hypothesis is rejected and alternative hypothesis is accepted. It means that the variables like desire to excel, regardless of social reward and educational status increases the vocational aspirations of Pre-university other backward (OBC) community students.

While, the non-significant negative relationship was found between vocational aspirations and unique accomplishment (r=-0.0094) at 0.05% level of significance. Hence the null hypothesis is accepted and alternative hypothesis is rejected. It means that variable unique accomplishment increases the vocational aspirations of Pre-university other backward (OBC) community students.

However, the non-significant positive relationship was found between vocational aspiration and Personality traits (r=0.0517), vocational aspiration and long-term involvement (r=0.0813), vocational aspiration and success in competition with standard of excellence (r=0.0574) and vocational aspiration and occupation status (r=0.0557) at 0.05% level of significance. Hence the null hypothesis is accepted and alternative hypothesis is rejected. It means that these variables are not supporting to increase the vocational aspirations of Pre-university other backward community students.

Hypothesis: There is no significant relationship between Vocational aspirations of Pre-University College SC/ST/Cat-I students and their Personality traits s, Achievement Motivation, Long term involvement, Unique accomplishment, Success in competition with standard of excellence, Desire to excel regardless of social reward, Social Status, Educational Status and Occupation Status.

To test the hypothesis, the Karl-Pearson's correlation coefficient technique was applied between dependent variable i.e. vocational aspirations and independent variables (Table 4.72).

Table 4.72 revels that:

The significant positive relationship was found between vocational aspirations and Educational Status (r=0.2960) at 0.05% level of significance. Hence, the null hypothesis is rejected and alternative hypothesis is accepted. It means that increases in educational status increases the vocational aspirations of Pre-university SC/ST/Cat-I students.

While, the non-significant negative relationship was found between vocational aspirations and Personality traits (r=-0.0659) at 0.05% level of significance. Hence, the null hypothesis is accepted and alternative hypothesis is rejected. It means that personality traits variable is decreases the vocational aspirations of Pre-university SC/ST/Cat-I students.

Table 4.72. Results of correlation coefficient between vocational aspirations and independent variables of Pre-University College SC/ST/Cat-I students of Dharwad district

Variables	*Vocational asperiations*	*Personality traits s*	*Long term involvement*	*Unique accomplishment*	*Success in competition with standard of excellence*	*Desire to excel regardless of social reward*	*Educational status*	*Occupational status*
Vocational aspirations	1.0000							
Personality traits s	-0.0659	1.0000						
Long term involvement	0.0984	0.0292	1.0000					
Unique accomplishment	0.1094	0.0261	0.1441*	1.0000				
Success in competition with standard of excellence	0.1206	0.1533	0.3191*	0.2737*	1.0000			
Desire to excel regardless of social reward	0.0224	0.0809	0.2396*	0.1662	0.2577*	1.0000		
Education status	0.2960**	0.0230	0.1552*	0.0425	0.1296	0.1756*	1.0000	
Occupation status	0.1250	0.1018	0.1156	0.0796	0.1380	0.1224	0.5419*	1.0000

* Significant at 0.05% level of significance.
** Significant at 0.01% level of significance.

However, the non-significant positive relationship was found between vocational aspiration and long-term involvement (r=0.0984), vocational aspiration and unique accomplishment (r=0.1094), vocational aspiration and success in competition with standard of excellence (r=0.1206), vocational aspiration and desire to excel regardless of social reward (r=0.0224) and vocational aspiration and occupation status (r=0.1250) at 0.05% level of significance. Hence the null hypothesis is accepted and alternative hypothesis is rejected. It means that these variables are not supporting to increase the vocational aspirations of Pre-university SC/ST/Cat-I students.

Hypothesis: There is no significant relationship between Vocational aspirations of Pre-University College rural students and their Personality traits s, Achievement Motivation, Long term involvement, Unique accomplishment, Success in competition with standard of excellence, Desire to excel regardless of social reward, Social Status, Educational Status and Occupation Status.

To test the hypothesis, the Karl-Pearson's correlation coefficient technique was applied between dependent variable i.e. vocational aspirations and independent variables (Table 6.73).

Table 4.73. Results of correlation coefficient between vocational aspirations and independent variables of Pre-University College rural students of Dharwad district

Variables	*Vocational asperiations*	*Personality traits s*	*Long term involvement*	*Unique accomplishment*	*Success in competition with standard of excellence*	*Desire to excel regardless of social reward*	*Educational status*	*Occupational status*
Vocational aspirations	1.0000							
Personality traits s	0.1181*	1.0000						
Long term involvement	0.1227*	-0.0005	1.0000					
Unique accomplishment	0.0626	0.0400	0.2098*	1.0000				
Success in competition with standard of excellence	0.0537	0.0364	0.2609*	0.2251*	1.0000			
Desire to excel regardless of social reward	0.1153*	-0.0290	0.2270*	0.0076	0.1209*	1.0000		
Education status	0.1434*	-0.0715	0.0240	0.0062	-0.0592	-0.0044	1.0000	
Occupation status	0.0060	-0.0496	-0.1183*	-0.0672	-0.0031	-0.1378*	0.1725*	1.0000

*Significant at 0.05% level of significance.

Table 4.73 reveals that:

The significant positive relationship was found between vocational aspirations and Personality traits (r=0.1181), vocational aspirations and long-term involvement (r=0.1227), vocational aspirations and desire to excel regardless of social reward (r=0.1153) and vocational aspirations and Educational Status (r=0.1434) at 0.05% level of significance. Hence the null hypothesis is rejected and alternative hypothesis is accepted. It means that the variables like personality traits, long term involvement, desire to excel regardless of social reward and educational status increases the vocational aspirations of Pre-university Rural students.

However, the non-significant positive relationship was found between vocational aspiration and unique accomplishment (r=0.0626), vocational aspiration and success in competition with standard of excellence (r=0.0537)) and vocational aspiration and occupation status (r=0.0060) at 0.05% level of significance. Hence the null hypothesis is accepted and alternative hypothesis is rejected. It means that these variables are not supporting to increase the vocational aspirations of Pre-university Rural students.

Hypothesis: There is no significant relationship between Vocational aspirations of Pre-University College urban students and their Personality traits s, Achievement Motivation, Long term involvement, Unique accomplishment, Success in competition with standard of excellence, Desire to excel regardless of social reward, Social Status, Educational Status and Occupation Status.

To test the hypothesis, the Karl-Pearson's correlation coefficient technique was applied between dependent variable i.e. vocational aspirations and independent variables (Table 4.74).

Table 4.74 reveals that:

The significant positive relationship was found between vocational aspirations and Desire to excel regardless of social reward (r=0.0974), vocational aspirations and Educational Status (r=0.2201) and vocational aspirations and Occupation status (r=0.1430) at 0.05% level of significance. Hence the null hypothesis is rejected and alternative hypothesis is accepted. It means that the variables like desire to excel, regardless of social reward, educational status and occupational status increases the vocational aspirations of Pre-university Urban students.

Table 4.74. Results of correlation coefficient between vocational aspirations and independent variables of Pre-University College urban students of Dharwad district

Variables	*Vocational asperiations*	*Personality traits s*	*Long term involvement*	*Unique accomplishment*	*Success in competition with standard of excellence*	*Desire to excel regardless of social reward*	*Educational status*	*Occupational status*
Vocational aspirations	1.0000							
Personality traits s	-0.0959*	1.0000						
Long term involvement	0.0641	0.0411	1.0000					
Unique accomplishment	0.0086	0.0913	0.1893*	1.0000				
Success in competition with standard of excellence	0.0215	0.1244*	0.3494*	0.3296*	1.0000			
Desire to excel regardless of social reward	0.0974*	0.0815	0.2492*	0.1813*	0.2673*	1.0000		
Education status	0.2201**	0.0669	0.1606*	-0.0581	0.1047*	0.1657*	1.0000	
Occupation status	0.1430*	0.0766	-0.0207	0.0953*	0.0222	0.1183*	0.4150*	1.0000

*Significant at 0.05% level of significance.
**Significant at 0.01% level of significance.

While, the significant negative relationship was found between vocational aspirations and Personality traits (r=-0.0959) at 0.05% level of significance. Hence, the null hypothesis is rejected and alternative hypothesis is accepted. It means that this variable is significantly decreases the vocational aspirations of Pre-university Urban students.

However, the non-significant positive relationship was found between vocational aspiration and Long-term involvement (r=0.0641), vocational aspiration and Unique accomplishment (r=0.0086)) and vocational aspiration and Success in competition with standard of excellence (r=0.0215) at 0.05% level of significance. Hence the null hypothesis is accepted and alternative hypothesis is rejected. It means that these variables are not supporting to increase the vocational aspirations of Pre-university Urban students.

Hypothesis: There is no significant relationship between Vocational aspirations of Pre-University College total, male and female students and their Personality traits and its dimensions (A, B, C, D, E, F, G, H, I, J, O, Q2, Q3, Q4) as a whole.

To test the hypothesis, the Karl-Pearson's correlation coefficient technique was applied between dependent variable i.e. vocational aspirations and independent variables (Table 4.75).

Table 4.75. Results of correlation coefficient between Vocational aspirations of Pre-University College total, male and female students and their Personality traits and its dimensions

Variables	*Vocational aspirations*		
	Male Correlation coefficient	*Female Correlation coefficient*	*Total Correlation coefficient*
Personality traits s	-0.1065*	0.1256*	0.0905*
Factors			
A	0.1457*	-0.0451	0.0897*
B	0.1116*	-0.0790	0.0500
C	0.1414*	-0.0578	0.0547
D	-0.0356	0.0590	0.0254
E	0.0603	0.0750	0.0700*
F	-0.0495	-0.0973*	-0.0500
G	0.0046	-0.0310	-0.0500
H	0.0572	0.0768	0.0987*
I	0.0512	-0.0041	0.0000
J	0.0096	0.0047	0.0500
O	-0.0948*	-0.1487*	-0.1300*
Q2	-0.1077*	-0.0951*	-0.0600
Q3	0.0784	-0.0356	0.0500
Q4	0.0548	-0.0310	-0.0200

*Significant at 0.05% level of significance

Table 4.75 reveals that:

- The relationship between vocational aspirations and Personality traits (r=0.0905), vocational aspirations and factor A of Personality traits (r=0.0897), vocational aspirations and factor E of Personality traits (r=0.0700) and vocational aspirations and factor H of Personality traits (r=0.0987) of Pre-university College total students is found to be positive and significant at 0.05% level of significance. It can be concluded that increase in the personality traits A, E, and H factors increases the vocational aspiration of the students. But the relationship between vocational aspirations and factor O of Personality traits (r=-0.1300) of Pre-university College total students is found to be negative and significant at 0.05% level of significance. Hence the null hypothesis is rejected and alternative hypothesis is accepted. However, other factors of Personality traits have not significant relationship with vocational aspirations of Pre-university College total students at 0.05% level of significance.
- The relationship between vocational aspirations and factor A of Personality traits (r=0.1457), vocational aspirations and factor B of Personality traits (r=0.1116) and vocational aspirations and factor C of Personality traits (r=0.1414) of Pre-university College male students is found to be positive and significant at 0.05% level of significance. It can be concluded that the personality factors A, B, and C increases the vocational aspirations of male students. But the relationship between vocational aspirations and Personality traits (r=-0.1065), vocational aspirations and factor O of Personality traits (r=-0.0948) and vocational aspirations and factor Q2 of Personality traits (r=-0.1077) of Pre-university College male students is found to be negative and significant at 0.05% level of significance. Hence the null hypothesis is rejected and alternative hypothesis is accepted. However other factors of Personality traits have not significant relationship with vocational aspirations of Pre-university College male students at 0.05% level of significance.

- The relationship between vocational aspirations and Personality traits (r=0.1256) of Pre-university College female students is found to be positive and significant at 0.05% level of significance. It can be concluded that the increase in the personality factor C increases the vocational aspirations of female students. But the relationship between vocational aspirations and factor F of Personality traits (r=-0.0973), vocational aspirations and factor O of Personality traits (r=-0.1487) and vocational aspirations and factor Q2 of Personality traits (r=-0.0951) of Pre-university College female students is found to be negative and significant at 0.05% level of significance. Hence the null hypothesis is rejected and alternative hypothesis is accepted. However other factors of personality traits have not significant relationship with vocational aspirations of Pre-university College female students at 0.05% level of significance.

Hypothesis: There is no significant relationship between Vocational aspirations of Pre-University College Arts, Science and commerce students and their Personality traits and its dimensions (A, B, C, D, E, F, G, H, I, J, O, Q2, Q3, Q4) as a whole.

To test the hypothesis, the Karl-Pearson's correlation coefficient technique was applied between dependent variable i.e. vocational aspirations and independent variables (Table 4.76).

Table 4.76 reveals that:

- The relationship between vocational aspirations and of Personality traits (r=0.1088), vocational aspirations and factor A of Personality traits (r=0.1528), vocational aspirations and factor C of Personality traits (r=0.1167), vocational aspirations and factor E of Personality traits (r=0.0925), vocational aspirations and factor G of Personality traits (r=0.0980) and vocational aspirations and factor Q3 of Personality traits (r=0.1050) of Pre-university College students with arts subject is found to be positive and significant at 0.05% level of significance. It can be concluded that increase in personality traits factors A, C, E, G and Q3 increases vocational aspirations of students with arts subject. But the relationship between vocational aspirations and factor O of Personality traits (r=-0.1580) of Pre-university College arts students is found to be negative and significant at 0.05% level of significance. Hence, the null hypothesis is rejected and alternative hypothesis is accepted. However, other factors of Personality traits have not significant relationship with vocational aspirations of Pre-university College arts students at 0.05% level of significance.

Table 4.76. Results of correlation coefficient between Vocational aspirations of Pre-University College Arts, Science and commerce students and their Personality traits and its dimensions

Variables	*Vocational aspirations*		
	Arts students Correlation coefficient	*Science students Correlation coefficient*	*Commerce students Correlation coefficient*
Personality traits s	0.1088*	-0.1205*	-0.1824*
Factors			
A	0.1528*	-0.0402	0.0820
B	0.0547	-0.0527	-0.0574
C	0.1167*	-0.0203	-0.0491
D	-0.0820	0.0514	-0.0300
E	0.0925*	0.1376*	0.1695*
F	-0.0567	-0.0099	-0.1837*
G	0.0980*	-0.0399	-0.0809
H	0.0501	0.1283	0.1188
I	0.0651	-0.0519	-0.1388
J	0.0521	0.0680	-0.0235
O	-0.1580*	-0.1482*	0.0930
Q2	0.0062	-0.0648	-0.1885*
Q3	0.1050*	-0.1473*	-0.1993*
Q4	0.0258	-0.0588	-0.0795

* Significant at 0.05% level of significance

- The relationship between vocational aspirations and factor E of Personality traits (r=0.1376) of Pre-university College students with science subject is found to be positive and significant at 0.05% level of significance. It can be concluded that increase in personality traits factor E increases the vocational aspiration of students with science subject. But the relationship between vocational aspirations and Personality traits (r=-0.1205), factor O of Personality traits (r=-0.1482) and factor E of Personality traits (r=-0.1473) of Pre-university College students with science subject is found to be negative and significant at 0.05% level of significance. Hence, the null hypothesis is rejected and alternative hypothesis is accepted. However, other factors of Personality traits have not significant relationship with vocational aspirations of Pre-university College students with science subject at 0.05% level of significance.
- The relationship between vocational aspirations and factor E of Personality traits (r=0.1695) of Pre-university College students with commerce subject is found to be positive and significant at 0.05% level of significance. It can be concluded that increase in personality traits factor E increases the vocational aspirations of students of commerce. But the relationship between vocational aspirations and Personality traits (r=-0.1824), vocational aspirations and factor F of Personality traits (r=-0.1837), vocational aspirations and factor Q2 of Personality traits (r=-0.1885) and vocational aspirations and factor Q3 of Personality traits (r=-0.1993) of Pre-university College students with commerce subject is found to be negative and significant at 0.05% level of significance. Hence the null hypothesis is rejected and alternative hypothesis is accepted. However, other factors of Personality traits have not significant relationship with vocational aspirations of Pre-university College students with commerce subject at 0.05% level of significance.

Hypothesis: There is no significant relationship between Vocational aspirations of Pre-University College Kannada and English medium students and their Personality traits and its dimensions (A, B, C, D, E, F, G, H, I, J, O, Q2, Q3, Q4) as a whole.

To test the hypothesis, the Karl-Pearson's correlation coefficient technique was applied between dependent variable i.e. vocational aspirations and independent variables (Table 4.77).

Table 4.77. Results of correlation coefficient between Vocational aspirations of Pre-University College Kannada and English medium students and their Personality traits and its dimensions

Variables	*Vocational aspirations*	
	Kannada medium students Correlation coefficient	*English medium students Correlation coefficient*
Personality traits s	0.1408*	-0.1398*
Factors		
A	0.1439*	-0.0361
B	0.0324	-0.0371
C	0.0839*	-0.0040
D	-0.0677	0.0516
E	0.0747	0.1953*
F	-0.0457	-0.0339
G	0.1070*	0.1678*
H	0.0518	0.0798
I	0.0488	-0.0802
J	0.0015	0.0274
O	-0.1351*	-0.1277*
Q2	-0.0526	-0.0577
Q3	0.0701	-0.1157*
Q4	-0.0546	-0.0315

*Significant at 0.05% level of significance.

The above table reveals that:

1. The relationship between vocational aspirations and of Personality traits (r=0.1408), vocational aspirations and factor A of Personality traits (r=0.1439), vocational

aspirations and factor C of Personality traits (r=00.0839) and vocational aspirations and factor G of Personality traits (r=0.1070) of Pre-university College Kannada medium students is found to be positive and significant at 0.05% level of significance. It can be concluded that increase in personality traits factors A, C and G increases the vocational aspirations of students studying in Kannada medium colleges. But the relationship between vocational aspirations and factor O of Personality traits (r=-0.1351) of Pre-university College Kannada medium students is found to be negative and significant at 0.05% level of significance. Hence the null hypothesis is rejected and alternative hypothesis is accepted. However, other factors of Personality traits have not significant relationship with vocational aspirations of Pre-university College Kannada medium students at 0.05% level of significance.

2. The relationship between vocational aspirations and factor E of Personality traits (r=0.1953), and vocational aspirations and factor G of Personality traits (r=0.1678) of Pre-university College English medium students is found to be positive and significant at 0.05% level of significance. It can be concluded that increase in personality trait factor E and G increases vocational aspirations of students studying in English medium colleges. But the relationship between vocational aspirations and Personality traits (r=-0.1398), vocational aspirations and factor O of Personality traits (r=-0.1277) and vocational aspirations and factor Q3 of Personality traits (r=-0.1157) of Pre-university College English medium students is found to be negative and significant at 0.05% level of significance. Hence the null hypothesis is rejected and alternative hypothesis is accepted. However, other factors of Personality traits have not significant relationship with vocational aspirations of Pre-university College English medium students at 0.05% level of significance.

Hypothesis: There is no significant relationship between Vocational aspirations of Pre-University government, aided and unaided Students College and their Personality traits and its dimensions (A, B, C, D, E, F, G, H, I, J, O, Q2, Q3, Q4) as a whole.

To test the hypothesis, the Karl-Pearson's correlation coefficient technique was applied between dependent variable i.e. vocational aspirations and independent variables (Table 4.78).

Table 4.78. Results of correlation coefficient between Vocational aspirations of Pre-University government, aided and unaided Students College and their Personality traits and its dimensions

Variables	*Vocational aspirations*		
	Government college Correlation coefficient	*Aided college Correlation coefficient*	*Unaided college Correlation coefficient*
Personality traits s	0.1743*	-0.0976*	-0.0440
Factors			
A	0.1770*	0.0321	0.0414
B	0.0844	0.0515	-0.0266
C	0.0264	-0.0508	0.1331*
D	-0.1454	0.0449	-0.0027
E	0.1758*	0.0542	0.0976
F	-0.1571*	0.1064*	-0.1165*
G	0.1508*	0.0223	-0.1167*
H	-0.0579	0.0581	0.1060
I	0.0810	-0.0521	-0.0836
J	0.0068	-0.0003	-0.0526
O	-0.2343*	-0.1391*	-0.0755
Q2	0.0503	-0.0546	-0.0909
Q3	0.0630	-0.0221	-0.0047
Q4	0.0862	-0.1262*	-0.0419

* Significant at 0.05% level of significance.

Table 4.78 reveals that:

1. The relationship between vocational aspirations and Personality traits (r=0.1743), vocational aspirations and

factor A of Personality traits (r=0.1770), vocational aspirations and factor E of Personality traits (r=0.1758) and vocational aspirations and factor G of Personality traits (r=0.1508) of Pre-university Government College students is found to be positive and significant at 0.05% level of significance. It can be concluded that increase in personality trait factors A, E and G increases vocational aspirations of students studying Government colleges. But the relationship between vocational aspirations and factor F of Personality traits (r=-0.1571) and vocational aspirations and factor F of Personality traits (r=-0.2343) of Pre-university Government College students is found to be negative and significant at 0.05% level of significance. Hence the null hypothesis is rejected and alternative hypothesis is accepted. However, other factors of Personality traits have not significant relationship with vocational aspirations of Pre-university Government College students at 0.05% level of significance.

2. The relationship between vocational aspirations and factor F of Personality traits (r=0.1064) of Pre-university Aided College students is found to be positive and significant at 0.05% level of significance. It can be concluded that increase in personality trait factor F increases the vocational aspiration of aided college students. But the relationship between vocational aspirations and Personality traits (r=-0.0976), vocational aspirations and factor O of Personality traits (r=-0.1391) and vocational aspirations and factor Q4 of Personality traits (r=-0.1262) of Pre-university Aided College students is found to be negative and significant at 0.05% level of significance. Hence the null hypothesis is rejected and alternative hypothesis is accepted. However other factors of Personality traits have not significant relationship with vocational aspirations of Pre-university Aided College students at 0.05% level of significance.

3. The relationship between vocational aspirations and factor C of Personality traits (r=0.1331) of Pre-university

Unaided College students is found to be positive and significant at 0.05% level of significance. It can be concluded that increase in the personality trait factor C increases the vocational aspiration of unaided college students. But relationship between vocational aspirations and factor F of Personality traits (r=-0.1165) and vocational aspirations and factor G of Personality traits (r=-0.1167) of Pre-university Unaided College students is found to be negative and significant at 0.05% level of significance. Hence, the null hypothesis is rejected and alternative hypothesis is accepted. However, other factors of Personality traits have not significant relationship with vocational aspirations of Pre-university Unaided College students at 0.05% level of significance.

Hypothesis: There is no significant relationship between Vocational aspirations of Pre-University College GM, OBC and SC/ST/Cat-I students and their Personality traits and its dimensions (A, B, C, D, E, F, G, H, I, J, O, Q2, Q3, Q4) as a whole.

To test the hypothesis, the Karl-Pearson's correlation coefficient technique was applied between dependent variable i.e. vocational aspirations and independent variables (Table 4.79).

Table 4.79 reveals that:

- The relationship between vocational aspirations and factor E of Personality traits (r=0.1739) and vocational aspirations and factor H of Personality traits (r=0.1716) of Pre-university General merit students is found to be positive and significant at 0.05% level of significance. It can be concluded that increase in the personality trait factor E and H increases the vocational aspirations of students belong to General merit. But the relationship between vocational aspirations and Personality traits (r=-0.1808), vocational aspirations and factor I of Personality traits (r=-0.1998), vocational aspirations and factor O of Personality traits (r=-0.1275), vocational aspirations and factor Q2 of Personality traits (r=-0.1237) and vocational aspirations and factor Q4 of Personality traits (r=-0.1610) of Pre-university General merit students is found to be negative and significant at 0.05% level of significance. Hence the null hypothesis is rejected and alternative hypothesis is accepted. However other factors of Personality traits have not significant relationship with vocational aspirations of Pre-university General merit students at 0.05% level of significance.

Table 4.79. Results of correlation coefficient between Vocational aspirations of Pre-University College GM, OBC and SC/ST/ Cat-I students and their Personality traits and its dimensions

Variables	*Vocational aspirations*		
	GM category Correlation Correlation coefficient	*OBC category Correlation Correlation coefficient*	*SC / ST / Cat-I category Correlation Correlation coefficient*
Personality traits s	-0.1808*	0.1117*	-0.0659
Factors			
A	-0.0049	0.1084*	-0.0563
B	0.0536	0.0570	-0.0579
C	0.0076	0.1118*	-0.1269
D	-0.0268	-0.0371	0.1004
E	0.1739*	0.0916*	0.0024
F	0.0548	-0.0337	-0.1507
G	-0.0234	0.0604	-0.0859
H	0.1716*	0.0756	-0.0698
I	-0.1998*	-0.0058	0.0742
J	0.0559	0.0573	-0.1368
O	-0.1275*	-0.0867*	-0.2192*
Q2	-0.1237*	-0.0461	-0.0034
Q3	-0.0288	0.0280	-0.0230
Q4	-0.1610*	0.0078	-0.0273

* Significant at 0.05% level of significance.

- The relationship between vocational aspirations and Personality traits (r=0.1117), vocational aspirations and factor A of Personality traits (r=0.1084), vocational aspirations and factor C of Personality traits (r=0.1118) and vocational aspirations and factor E of Personality traits (r=0.0916) of Pre-university Other backward community students is found to be positive and significant at 0.05% level of significance. It can be concluded that the increase in personality trait factors A, C and E of increases vocational aspirations of students belong to OBC. But the relationship between vocational aspirations and factor O of Personality traits (r=-0.0867) of Pre-university Other backward cast students is found to be negative and significant at 0.05% level of significance. Hence, the null hypothesis is rejected and alternative hypothesis is accepted. However, other factors of Personality traits have not significant relationship with vocational aspirations of Pre-university Other backward community students at 0.05% level of significance.
- The relationship between vocational aspirations and factor O of Personality traits (r=-0.2192) of Pre-university SC/ST/Cat-I students is found to be negative and significant at 0.05% level of significance. It can be concluded that increase in personality trait factor O decreases the vocational aspirations of SC/ST/Cat-I students. Hence the null hypothesis is rejected and alternative hypothesis is accepted. However, all the other factors of Personality traits have not significant relationship with vocational aspirations of Pre-university SC/ST/Cat-I students at 0.05% level of significance.

Hypothesis: There is no significant relationship between Vocational aspirations of Pre-University College Rural and Urban students and their Personality traits and its dimensions (A, B, C, D, E, F, G, H, I, J, O, Q2, Q3, Q4) as a whole.

To test the hypothesis, the Karl-Pearson's correlation coefficient technique was applied between dependent variable i.e. vocational aspirations and independent variables (Table 4.80).

Table 4.80. Results of correlation coefficient between Vocational aspirations of Pre-University College Rural and Urban students and their Personality traits and its dimensions

Variables	*Vocational aspirations*	
	Rural students *Correlation coefficient*	*Urban students* *Correlation coefficient*
Personality traits s	0.1181*	-0.0959*
Factors		
A	0.1637*	-0.0307
B	0.0544	0.0041
C	0.0882	0.0022
D	-0.1361*	0.0316
E	0.1077*	0.0577
F	-0.1054*	0.0530
G	0.1316*	-0.0584
H	0.0473	0.0679
I	0.0635	-0.1092*
J	0.0447	-0.0519
O	-0.1512*	-0.0600
Q2	0.0506	0.1108*
Q3	0.0790	-0.1457*
Q4	-0.0216	-0.0256

* Significant at 0.05% level of significance.

Table 4.80 reveals that:

- ➤ The relationship between vocational aspirations and Personality traits (r=0.1181), vocational aspirations and factor A of Personality traits (r=0.1637), vocational aspirations and factor E of Personality traits (r=0.1077) and vocational aspirations and factor G of Personality traits (r=0.1316) of Pre-university Rural students is found to be positive and significant at 0.05% level of significance. It can be concluded that increase in personality trait factors A, E and G increases the vocational aspirations of studying in rural areas. But the relationship between vocational aspirations and factor D of Personality traits (r=-0.1361), vocational aspirations and factor F of Personality traits (r=-0.1054), and vocational aspirations and factor O of Personality traits (r=-0.1512) of Pre-university Rural students is found to be negative and significant at 0.05% level of significance. Hence the null hypothesis is rejected and alternative hypothesis is accepted. However other factors of Personality traits have not significant relationship with vocational aspirations of Pre-university Rural students at 0.05% level of significance.

- The relationship between vocational aspirations and factor Q2 of Personality traits (r=0.1108) of Pre-university Urban students is found to be positive and significant at 0.05% level of significance. It can be concluded that the increase personality trait factor Q2 increases the vocational aspirations of students studying in urban areas. But the relationship between vocational aspirations and Personality traits (r=-0.0959) and vocational aspirations and factor I of Personality traits (r=-0.1092) of Pre-university Urban students is found to be negative and significant at 0.05% level of significance. Hence the null hypothesis is rejected and alternative hypothesis is accepted. However other factors of Personality traits have not significant relationship with vocational aspirations of Pre-university Urban students at 0.05% level of significance.

Regression Analysis

Prediction of vocational aspirations-contributing predictor variables

In this section, selected independent variables from the preceding chapter have been carried forward for a multiple regression analysis to determine the relative importance of each variable, the total variance explained by all variables and the net contribution of each variable.

Correlation coefficient merely gives an indication as to the nature of the relationship existing between the variables. But the regression coefficient gives a measure of the change in the dependent variable for some unit change in the independent variable. Thus it is as estimation coefficient, that is to say, for a given value of the independent variable. We can predict what the value of the dependent variable would be. In short, the regression coefficient indicates the trend of variation of the dependent variable in relation to the variations in the independent variable.

Multiple regression analysis enables us to measure the joint effect of any number of independent variables upon a dependent variable. The multiple regression equation describes the average relationship between these variables and this relationship is used to predict the dependent variable.

A vocational aspiration is one of the important areas which has the highest number of correlates. It would be interesting to see how many factors that correlated significantly with vocational aspirations at the simple zero order correlation would turn out to be significant predictors of this area.

The significant zero order correlations between selected independent variables pertaining to the students on one hand and vocational aspirations on the other hand can not be taken to be final and ultimate. This relationship for the zero order correlation between two variables is sometimes misleading and may be erroneous if there is little or no correlation between the variables other than that brought about by their common dependence upon a third variable or several variables (Garret 1973, P.403). Correlation and multiple regressions disclose the degree to which each independent variable is related to vocational aspirations. While the effect of all other independent variables are controlled to identify the type of relationship between independent variables with vocational aspirations of the Pre-university College students, step wise multiple regression analysis is carried out.

Hypothesis: Achievement motivation, personality traits s, Social status, Educational status, and Occupational status are would not be a significant predictor of vocational aspirations of Pre-university College students as a total

To test this hypothesis, the step wise multiple linear regression analysis is applied for identifying the potent factors that predict the vocational aspirations of the Pre-university college students and results are presented in Table 4.81.

Table 4.81. Stepwise regression of predictor variables of vocational aspirations of Pre-University College students (n=1000)

Independent Variables	*Regression Coefficient*	*SE of Coefficient*	*t-value*
Intercept	36.8284	2.4412	15.0860**
Educational Status (X8)	0.8235	0.2128	3.8700**
Social Status (X7)	0.2321	0.0706	3.2892**
Achievement Motivation (X2)	0.2241	0.0752	2.9778*

R=0.3425, R^2=0.1173, F=16.4941, p<0.01, S, Std. Error of estimate: 9.0718.
* Significant at 0.05% level of significance.
** Significant at 0.05% level of significance.

The step-wise regression equation predicting the vocational aspirations (Y1) of Pre-University College students in total turn out to be:

Vocational aspirations (Y1) = 36.8284+ 0.8235X8+0.2321X7+ 0.2241X2

The multiple R of the stepwise regression equation is 0.3425. For testing multiple correlation coefficients the F-ratio (16.4941) was found to be significant at 0.01% level. Thus the null hypothesis is rejected and alternative hypothesis is accepted. Significant R suggests that estimation of vocational aspirations is possible on the basis of the predictors Educational Status (X8), Social Status (X7) and Achievement Motivation (X2). Further, the step wise regression equation shows that Educational Status (X8), Social Status (X7) and Achievement Motivation (X2) can be used predict vocational aspirations and they predict at much three independent variables could predict.

The coefficient of multiple determination of R^2 is 0.1173. It can be therefore, be said that nearly 11.73 percent of the variance in vocational aspirations of Pre-University College students in total accounted for whatever is measured by Educational Status (X8), Social Status (X7) and Achievement Motivation (X2) taken together. Among the educational status is the highest contributor to predict the vocational aspiration which is followed by social status and achievement motivation in their significance to predict. The remaining percentage of the variance must be attributed to variables not measured in the regression equation.

The SE_{est} for the regression equation is 9.0718. This means that each time the regression equation for the sample is used to predict a vocational aspirations, the vocational aspirations will not miss the actual dimension of vocational aspirations of Pre-University College total students by more that ±9.0718.

The relative contributions of Educational Status (X8), Social Status (X7) and Achievement Motivation (X2) independent variables in terms of proportions of variance predicted by each were determined and are given in Table 4.82.

Table 4.82. Contribution of predictor variables in predicting dimension of vocational aspirations of Pre-University College total students of Dharwad district

Predictors	*Beta*	*r*	*Beta × r*	*% of contribution*
Educational Status (X8)	0.1769	0.2848	0.0504	5.0373
Social Status (X7)	0.1436	0.2561	0.0368	3.6770
Achievement Motivation (X2)	0.2435	0.1238	0.0302	3.0154
			0.1173	11.7297

It is evident from above table that 11.7297 percent of variance in the criterion variable is accounted for by variance in of 4.0373 percent in the variable Educational Status (X8), of 3.6770 in the variable Social Status (X7) and of 3.0154 in the variable Achievement Motivation (X2). Thus, it seems that Educational Status (X8) contributes better than the two remaining potent predictors. The next predictor that contributes for predicting the vocational aspirations of the Pre-university College students is Social Status (X7). It is observed from the analysis that total Educational Status (X8), Social Status (X7) and Achievement Motivation (X2) are important in explaining the vocational aspirations of students.

Hypothesis: Achievement motivation, personality traits s, Social status, Educational status, and Occupational status are would not be a significant predictor of vocational aspirations of Pre-university College male students.

To test this hypothesis, the step wise multiple linear regression analysis is applied for identifying the potent factors that predict the vocational aspirations of the Pre-university college students and results are presented in Table 4.83.

Table 4.83. Stepwise regression of predictor variables of vocational aspirations of Pre-University College male students (n=500)

Independent Variables	*Regression Coefficient*	*SE of Coefficient*	*t-value*
Intercept	39.7802	3.5787	11.1158
Achievement Motivation (X2)	0.1883	0.0536	3.5154**
Social Status (X7)	0.0530	0.0585	2.8712**
Personality traits (X1)	0.3180	0.1228	2.5901*
Educational Status (X8)	0.7187	0.3200	2.2458*

R=0.2906, R^2=0.0845, F=5.6859, p<0.05, S, Std. Error of estimate: 10.0060
* Significant at 0.05% level of significance.
** Significant at 0.05% level of significance.

The step-wise regression equation predicting the vocational aspirations (Y1) of Pre-University College male students turn out to be:

Vocational aspirations (Y1) = 39.7802+ 0.1883X2 + 0.0530X7+0.3180X1+0.7187X8

The multiple R of the stepwise regression equation is 0.2906. For testing multiple correlation coefficients the F-ratio (5.6859) was found to be significant at 0.05% level. Thus the null hypothesis is rejected and alternative hypothesis is accepted. Significant R suggests that estimation of vocational aspirations is possible on the basis of the predictors Achievement Motivation (X2), Social Status (X7), Personality traits (X1) and Educational Status (X8). Among these, achievement motivation is the highest contributor to predict the vocational aspirations which followed social status and personality trait and educational status. Further, the stepwise regression equation shows that Achievement Motivation (X2), Social Status (X7), Personality traits (X1) and Educational Status (X8) can be used predict vocational aspirations and they predict at much four independent variables could predict.

The coefficient of multiple determination of R^2 is 0.0845. It can be therefore, be said that nearly 8.75 percent of the variance

in vocational aspirations of Pre-University College male students accounted for whatever is measured by Achievement Motivation (X2), Social Status (X7), Personality traits (X1) and Educational Status (X8) taken together. The remaining percentage of the variance must be attributed to variables not measured in the regression equation

The SE_{est} for the regression equation is 10.0060. This means that each time the regression equation for the sample is used to predict a vocational aspirations, the vocational aspirations will not miss the actual dimension of vocational aspirations of Pre-University College male students by more that ±10.0060.

Table 4.84. Contribution of predictor variables in predicting dimension of vocational aspirations of Pre-University College male students of Dharwad district

Predictors	*Beta*	*r*	*Beta x r*	*% of contribution*
Achievement Motivation (X2)	0.2099	0.2367	0.0497	4.9682
Social Status (X7)	0.1834	0.2538	0.0466	4.6555
Personality traits (X1)	-0.1536	-0.1065	0.0564	1.6357
Educational Status (X8)	0.1108	0.0415	0.0046	0.4593
			0.1172	11.7187

It is evident from Table 4.84 that, 11.7187 percent of variance in the criterion variable is accounted for by variance in of 4.9682 percent in the variable Achievement Motivation (X2), of 4.6555 in the variable Social Status (X7), of 1.6357 in the variable Personality traits (X1) and of 0.4593 of 1.6357 in the variable Educational Status (X8). Thus, it seems that Achievement Motivation (X2) contributes better than the three remaining potent predictors. The next predictor that contributes for predicting the vocational aspirations of the Pre-university College male students is Social Status (X7). It is observed from the analysis that the Achievement Motivation (X2), Social Status (X7), Personality traits (X1) and Educational Status (X8) are important in explaining the vocational aspirations of male students.

Hypothesis: Achievement motivation, personality traits s, Social status, Educational status, and Occupational status are would not be a significant predictor of vocational aspirations of Pre-university College female students

To test this hypothesis, the step wise multiple linear regression analysis is applied for identifying the potent factors that predict the vocational aspirations of the Pre-university college students and results are presented in Table 4.85.

Table 4.85. Stepwise regression of predictor variables of vocational aspirations of Pre-University College female students (n=500)

Independent Variables	*Regression Coefficient*	*SE of Coefficient*	*t-value*
Intercept	33.6656	1.8843	17.8666**
Educational Status (X8)	0.9832	0.1408	6.9813*
Achievement Motivation (X2)	0.4287	0.0991	4.3268**

R=0.2930, R^2=0.0859, F=5.7879, $p<0.05$, S, Std.Error of estimate: 7.9910

* Significant at 0.05% level of significance

** Significant at 0.05% level of significance

The step-wise regression equation predicting the vocational aspirations (Y1) of Pre-University College female students turn out to be:

Vocational aspirations (Y1) = 33.6656+ 0.9832X8+0.4287X2

The multiple R of the stepwise regression equation is 0.2930. For testing multiple correlation coefficients the F-ratio (5.7879) was found to be significant at 0.05% level. Thus, the null hypothesis is rejected and alternative hypothesis is accepted. Significant R suggests that estimation of vocational aspirations is possible on the basis of the predictors Educational Status (X8) and Achievement Motivation (X2). Further, the stepwise regression equation shows that Educational Status (X8) and Achievement Motivation (X2) can be used predict vocational aspirations and they predict at much two independent variables could predict.

The coefficient of multiple determination of R^2 is 0.0859. It can be therefore, be said that nearly 8.59 percent of the variance

in vocational aspirations of Pre-University College female students accounted for whatever is measured by Educational Status (X8) and Achievement Motivation (X2) taken together. The remaining percentage of the variance must be attributed to variables not measured in the regression equation

The SE_{est} for the regression equation is 7.9910. This means that each time the regression equation for the sample is used to predict a vocational aspirations, the vocational aspirations will not miss the actual dimension of vocational aspirations of Pre-University College female students by more that ±7.9910.

Table 4.86. Contribution of predictor variables in predicting dimension of vocational aspirations of Pre-University College female students of Dharwad district

Predictors	*Beta*	*r*	*Beta x r*	*% of contribution*
Educational Status (X8)	0.1541	0.3256	0.0502	5.0176
Achievement Motivation (X2)	0.1536	0.2323	0.0357	3.5682
			0.0859	8.5857

It is evident from Table 4.86 that, 8.5857 percent of variance in the criterion variable is accounted for by variance in of 5.0176 percent in the variable Educational Status (X8) and of 3.5682 in the variable Achievement Motivation (X2). Thus, it seems that Educational Status (X8) contributes better than the remaining potent predictors. The next predictor that contributes for predicting the vocational aspirations of the Pre-university College female students is Achievement Motivation (X2). It is observed from the analysis that the Educational Status (X8) and Achievement Motivation (X2) are important in explaining the vocational aspirations of female students.

Hypothesis: Achievement motivation, personality traits s, Social status, Educational status, and Occupational status are would not be a significant predictor of vocational aspirations of Pre-university College arts students

To test this hypothesis, the step wise multiple linear regression analysis is applied for identifying the potent factors that predict the vocational aspirations of the Pre-university college students and results are presented in Table 4.87 :

Table 4.87. Stepwise regression of predictor variables of vocational aspirations of Pre-University College arts students (n=555)

Independent Variables	*Regression Coefficient*	*SE of Coefficient*	*t-value*
Intercept	31.4330	3.4678	9.0642**
Personality traits (X1)	0.0513	0.0598	2.5862**
Educational Status (X8)	0.3945	0.1621	2.4335*
Achievement Motivation (X2)	0.2715	0.1128	2.4068*

R=0.1817, R^2=0.0330, F=6.2750 p<0.05, S, Std. Error of estimate: 8.9310

*** Significant at 0.05% level of significance.**

**** Significant at 0.05% level of significance.**

The step-wise regression equation predicting the vocational aspirations (Y1) of Pre-University College arts students turn out to be:

Vocational aspirations (Y1) = 31.4330 + 0.0513X1 + 0.3945X8+0.2715X2

The multiple R of the stepwise regression equation is 0.1817. For testing multiple correlation coefficients the F-ratio (6.2750) was found to be significant at 0.05% level. Thus, the null hypothesis is rejected and alternative hypothesis is accepted. Significant R suggests that estimation of vocational aspirations is possible on the basis of the predictors Personality traits (X1), Educational Status (X8) and Achievement Motivation (X2). Further, the stepwise regression equation shows that Personality traits (X1), Educational Status (X8) and Achievement Motivation (X2) can be used predict vocational aspirations and they predict at much three independent variables could predict.

The coefficient of multiple determination of R^2 is 0.0330. It can be therefore, be said that nearly 3.30 percent of the variance in vocational aspirations of Pre-University College arts students accounted for whatever is measured by Personality traits (X1),

Educational Status (X8) and Achievement Motivation (X2) taken together. The remaining percentage of the variance must be attributed to variables not measured in the regression equation

The SE_{est} for the regression equation is 8.9310. This means that each time the regression equation for the sample is used to predict a vocational aspirations, the vocational aspirations will not miss the actual dimension of vocational aspirations of Pre-University College arts students by more that ±8.9310.

Table 4.88. Contribution of predictor variables in predicting dimension of vocational aspirations of Pre-University College arts students of Dharwad district

Predictors	*Beta*	*r*	*Beta x r*	*% of contribution*
Personality traits (X1)	0.1084	0.1088	0.0518	1.1788
Educational Status (X8)	0.1020	0.1038	0.0506	1.0591
Achievement Motivation (X2)	0.1009	0.1056	0.0507	1.0657
			0.0330	3.3036

It is evident from Table 4.88 that, 3.3036 percent of variance in the criterion variable is accounted for by variance in of 1.1788 percent in the variable Personality traits (X1), of 1.0591 in the Educational Status (X8) and of 1.0657 in the variable Achievement Motivation (X2). Thus, it seems that Personality traits (X1) contributes better than the remaining potent predictors. The next predictor that contributes for predicting the vocational aspirations of the Pre-university College arts students is Educational Status (X8). It is observed from the analysis that the Personality traits (X1), Educational Status (X8) and Achievement Motivation (X2) are important in explaining the vocational aspirations of arts students.

Hypothesis: Achievement motivation, personality traits s, Social status, Educational status, and Occupational status are would not be a significant predictor of vocational aspirations of Pre-university College science students

To test this hypothesis, the step wise multiple linear regression analysis is applied for identifying the potent factors that predict the vocational aspirations of the Pre-university college students and results are presented in Table 4.89:

Table 4.89. Stepwise regression of predictor variables of vocational aspirations of Pre-University College Science students (n=298)

Independent Variables	*Regression Coefficient*	*SE of Coefficient*	*t-value*
Intercept	42.8405	2.6129	16.3959**
Social Status (X7)	0.5170	0.1311	3.9450**
Achievement Motivation (X2)	0.2106	0.1045	2.0144*

R=0.2440, R^2=0.0595, F=4.3370, p<0.05, S, Std. Error of estimate: 8.4360

* Significant at 0.05% level of significance.

** Significant at 0.05% level of significance.

The step-wise regression equation predicting the vocational aspirations (Y1) of Pre-University College science students turn out to be:

Vocational aspirations (Y1) = 42.8405+ 0.5170X7+0.2106X2

The multiple R of the stepwise regression equation is 0.2440. For testing multiple correlation coefficients the F-ratio (4.3370) was found to be significant at 0.05% level. Thus, the null hypothesis is rejected and alternative hypothesis is accepted. Significant R suggests that estimation of vocational aspirations is possible on the basis of the predictors Social Status (X7) and Achievement Motivation (X2). Further, the stepwise regression equation shows that Social Status (X7) and Achievement Motivation (X2) can be used predict vocational aspirations and they predict at much two independent variables could predict.

The coefficient of multiple determination of R^2 is 0.0595. It can be therefore, be said that nearly 5.95 percent of the variance in vocational aspirations of Pre-University College science students accounted for whatever is measured by Social Status (X7) and Achievement Motivation (X2) taken together. The remaining percentage of the variance must be attributed to variables not measured in the regression equation

The SE_{est} for the regression equation is 8.4360. This means that each time the regression equation for the sample is used to predict a vocational aspirations, the vocational aspirations will not miss the actual dimension of vocational aspirations of Pre-University College science students by more that ±8.4360.

Table 4.90. Contribution of predictor variables in predicting dimension of vocational aspirations of Pre-University College science students of Dharwad district

Predictors	*Beta*	*r*	*Beta x r*	*% of contribution*
Social Status (X7)	0.2244	0.2223	0.0499	4.9878
Achievement Motivation (X2)	0.1146	0.0843	0.0097	0.9666
			0.0595	5.9544

It is evident from Table 4.90 that 5.9544 percent of variance in the criterion variable is accounted for by variance in of 4.9878 percent in the variable Social Status (X7) and of 0.9666 in the variable Achievement Motivation (X2). Thus, it seems that Social Status (X7) contributes better than the remaining potent predictors. The next predictor that contributes for predicting the vocational aspirations of the Pre-university College science students is Achievement Motivation (X2). It is observed from the analysis that the Social Status (X7) and Achievement Motivation (X2) are important in explaining the vocational aspirations of science students.

Hypothesis: Achievement motivation, personality traits s, Social status, Educational status, and Occupational status are would not be a significant predictor of vocational aspirations of Pre-university College Commerce students

To test this hypothesis, the step wise multiple linear regression analysis is applied for identifying the potent factors that predict the vocational aspirations of the Pre-university college students and results are presented in Table 4.91:

Table 4.91. Stepwise regression of predictor variables of vocational aspirations of Pre-University College Commerce students (n=147)

Independent Variables	*Regression Coefficient*	*SE of Coefficient*	*t-value*
Intercept	54.1944	6.0751	8.9207**
Educational Status (X8)	0.5702	0.2660	2.1438*
Personality traits (X1)	-0.0954	0.0377	-2.5341*

R=0.1833, R^2=0.0336, F=3.3817, $p<0.05$, S, Std. Error of estimate: 8.8103

* Significant at 0.05% level of significance

** Significant at 0.05% level of significance

The step-wise regression equation predicting the vocational aspirations (Y1) of Pre-University College commerce students turn out to be:

Vocational aspirations (Y1) = 54.1944+0.5702X8-0.0954X1

The multiple R of the stepwise regression equation is 0.1833. For testing multiple correlation coefficients the F-ratio (3.3817) was found to be significant at 0.05% level. Thus the null hypothesis is rejected and alternative hypothesis is accepted. Significant R suggests that estimation of vocational aspirations is possible on the basis of the predictors Educational Status (X8) and Personality traits (X1). Further the stepwise regression equation shows that Educational Status (X8) and Personality traits (X1) can be used predict vocational aspirations and they predict at much two independent variables could predict.

The coefficient of multiple determination of R^2 is 0.0336. It can be therefore, be said that nearly 3.36 percent of the variance in vocational aspirations of Pre-University College commerce students accounted for whatever is measured by Educational Status (X8) and Personality traits (X1) taken together. The remaining percentage of the variance must be attributed to variables not measured in the regression equation.

The SE_{est} for the regression equation is 8.8103. This means that each time the regression equation for the sample is used to predict a vocational aspirations, the vocational aspirations will not miss the actual dimension of vocational aspirations of Pre-University College commerce students by more that ±8.8103.

Table 4.92. Contribution of predictor variables in predicting dimension of vocational aspirations of Pre-University College commerce students of Dharwad district

Predictors	*Beta*	*r*	*Beta x r*	*% of contribution*
Educational Status (X8)	0.1758	0.1453	0.0255	2.5544
Personality traits (X1)	-0.2077	-0.0388	0.0081	0.8057
			0.0336	3.3601

It is evident from Table 4.92 that 3.3601 percent of variance in the criterion variable is accounted for by variance in of 2.5544

percent in the variable Educational Status (X8) and of 0.8057 in the variable Personality traits (X1). Thus it seems that Personality traits (X1) contributes better than the remaining potent predictors. The next predictor that contributes for predicting the vocational aspirations of the Pre-university College commerce students is Personality traits (X1). It is observed from the analysis that the Educational Status (X8) and Personality traits (X1) are important in explaining the vocational aspirations of commerce students.

Hypothesis: Achievement motivation, personality traits s, Social status, Educational status, and Occupational status are would not be a significant predictor of vocational aspirations of Pre-university College Kannada medium students

To test this hypothesis, the step wise multiple linear regression analysis is applied for identifying the potent factors that predict the vocational aspirations of the Pre-university college students and results are presented in Table 4.93.

Table 4.93. Stepwise regression of predictor variables of vocational aspirations of Pre-University College Kannada medium students (n=670)

Independent Variables	*Regression Coefficient*	*SE of Coefficient*	*t-value*
Intercept	33.5468	3.2311	10.3826**
Educational Status (X8)	0.5028	0.1485	3.3856**
Achievement Motivation (X2)	0.2284	0.1022	2.2343*
Personality traits (X1)	0.0391	0.0589	2.0654*

R=0.1910, R^2=0.0365, F=8.4293, p<0.01, S, Std. Error of estimate: 9.0158

* Significant at 0.05% level of significance

** Significant at 0.05% level of significance

The step-wise regression equation predicting the vocational aspirations (Y1) of Pre-University College Kannada medium students turn out to be:

Vocational aspirations (Y1) = 33.5468 + 0.5028X8 + 0.2284X2+0.0391X1

The multiple R of the stepwise regression equation is 0.1910. For testing multiple correlation coefficients the F-ratio (8.4293) was found to be significant at 0.01% level. Thus the null hypothesis is rejected and alternative hypothesis is accepted. Significant R suggests that estimation of vocational aspirations is possible on the basis of the predictors Educational Status (X8), Achievement Motivation (X2) and Personality traits (X1). Further the stepwise regression equation shows that Educational Status (X8), Achievement Motivation (X2) and Personality traits (X1) can be used predict vocational aspirations and they predict at much three independent variables could predict.

The coefficient of multiple determination of R^2 is 0.0365. It can be therefore, be said that nearly 3.65 percent of the variance in vocational aspirations of Pre-University College Kannada medium students accounted for whatever is measured by Educational Status (X8), Achievement Motivation (X2) and Personality traits (X1) taken together. The remaining percentage of the variance must be attributed to variables not measured in the regression equation.

The SE_{est} for the regression equation is 9.0158. This means that each time the regression equation for the sample is used to predict a vocational aspirations, the vocational aspirations will not miss the actual dimension of vocational aspirations of Pre-University College Kannada medium students by more that ±9.0158.

Table 4.94. Contribution of predictor variables in predicting dimension of vocational aspirations of Pre-University College Kannada medium students of Dharwad district

Predictors	*Beta*	*r*	*Beta x r*	*% of contribution*
Educational Status (X8)	0.1293	0.1333	0.0572	1.7233
Achievement Motivation (X2)	0.0854	0.0955	0.0082	0.8153
Personality traits (X1)	0.0788	0.1407	0.0511	1.1089
			0.0365	3.6475

It is evident from Table 4.94 that 3.6475 percent of variance in the criterion variable is accounted for by variance in of 1.7233

percent in the variable Educational Status (X8) of 0.8153 in the variable Achievement Motivation (X2) and of 1.1089 in the variable Personality traits (X1). Thus, it seems that Educational Status (X8) contributes better than the remaining potent predictors. The next predictor that contributes for predicting the vocational aspirations of the Pre-university College Kannada medium students is Personality traits (X1). It is observed from the analysis that the Educational Status (X8), Achievement Motivation (X2) and Personality traits (X1) are important in explaining the vocational aspirations of Kannada medium students.

Hypothesis: Achievement motivation, personality traits s, Social status, Educational status, and Occupational status are would not be a significant predictor of vocational aspirations of Pre-university College English medium students

To test this hypothesis, the step wise multiple linear regression analysis is applied for identifying the potent factors that predict the vocational aspirations of the Pre-university college students and results are presented in Table 4.95.

Table 4.95. Stepwise regression of predictor variables of vocational aspirations of Pre-University College English medium students (n=330)

Independent Variables	*Regression Coefficient*	*SE of Coefficient*	*t-value*
Intercept	46.0455	3.3319	13.8194**
Social Status (X7)	0.4725	0.1198	3.9447**
Achievement Motivation (X2)	0.2855	0.1030	2.7714**
Personality traits (X1)	-0.0455	0.0591	-2.3788*

R=0.2793, R^2=0.0780, F=9.2496, p<0.01, S, Std. Error of estimate: 8.3924

* Significant at 0.05% level of significance

** Significant at 0.05% level of significance

The step-wise regression equation predicting the vocational aspirations (Y1) of Pre-University College English medium students turn out to be:

Vocational aspirations (Y1) = 46.0455+0.4725X7+0.2855X2-0.0455X1

The multiple R of the stepwise regression equation is 0.2793. For testing multiple correlation coefficients the F-ratio (9.2496) was found to be significant at 0.01% level. Thus, the null hypothesis is rejected and alternative hypothesis is accepted. Significant R suggests that estimation of vocational aspirations is possible on the basis of the predictors Social Status (X7), Achievement Motivation (X2) and Personality traits (X1). Further, the stepwise regression equation shows that Social Status (X7), Achievement Motivation (X2) and Personality traits (X1) can be used predict vocational aspirations and they predict at much three independent variables could predict.

The coefficient of multiple determination of R^2 is 0.0780. It can be therefore, be said that nearly 7.80 percent of the variance in vocational aspirations of Pre-University College English medium students accounted for whatever is measured by Social Status (X7), Achievement Motivation (X2) and Personality traits (X1) taken together. The remaining percentage of the variance must be attributed to variables not measured in the regression equation

The SE_{est} for the regression equation is 8.3924. This means that each time the regression equation for the sample is used to predict a vocational aspirations, the vocational aspirations will not miss the actual dimension of vocational aspirations of Pre-University College English medium students by more that ±8.3924.

Table 4.96. Contribution of predictor variables in predicting dimension of vocational aspirations of Pre-University College English medium students of Dharwad district

Predictors	*Beta*	*r*	*Beta x r*	*% of contri-bution*
Social Status (X7)	0.2136	0.2171	0.0464	4.6386
Achievement Motivation (X2)	0.1521	0.0877	0.0533	1.3343
Personality traits (X1)	-0.1307	-0.1398	0.0583	1.8272
			0.0780	7.8001

It is evident from Table 4.76 that 7.8001 percent of variance in the criterion variable is accounted for by variance in of 4.6386

percent in the variable Social Status (X7), of 1.3343 in the variable Achievement Motivation (X2) and of 1.8272 in the variable Personality traits (X1). Thus it seems that Social Status (X7) contributes better than the remaining potent predictors. The next predictor that contributes for predicting the vocational aspirations of the Pre-university College English medium students is Personality traits (X1). It is observed from the analysis that the Social Status (X7), Achievement Motivation (X2) and Personality traits (X1) are important in explaining the vocational aspirations of English medium students.

Hypothesis: Achievement motivation, personality traits s, Social status, Educational status, and Occupational status are would not be a significant predictor of vocational aspirations of Pre-university government College students

To test this hypothesis, the step wise multiple linear regression analysis is applied for identifying the potent factors that predict the vocational aspirations of the Pre-university college students and results are presented in Table 4.97.

Table 4.97. Stepwise regression of predictor variables of vocational aspirations of Pre-University government College students (n=187)

Independent Variables	*Regression Coefficient*	*SE of Coefficient*	*t-value*
Intercept	38.8837	3.6017	10.7958**
Educational Status (X8)	0.5597	0.2521	2.2198*
Achievement Motivation (X2)	0.4170	0.1978	2.1083*

R=0.2144, R^2=0.0460, F=4.4794, $p<0.05$, S, Std. Error of estimate: 9.1869

* Significant at 0.05% level of significance

** Significant at 0.05% level of significance

The step-wise regression equation predicting the vocational aspirations (Y1) of Pre-University Government college students turn out to be:

Vocational aspirations (Y1) = 38.8837+0.5597X8+0.4170X2

The multiple R of the stepwise regression equation is 0.2144. For testing multiple correlation coefficients the F-ratio (4.4794) was found to be significant at 0.05% level. Thus the null hypothesis is rejected and alternative hypothesis is accepted. Significant R suggests that estimation of vocational aspirations is possible on the basis of the predictors Educational Status (X8) and Achievement Motivation (X2). Further the stepwise regression equation shows that Educational Status (X8) and Achievement Motivation (X2) can be used predict vocational aspirations and they predict at much two independent variables could predict.

The coefficient of multiple determination of R^2 is 0.0460. It can be therefore, be said that nearly 4.60 percent of the variance in vocational aspirations of Pre-University Government college students accounted for whatever is measured by Educational Status (X8) and Achievement Motivation (X2) taken together. The remaining percentage of the variance must be attributed to variables not measured in the regression equation.

The SE_{est} for the regression equation is 9.1869. This means that each time the regression equation for the sample is used to predict a vocational aspirations, the vocational aspirations will not miss the actual dimension of vocational aspirations of Pre-University Government college students by more that ±9.1869.

Table 4.98. Contribution of predictor variables in predicting dimension of vocational aspirations of Pre-University government College students of Dharwad district

Predictors	*Beta*	*r*	*Beta x r*	*% of contribution*
Educational Status (X8)	0.1614	0.1454	0.0235	2.3462
Achievement Motivation (X2)	0.1530	0.1470	0.0225	2.2491
			0.0460	4.5953

It is evident from Table 4.98 that, 4.5953 percent of variance in the criterion variable is accounted for by variance in of 2.3462 percent in the variable Educational Status (X8) and of 2.2491 in the variable Achievement Motivation (X2). Thus it seems that Educational Status (X8) contributes better than the remaining potent predictors. The next predictor that contributes for predicting the vocational aspirations of the Pre-university Government college students is Achievement Motivation (X2). It is observed from the analysis that the Educational Status (X8) and Achievement Motivation (X2) are important in explaining the vocational aspirations of Government students.

Hypothesis: Achievement motivation, personality traits s, Social status, Educational status, and Occupational status are would not be a significant predictor of vocational aspirations of Pre-university aided College students

To test this hypothesis, the step wise multiple linear regression analysis is applied for identifying the potent factors that predict the vocational aspirations of the Pre-university college students and results are presented in Table 4.99.

Table 4.99. Stepwise regression of predictor variables of vocational aspirations of Pre-University aided College students (n=466)

Independent Variables	*Regression Coefficient*	*SE of Coefficient*	*t-value*
Intercept	36.0863	2.4614	14.6611**
Educational Status (X8)	0.6583	0.1811	3.6360**
Achievement Motivation (X2)	0.3895	0.1320	2.9500**

R=0.2145, R^2=0.0461, F=10.7309, p<0.01, S, Std. Error of estimate: 9.5443
* Significant at 0.05% level of significance
** Significant at 0.05% level of significance

The step-wise regression equation predicting the vocational aspirations (Y1) of Pre-University Aided college students turn out to be:

Vocational aspirations (Y1) = 36.0863+0.6583X8+0.3895X2

The multiple R of the stepwise regression equation is 0.2145. For testing multiple correlation coefficients the F-ratio (10.7309) was found to be significant at 0.01% level. Thus, the null hypothesis is rejected and alternative hypothesis is accepted. Significant R suggests that estimation of vocational aspirations is possible on the basis of the predictors Educational Status (X8) and Achievement Motivation (X2). Further, the stepwise regression equation shows that Educational Status (X8) and Achievement Motivation (X2) can be used predict vocational aspirations and they predict at much two independent variables could predict.

The coefficient of multiple determination of R^2 is 0.0461. It can be therefore, be said that nearly 4.61 percent of the variance in vocational aspirations of Pre-University Aided college students accounted for whatever is measured by Educational Status (X8) and Achievement Motivation (X2) taken together. The remaining percentage of the variance must be attributed to variables not measured in the regression equation

The SE_{est} for the regression equation is 9.5443. This means that each time the regression equation for the sample is used to predict a vocational aspirations, the vocational aspirations will not miss the actual dimension of vocational aspirations of Pre-University Aided college students by more that ±9.5443.

Table 4.100. Contribution of predictor variables in predicting dimension of vocational aspirations of Pre-University aided College students of Dharwad district

Predictors	*Beta*	*r*	*Beta x r*	*% of contribution*
Educational Status (X8)	0.1651	0.1676	0.0277	2.7661
Achievement Motivation (X2)	0.1339	0.1370	0.0583	1.8349
			0.0460	4.6010

It is evident from Table 4.100 that, 4.6010 percent of variance in the criterion variable is accounted for by variance in of 2.7661 percent in the variable Educational Status (X8) and of 1.8349 in the variable Achievement Motivation (X2). Thus it seems that Educational Status (X8) contributes better than the remaining potent predictors. The next predictor that contributes for predicting the vocational aspirations of the Pre-university Aided college students is Achievement Motivation (X2). It is observed from the analysis that the Educational Status (X8) and Achievement Motivation (X2) are important in explaining the vocational aspirations of Aided students.

Hypothesis: Achievement motivation, personality traits s, Social status, Educational status, and Occupational status are would not be a significant predictor of vocational aspirations of Pre-university unaided College students

To test this hypothesis, the step wise multiple linear regression analysis is applied for identifying the potent factors that predict the vocational aspirations of the Pre-university college students and results are presented in Table 4.101.

Table 4.101. Stepwise regression of predictor variables of vocational aspirations of Pre-University unaided College students (n=347)

Independent Variables	*Regression Coefficient*	*SE of Coefficient*	*t-value*
Intercept	41.8050	3.4841	11.9988**
Educational Status (X8)	0.5234	0.1529	3.4229**
Achievement Motivation (X2)	0.2010	0.0956	2.1032*
Social Status (X7)	0.4077	0.2037	2.0011*

R=0.3641, R^2=0.1326, F=17.5794, p<0.01, S, Std.Error of estimate: 7.8961

* Significant at 0.05% level of significance

** Significant at 0.05% level of significance

The step-wise regression equation predicting the vocational aspirations (Y1) of Pre-University Unaided college students turn out to be:

Vocational aspirations (Y1) = 41.8050 + 0.5234X8 + 0.2010X2+0.4077X7

The multiple R of the stepwise regression equation is 0.3641. For testing multiple correlation coefficients the F-ratio (17.5794) was found to be significant at 0.01% level. Thus, the null hypothesis is rejected and alternative hypothesis is accepted. Significant R suggests that estimation of vocational aspirations is possible on the basis of the predictors Educational Status (X8), Achievement Motivation (X2) and Social Status (X7). Further, the stepwise regression equation shows that Educational Status (X8), Achievement Motivation (X2) and Social

Status (X7) can be used predict vocational aspirations and they predict at much three independent variables could predict.

The coefficient of multiple determination of R^2 is 0.1326. It can be therefore, be said that nearly 13.26 percent of the variance in vocational aspirations of Pre-University Unaided college students accounted for whatever is measured by Educational Status (X8), Achievement Motivation (X2) and Social Status (X7) taken together. The remaining percentage of the variance must be attributed to variables not measured in the regression equation

The SE_{est} for the regression equation is 7.8961. This means that each time the regression equation for the sample is used to predict a vocational aspirations, the vocational aspirations will not miss the actual dimension of vocational aspirations of Pre-University Unaided college students by more that ±7.8961.

Table 4.102. Contribution of predictor variables in predicting dimension of vocational aspirations of Pre-University unaided College students of Dharwad district

Predictors	*Beta*	*r*	*Beta x r*	*% of contribution*
Predictors contribution	Beta	r	Beta x r	% of
Educational Status (X8)	0.2185	0.3101	0.0678	6.7752
Achievement Motivation (X2)	0.1616	0.0592	0.0096	0.9574
Social Status (X7)	0.1740	0.3176	0.0553	5.5269
			0.1326	13.2595

It is evident from Table 4.102 that 13.2595 percent of variance in the criterion variable is accounted for by variance in of 6.7752 percent in the variable Educational Status (X8), of 5.5269 percent in the variable Social Status (X7) and of 0.9574 in the variable Achievement Motivation (X2). Thus, it seems that Educational Status (X8) contributes better than the remaining potent predictors. The next predictor that contributes for predicting the vocational aspirations of the Pre-university Unaided college students is Social Status (X7). It is observed from the analysis that the Educational Status (X8), Achievement Motivation (X2) and Social Status (X7) are important in explaining the vocational aspirations of unaided students.

Hypothesis: Achievement motivation, personality traits s, Social status, Educational status, and Occupational status are would not be a significant predictor of vocational aspirations of Pre-university College GM students.

To test this hypothesis, the step wise multiple linear regression analysis is applied for identifying the potent factors that predict the vocational aspirations of the Pre-university college students and results are presented in Table 4.103.

Table 4.103. Stepwise regression of predictor variables of vocational aspirations of Pre-University College GM students (n=272)

Independent Variables	*Regression Coefficient*	*SE of Coefficient*	*t-value*
Intercept	34.2117	2.8551	11.9826**
Social Status (X7)	0.9059	0.2355	3.8474**
Educational Status (X8)	0.3443	0.1255	2.7426**
Achievement Motivation (X2)	0.8926	0.4067	2.1948*

R=0.4565, R^2=0.2084, F=23.6888, p<0.01, S, Std. Error of estimate: 8.5845
* Significant at 0.05% level of significance.
** Significant at 0.05% level of significance.

The step-wise regression equation predicting the vocational aspirations (Y1) of Pre-University College GM students turn out to be:

Vocational aspirations (Y1) = 34.2117 + 0.9059X7 + 0.3443X8+0.8926X2

The multiple R of the stepwise regression equation is 0.4565. For testing multiple correlation coefficients the F-ratio (23.6888) was found to be significant at 0.01% level. Thus, the null hypothesis is rejected and alternative hypothesis is accepted. Significant R suggests that estimation of vocational aspirations is possible on the basis of the predictors Social Status (X7), Educational Status (X8) and Achievement Motivation (X2). Further, the stepwise regression equation shows that Social Status (X7), Educational Status (X8) and Achievement Motivation (X2) can be used predict vocational aspirations and they predict at much three independent variables could predict.

The coefficient of multiple determination of R^2 is 0.2084. It can be therefore, be said that nearly 20.84 percent of the variance in vocational aspirations of Pre-University College GM students accounted for whatever is measured by Social Status (X7), Educational Status (X8) and Achievement Motivation (X2) taken together. The remaining percentage of the variance must be attributed to variables not measured in the regression equation

The SE_{est} for the regression equation is 8.5845. This means that each time the regression equation for the sample is used to predict a vocational aspirations, the vocational aspirations will not miss the actual dimension of vocational aspirations of Pre-University College GM students by more that ±8.5845.

Table 4.104. Contribution of predictor variables in predicting dimension of vocational aspirations of Pre-University College GM students of Dharwad district

Predictors	*Beta*	*r*	*Beta x r*	*% of contri-bution*
Social Status (X7)	0.3739	0.3089	0.1155	11.5494
Educational Status (X8)	0.2094	0.3025	0.0633	6.3337
Achievement Motivation (X2)	0.1586	0.1862	0.0295	2.9534
			0.2084	20.8366

It is evident from Table 4.104 that, 20.8366 percent of variance in the criterion variable is accounted for by variance in of 11.5494 percent in the variable Social Status (X7), of 6.3337 percent in the variable Educational Status (X8) and of 2.9534 in the variable Achievement Motivation (X2). Thus, it seems that Social Status (X7) contributes better than the remaining potent predictors. The next predictor that contributes for predicting the vocational aspirations of the Pre-university College GM students is Educational Status (X8). It is observed from the analysis that the Social Status (X7), Educational Status (X8) and Achievement Motivation (X2) are important in explaining the vocational aspirations of GM students.

Hypothesis: Achievement motivation, personality traits s, Social status, Educational status, and Occupational status are would not be a significant predictor of vocational aspirations of Pre-university College OBC students.

To test this hypothesis, the step wise multiple linear regression analysis is applied for identifying the potent factors that predict the vocational aspirations of the Pre-university college students and results are presented in Table 4.105.

Table 4.105. Stepwise regression of predictor variables of vocational aspirations of Pre-University College OBC students (n=594)

Independent Variables	*Regression Coefficient*	*SE of Coefficient*	*t-value*
Intercept	34.5559	3.2461	10.6455**
Educational Status (X8)	0.7928	0.1519	5.2181**
Personality traits (X1)	0.0845	0.0599	4.2452**
Achievement Motivation (X2)	0.4108	0.1007	4.0801**

R=0.3119, R^2= 0.0973, F=21.2653, p<0.01, S, Std. Error of estimate: 9.0838

* Significant at 0.05% level of significance.

** Significant at 0.05% level of significance.

The step-wise regression equation predicting the vocational aspirations (Y1) of Pre-University College OBC students turn out to be:

Vocational aspirations (Y1) = 34.5559 + 0.7928X8 + 0.0845X7+0.4108X2

The multiple R of the stepwise regression equation is 0.3119. For testing multiple correlation coefficients the F-ratio (21.2653) was found to be significant at 0.01% level. Thus, the null hypothesis is rejected and alternative hypothesis is accepted. Significant R suggests that estimation of vocational aspirations is possible on the basis of the predictors Educational Status (X8), Personality traits (X1) and Achievement Motivation (X2). Further, the stepwise regression equation shows that Educational Status (X8), Personality traits (X1) and Achievement Motivation (X2) can be used predict vocational aspirations and they predict at much three independent variables could predict.

The coefficient of multiple determination of R^2 is 0.0973. It can be therefore, be said that nearly 9.73 percent of the variance

in vocational aspirations of Pre-University College OBC students accounted for whatever is measured by Educational Status (X8), Personality traits (X1) and Achievement Motivation (X2) taken together. The remaining percentage of the variance must be attributed to variables not measured in the regression equation

The SE_{est} for the regression equation is 9.0838. This means that each time the regression equation for the sample is used to predict a vocational aspirations, the vocational aspirations will not miss the actual dimension of vocational aspirations of Pre-University College OBC students by more that ±9.0838.

Table 4.106. Contribution of predictor variables in predicting dimension of vocational aspirations of Pre-University College OBC students of Dharwad district

Predictors	*Beta*	*r*	*Beta x r*	*% of contribution*
Educational Status (X8)	0.2098	0.2181	0.0458	4.5752
Personality traits (X1)	0.1705	0.2117	0.0361	3.6087
Achievement Motivation (X2)	0.1652	0.0935	0.0554	
	1.5441	0.0973	9.7280	

It is evident from Table 4.106 that, 9.7280 percent of variance in the criterion variable is accounted for by variance in of 4.5752 percent in the variable Educational Status (X8), of 3.6087 percent in the variable Personality traits (X1) and of 1.5441 in the variable Achievement Motivation (X2). Thus, it seems that Educational Status (X8) contributes better than the remaining potent predictors. The next predictor that contributes for predicting the vocational aspirations of the Pre-university College OBC students is Personality traits (X1). It is observed from the analysis that the Educational Status (X8), Personality traits (X1) and Achievement Motivation (X2) are important in explaining the vocational aspirations of OBC students.

Hypothesis: Achievement motivation, personality traits s, Social status, Educational status, and Occupational status are would not be a significant predictor of vocational aspirations of Pre-university College SC/ST/Cat-I students

To test this hypothesis, the step wise multiple linear regression analysis is applied for identifying the potent factors that predict the vocational aspirations of the Pre-university college students and results are presented in Table 4.107.

Table 4.107. Stepwise regression of predictor variables of vocational aspirations of Pre-University College SC/ST/Cat-I students (n=134)

Independent Variables	*Regression Coefficient*	*SE of Coefficient*	*t-value*
Intercept	41.0001	5.4352	7.5434**
Personality traits (X1)	0.0753	0.0272	2.7684**
Achievement Motivation (X2)	0.2844	0.1204	2.3621*
Educational Status (X8)	0.7228	0.3237	2.2329*

R=0.1794, R^2=0.0322, F=6.5597, p<0.05, S, Std. Error of estimate: 9.6516

* Significant at 0.05% level of significance.

** Significant at 0.05% level of significance.

The step-wise regression equation predicting the vocational aspirations (Y1) of Pre-University College SC/ST/CAT-I students turn out to be:

Vocational aspirations (Y1) = 41.0001 + 0.0753X1 + 0.2844X2+0.7228X8

The multiple R of the stepwise regression equation is 0.1794. For testing multiple correlation coefficients the F-ratio (6.5597) was found to be significant at 0.05% level. Thus, the null hypothesis is rejected and alternative hypothesis is accepted. Significant R suggests that estimation of vocational aspirations is possible on the basis of the predictors Personality traits (X1), Achievement Motivation (X2) and Educational Status (X8). Further, the stepwise regression equation shows that Education Personality traits (X1), Achievement Motivation (X2) and Educational Status (X8) can be used predict vocational aspirations and they predict at much three independent variables could predict.

The coefficient of multiple determination of R^2 is 0.0322. It can be therefore, be said that nearly 3.22 percent of the variance in vocational aspirations of Pre-University College SC/ST/CAT-

I students accounted for whatever is measured by Personality traits (X1), Achievement Motivation (X2) and Educational Status (X8) taken together. The remaining percentage of the variance must be attributed to variables not measured in the regression equation

The SE_{est} for the regression equation is 9.6516. This means that each time the regression equation for the sample is used to predict a vocational aspirations, the vocational aspirations will not miss the actual dimension of vocational aspirations of Pre-University College SC/ST/CAT-I students by more that ±9.6516.

Table 4.108. Contribution of predictor variables in predicting dimension of vocational aspirations of Pre-University College SC/St/Cat-I students of Dharwad district

Independent Variables	*Regression Coefficient*		*SE of Coefficient*	*t-value*
Personality traits (X1)	0.1111	-0.0659	-0.0073	-0.7321
Achievement Motivation (X2)	0.0947	0.1350	0.0528	1.2790
Educational Status (X8)	0.0902	0.2960	0.0267	2.6703
			0.0322	3.2172

It is evident from Table 4.108 that, 3.2172 percent of variance in the criterion variable is accounted for by variance in of 1.2790 percent in the variable Achievement Motivation (X2), of 2.6703 percent in the variable Educational Status (X8) and of -0.7321 in the variable Personality traits (X1). Thus, it seems that Educational Status (X8) contributes better than the remaining potent predictors. The next predictor that contributes for predicting the vocational aspirations of the Pre-university College SC/ST/CAT-I students is Achievement Motivation (X2). It is observed from the analysis that the Personality traits (X1), Achievement Motivation (X2) and Educational Status (X8) are important in explaining the vocational aspirations of SC/ST/CAT-I students.

Hypothesis: Achievement motivation, personality traits s, Social status, Educational status, and Occupational status are would not be a significant predictor of vocational aspirations of Pre-university College rural students.

To test this hypothesis, the step wise multiple linear regression analysis is applied for identifying the potent factors that predict the vocational aspirations of the Pre-university college students and results are presented in Table 4.109.

Table 4.109. Stepwise regression of predictor variables of vocational aspirations of Pre-University College rural students (n=500)

Independent Variables	*Regression Coefficient*	*SE of Coefficient*	*t-value*
Intercept	30.8356	3.6465	8.4563**
Educational Status (X8)	0.5755	0.1728	3.3296**
Achievement Motivation (X2)	0.3491	0.1188	2.9390**
Personality traits (X1)	0.0479	0.0210	2.2794*

R=0.2240, R^2=0.0502, F=8.7722, p<0.05, S, Std. Error of estimate: 9.0205

* Significant at 0.05% level of significance

** Significant at 0.05% level of significance

The step-wise regression equation predicting the vocational aspirations (Y1) of Pre-University College rural students turn out to be:

Vocational aspirations (Y1) = 30.8356 + 0.5755X8 + 0.3491X2+0.0479X1

The multiple R of the stepwise regression equation is 0.2240. For testing multiple correlation coefficients the F-ratio (8.7722) was found to be significant at 0.05% level. Thus, the null hypothesis is rejected and alternative hypothesis is accepted. Significant R suggests that estimation of vocational aspirations is possible on the basis of the predictors Educational Status (X8), Achievement Motivation (X2) and Personality traits (X1). Further, the stepwise regression equation shows that Educational Status (X8), Achievement Motivation (X2) and Personality traits (X1) can be used predict vocational aspirations and they predict at much three independent variables could predict.

The coefficient of multiple determination of R^2 is 0.0502. It can be therefore, be said that nearly 5.02 percent of the variance

in vocational aspirations of Pre-University College rural students accounted for whatever is measured by Educational Status (X8), Achievement Motivation (X2) and Personality traits (X1) taken together. The remaining percentage of the variance must be attributed to variables not measured in the regression equation

The SE_{est} for the regression equation is 9.0205. This means that each time the regression equation for the sample is used to predict a vocational aspirations, the vocational aspirations will not miss the actual dimension of vocational aspirations of Pre-University College rural students by more that ±9.0205.

Table 4.110. Contribution of predictor variables in predicting dimension of vocational aspirations of Pre-University College rural students of Dharwad district

Predictors	*Beta*	*r*	*Beta x r*	*% of contribution*
Educational Status (X8)	0.1463	0.1434	0.0210	2.0973
Achievement Motivation (X2)	0.1292	0.1348	0.0574	1.7411
Personality traits (X1)	0.1000	0.1181	0.0518	1.1808
			0.0502	5.0192

It is evident from Table 4.110 that, 5.0192 percent of variance in the criterion variable is accounted for by variance in of 2.0973 percent in the variable Educational Status (X8), of 1.7411 percent in the variable Achievement Motivation (X2) and of 1.1808 in the variable Personality traits (X1). Thus, it seems that Educational Status (X8) contributes better than the remaining potent predictors. The next predictor that contributes for predicting the vocational aspirations of the Pre-university College rural students is Achievement Motivation (X2). It is observed from the analysis that the Educational Status (X8), Achievement Motivation (X2) and Personality traits (X1) are important in explaining the vocational aspirations of rural students.

Hypothesis: Achievement motivation, personality traits s, Social status, Educational status, and Occupational status are would not be a significant predictor of vocational aspirations of Pre-university College urban students.

To test this hypothesis, the step wise multiple linear regression analysis is applied for identifying the potent factors that predict the vocational aspirations of the Pre-university college students and results are presented in the following table:

Table 4.111. Stepwise regression of predictor variables of vocational aspirations of Pre-University College urban students (n=500)

Independent Variables	*Regression Coefficient*	*SE of Coefficient*	*t-value*
Intercept	44.6355	3.0655	14.5604**
Educational Status (X8)	0.7517	0.1936	3.8824**
Occupation Status (X9)	0.6102	0.1811	3.3692**
Personality traits (X1)	-0.1001	0.0278	-3.6010**
Achievement Motivation (X2)	0.3110	0.0938	3.3163*

R=0.2970, R^2= 0.0882, F=12.0225, p<0.01, S, Std.Error of estimate: 8.7227

* Significant at 0.05% level of significance.

** Significant at 0.05% level of significance.

The step-wise regression equation predicting the vocational aspirations (Y1) of Pre-University College urban students turn out to be:

Vocational aspirations (Y1) = 44.6355+0.7517X8+0.6102X9-0.1001X1+0.3110X2.

The multiple R of the stepwise regression equation is 0.2970. For testing multiple correlation coefficients the F-ratio (12.0225) was found to be significant at 0.01% level. Thus, the null hypothesis is rejected and alternative hypothesis is accepted. Significant R suggests that estimation of vocational aspirations is possible on the basis of the predictors Educational Status (X8), Occupation Status (X9), Personality traits (X1) and Achievement Motivation (X2). Further, the stepwise regression equation shows that Educational Status (X8), Occupation Status (X9), Personality traits (X1) and Achievement Motivation (X2) can be used predict vocational aspirations and they predict at much four independent variables could predict.

The coefficient of multiple determination of R^2 is 0.0882. It can be therefore, be said that nearly 8.82 percent of the variance in vocational aspirations of Pre-University College urban students accounted for whatever is measured by Educational Status (X8), Occupation Status (X9), Personality traits (X1) and Achievement Motivation (X2) taken together. The remaining percentage of the variance must be attributed to variables not measured in the regression equation.

The SE_{est} for the regression equation is 8.7227. This means that each time the regression equation for the sample is used to predict a vocational aspirations, the vocational aspirations will not miss the actual dimension of vocational aspirations of Pre-University College urban students by more that ±8.7227.

Table 4.112. Contribution of predictor variables in predicting dimension of vocational aspirations of Pre-University College urban students of Dharwad district

Predictors	*Beta*	*r*	*Beta x r*	*% of contri-bution*
Educational Status (X8)	0.1884	0.1430	0.0269	2.6940
Occupation Status (X9)	0.1617	0.2201	0.0356	3.5579
Personality traits (X1)	-0.1495	-0.0959	0.0543	1.4341
Achievement Motivation (X2)	0.1475	0.0770	0.0514	1.1364
			0.0882	8.8224

It is evident from Table 4.112 that, 8.8224percent of variance in the criterion variable is accounted for by variance in of 2.6940 percent in the variable Educational Status (X8), of 3.5579 percent in the variable Occupation Status (X9), of 1.4341 percent in the variable Personality traits (X1), and of 1.1364 in the variable Achievement Motivation (X2). Thus, it seems that Occupation Status (X9) contributes better than the remaining potent predictors. The next predictor that contributes for predicting the vocational aspirations of the Pre-university College urban students is Educational Status (X8). It is observed from the analysis that the Educational Status (X8), Occupation Status (X9), Personality traits (X1) and Achievement Motivation (X2) are important in explaining the vocational aspirations of urban students.

5

Summary, Findings and Recommendations

Introduction

If an individual is to lead his life happily, one should be happy with work. If one is to be happy with work, one should choose an occupation that would give satisfaction. For every young child, the 'world of work' may appear remote. But as one grows and goes through the pressures and processes of socialization the 'world of work' comes into one's focus. Certain ideas about work take shape during pre-adolescent years. The process of vocational development is further accelerated in competitive societies like ours by the educational system, which is so designed, that the individual must make a beginning in the matter of vocational choice early in the high college days. The individual has to choose a particular curriculum and by so choosing one would be preparing for certain types of employment and all the same denying himself certain other types of vocational openings in the 'world of work' thus restricting one's aspirations.

Choosing a career goal is one of the most important decisions one may ever have to make. Also for many of the pupils the secondary college stage is the terminal stage of education. It is an important phase in their lives because of the conclusion of this period they are on the threshold of the 'world of work'. The amount of education one receives and the career one chooses will go a long way towards determining one's chances for steady employment in the future. The students at this juncture have to learn more about themselves what are their interests, abilities and aspirations. Here 'Aspirations' refer to an individual's goal or expectations or wants in regard to the welfare of one's future whereas 'vocation' is a particular kind of productive property known as person's vocation by which it means the kind of job one holds.

An individual who aspire to better him self academically, socially and economically would be satisfied only when his achievements come up to the goals he has set, regardless of how others view his achievement. This means to say that the persons ego is involved in his aspiration.

As the child develops his aspiration shaped by the influence of his imaginations and child fantasies. These are treated as unrealistic as they are based on child's fantasies and fallacies. When the child grows and attains education at college or college level, it becomes 'ambitious' but not unrealistic in aspiration. It is because the matured individual would be able to think realistically. At college level as a student the aspirations are developed with respect to his/ her education and vocation. That is why, any choice of subject are interest made towards one subject is due to aspiration, to achieve the set goal in his/ her life.

Everybody is destined to choose a vocation for one's basic need and it is imperative for the survival. However, an occupation for the sake of merely survival is a low rung concept. As Maslow's motivation theory holds the view that every one desires to depart for hither needs, so to excel in an opted occupation is a natural tendency. It is very difficult to discern the personal and professional growth, as these are deeply interwoven phenomenon. Any one lives one's greater part of life in chosen vocation. To live the life holistically and happily the occupation of an individual must be paired with love when a person enters in an aspired occupation, personal and professional progress goes hand in hand.

Occupation of an individual is considered as a major source of satisfaction in adult life and it links to real world. It is the identity of an individual when a simple query is made about any one "who is he/she" the answer flows in terms of persons occupation. Therefore, the vocation of a person is not only the means of livelihood but also the way of life. In order to succeed in a chosen vocation a realistic and pragmatic approach is highly desirable. It has become exceedingly difficult to adjust for the poorly skilled and educated individual to face challenges of the modern society. Exorbitant advancement in scientific and technological field has exerted enormous pressure on individual to sharpen and substantiate the vocational competencies. Undoubtedly, the education imparted to a child, which is commensurate with the interest and abilities can prepare for the right vocation to meet the contemporary challenges. There is a great need to match the education imparted to the students with their endowed potential. As after certain standard, Education is nothing but the preparation of an individual for the "World of Work". Vegetative growth in Academics without realistic vocational goal, which is not in accordance with one's abilities, interests and aptitude, can be responsible for the dropout at the later stages.

The pupils are at the Pre-university stage are in the twilight zone and at the terminal stage. Concept of vocation crystallizes at this level so they have to prepare accordingly. There is a great need of suitable guidance in order to choose the right vocation, which is commensurate with the personality. A holistic approach is essential at this juncture to optimize the potential and analyze the psychological strength and weaknesses in terms of vocational success at the later stages.

The objective of vocational education is to prepare students for vocations and enable them to enter the world of work with the necessary skills. For this reason, after completing 10 years of general education, the student sets about acquiring new practical knowledge of technical processes, regulating manual operations and also certain knacks and tricks of the trade. Last, but not the least, the student must develop civic attitudes.

Every vocational area has work that ranges from the less complex to the very theoretical. Therefore, if one is interested in medicine, electricity, construction or art, there is work to be done if one prepares. Many of these jobs require early planning and preparation. At present the teachers and institutions know that one cannot get a good job unless one has a minimum of education and a saleable job skill. Whatever a young person's interests and abilities, there is a place for one if one plans and prepares for it.

It is said that one's occupation is the watershed down, which the rest of one's life flows. If an individual is to lead his life happily one should be happy with work. If one is to be happy with work, one should choose an occupation that would give satisfaction. For every young child, the world of work may appear remote. But as one grows and goes through the pressures and processes of socialization the 'world of work' comes into one's focus. Certain ideas about work take shape during the pre-adolescent years. The process of vocational development is further accelerated in competitive societies like ours by the educational system which is so designed that the individual must make a beginning in the matter of vocational choice early in the high college days. The individual has to choose a particular curriculum and by so choosing one would be preparing oneself for certain types of employment and all the same denying himself certain other types of vocational openings in the 'world of work' thus restricting one's aspirations.

Need and Importance of the Study

The study of vocational aspiration has attracted the attention of educators more than the psychologists. We are still very much in the dark as to the characteristics of the individual who makes a wise selection of objective as contrasted to the barren or unrealistic chooser. Our professional ignorance of what constitutes a "good" choice explains part of our failure to identify the characteristics of the adequate vocational planner. Among all levels of intelligence, individuals show a wide difference in their capacity to set vocational goals, reasonable in the light of their potentialities. Such individual differences need to be explored. In the past there has been too little attention to the phenomenological study of choice and a resulting tendency to regard vocational choice as whimsical and devoid of significance, particularly when the choice was regarded as irrational. There is a continuing need to study the psychological. There is a continuing need to study the psychological factors in vocational aspirations. It is also a common observation that social factors also play a vital role in vocational aspirations.

Failure in one occupation has a greater demoralizing effect on an individual. In the crucial period of adolescence many formative forces related to psychological and social factors affect the growing individual. The urgent need of greater understanding of the factors, which influence the vocational aspirations of young people, prompted this study.

Though there are innumerable influencing factors, the present study is concerned with academic achievement motivation, personality and social status of urban and rural students. A review of the available literature reveals that there are a few studies that investigated the relationship between the above important variables and vocational aspirations of Indian youth, but the research in this area are not exhaustive.

The adolescent pupils belonging to different geographic localities such as the metropolitan, urban and rural areas would be exposed to different environmental and situational conditions that provide varied stimulation and learning experiences. The limited and restricted stimulation and opportunities for growth in the rural environments may handicap the individuals in certain significant ways. In contrast the urban environment is expected to offer richer and wider learning experiences. So it is possible that individuals hailing from different localities may be expected to show significant differences in their vocational aspirations.

Educators generally agree that major variables affecting classroom performance are academic achievement motivation and personality adjustment. The vocational application of psychological theory to education has not typically eventuated in a theory of academic achievement motivation or a unified and coherent body of information. As a result there is a little in the way of academic achievement motivation theory which is clearly of help to the classroom teacher or to education in general. And there is no doubt that adjustment influence daily living is seldom denial. It might be expected, then, that emotional stability or adjustment would be in some way related to the vocational aspirations. Based on a review of the aspiration literature in sociology, psychology and education, one expects variation in levels of vocational aspiration to correlate with measures of social status. The controversial findings of personality in relation to vocational aspirations need a carefully designed study to clarify the extent to which an individual's personality plays a part in the relationship of aspirations. On the whole the students' achievement motivation, their personality and social background may help the counsellors in understanding their vocational planning problems and to offer counselling assistance in a more effective way at this stage.

Therefore, there is a need to study vocational aspirations of students at Pre-university stage level as majority of them usually drop out at this stage and seek employment assistance. So the investigator is promoted to explore the relationship of vocational aspirations with some selected social and psychological variables of the students studying in +2 stage of Dharwad district.

Genesis of the Study

Throughout the life, an individual constantly makes decisions whether to listen to one radio programme or another, whether to vote for one candidate or another, whether to make along short or no vacation, whether to buy a Maruti, Santro, Zen etc. Whether it is a matter of deciding what to have for breakfast or deciding what college to enroll in the common characteristic is that a man must make a choice from among certain range of alternatives.

Getting right down to it, however, there aren't many really "big" decisions that have to be made in a mans lifetimes decisions which involve very long commitments which influence chances for living full, rich, satisfying lives which influence a mans thoughts, feelings and actions for years to come. One of these "big" decisions is marriage- whether to marry and if so, to whom. Another is choosing one's life work-whether to work at this job or that. It is plan that the selection of a particular kind of work has important implications both for the individual and for the total society. It means individual's vocational decision has important implications both for society and for his future life activity and satisfaction. Behind every decision about occupations many factors play an important role, one of the important factor is individual's vocational aspiration.

An interesting area for research in vocational education is development of vocational aspiration among students. This is of value for educational planning, curriculum designers, career guidance personnel and educational administrators. Vocational aspiration influence vocational maturity and vocational choices in later life which interns affect job satisfaction and optimization of job performance.

The study of vocational aspiration seems to have attracted the attention of educators more than a psychologists. Indian society is still very much in the dark as to the characteristics of the individual who makes a wise selection of objective. The professional ignorance of what constitutes a "good" choice explains part of the failure to identify the characteristics of the adequate vocational planner. Among all levels of intelligence, individuals show a wide difference in their capacity to set up vocational goals, reasonable in the light of their potentialities, such individual difference need to be explored.

The vocational fields which are considered on an hierarchical basis seem to be misleading. An individual, for example, may have genuine aspiration for medical profession despite his low intellectual abilities. According to literature and general view his choice behaviour would be considered as quite unrealistic. On the other hand this individual having genuine interest in the medical line may profit more if he is placed in this field. He may not prove to be suitable for as high a position as that of a medical specialist with 3 or 4 years of training after MBBS or a medical technologist, laboratory technician, pharmacist, but he may do well in the job of a vaccinator, basis health worker, sanitary inspector. Similarly in the engineering profession an individual with interest in the line but with low intelligence may not be considered fit for the position of an engineer, overseer, draftsman but may be suitable for an assignment of a fitter, turner, moulder, sheet metal worker, radio-mechanic, welder etc. Thus the 'field' as a whole cannot be classified in hierarchical order. These vocational fields are rather independent and within each vocational field area an individual may opt for a very high or a very low occupation. Therefore, it is of immense practical value to evaluate the subject's achievement motivation, personality, the social background of the individual in addition to his verbal future vocational plans to assist them and also their guardians in the vocational planning process. If an individual opts for a vocation of which he never thought or for which he has little liking or interest he may make himself vocationally misfit.

Adolescence is an ideal time to study the career development of young men/ women. It is during adolescence that many changes occur that strongly influence the development of career preferences and aspirations. Puberty and emerging sexuality, including a growing interest in hetero-social relationship, create an intensification of gender role identity. Greater autonomy and independence contribute to the process of identity development. Hence, there is a large scope for educational researches to explore this field. The present is therefore undertaken to study the vocational aspirations of the students.

Restatement of the Problem

The problem selected for the present investigation is restated as follows:

"Socio-Psychological Correlates of Vocational Aspirations"

Objectives of the Study

The present study has been undertaken with the following objectives.

(*a*) To study the relationship between vocational aspirations of Pre-university students and their achievement motivation.

(*b*) To study the relationship between vocational aspirations of Pre-university students and personality traits with its factors.

- (*a*) Reserved and outgoing
- (*b*) Less intelligent and more intelligent
- (*c*) Affected by feeling and emotionally stable
- (*d*) Phlegmatic and excitable
- (*e*) Obedient and assertive
- (*f*) Sober and happy-go-lucky
- (*g*) Expedient and conscientious
- (*h*) Shy and venturesome

(*i*) Tough minded and tender minded

(*j*) Vigorous and doubting

(*k*) Placid and apprehensive

(*l*) Group dependent and self sufficient

(*m*) Undisciplined self-conflict and controlled

(*n*) Relaxed and tense.

(*c*) To study the relationship between students belonging to different social status groups and their vocational aspirations.

(*d*) To study the relationship between sex and vocational aspirations.

(*e*) To study the relationship between locality and vocational aspirations.

(*f*) To study the relationship between different type of Pre-university college (Government/ Aided/Unaided) and vocational aspirations.

(*g*) To study the relationship between different medium of instruction (English/ Kannada) and vocational aspirations.

(*h*) To study the relationship between students belong to different categories.

Variables of the Study

Independent Variables

1. Personality: Personality with 14 dimensions
2. Achievement Motivation : Achievement motivation dimensions are:

   (*i*) Long term involvement

   (*ii*) Unique accomplishment

   (*iii*) Success in competition with standard of excellence

   (*iv*) Desire to excel regardless of social reward.
3. Social factors : includes educational and vocational status of parents.

Dependent Variable

Vocational aspirations

Moderate Variables

1. Sex (Male and female)
2. Type of management (Government/ Aided /Unaided)
3. Medium of instruction (Kannada/ English)
4. Birth order
5. Locality (Rural/Urban)
6. Subjects selected (Arts/Science/Commerce)
7. Categories (GM/OBC/SC/ST/Cat-I)

Tools Used for Collecting Data

1. Vocational Aspiration Scale – Grewal (1973)
2. High College Students Personality Questionnaire – By Cattell (1965)
3. Achievement Motivation Inventory constructed and Standardized by the researcher
4. Social Status Scale constructed by the researcher to collect data on education and occupation of parents

Statistical Techniques Used for the Analysis of the Data

The following techniques were used for analyzing the data as per the objectives of the study stated earlier

(*i*) Descriptive analysis
(*ii*) Differential analysis
(*iii*) Correlation analysis
(*iv*) Regression analysis

Findings of the Study

Findings of Differential Analysis

1. Pre-university College students belong to Arts subject has low vocational aspirations than Science students.
2. Pre-university College students belong to Arts subject has low vocational aspirations than Commerce students.
3. Pre-university College students belong to Commerce subject has low vocational aspirations than science students.

4. Kannada medium students of Pre-university College have low vocational aspirations when comparing to the students studying in English medium of instruction.
5. Students belong to unaided colleges have higher vocational aspirations than the students of government Pre-university colleges.
6. Students belong to unaided colleges have higher vocational aspirations than the students of colleges
7. Students belong to GM have higher vocational aspirations than the students belong to OBC category of Pre-university colleges.
8. Students belong to GM have higher vocational aspirations than the students belong to SC/ST/Cat-I category of Pre-university colleges
9. Students belong to urban Pre-university Colleges have higher vocational aspirations than the students belong to rural Pre-university Colleges.
10. Students with high achievement motivation have higher vocational aspirations than the students with low achievement motivation.
11. Students with high social status have higher vocational aspirations than the students of low social status.
12. The Group dependent, Average and Self-sufficient students of Pre-university Colleges have different vocational aspirations.
13. The Group dependent students are higher in vocational aspiration than Average students of Pre-university Colleges.
14. The Group dependent are higher in vocational aspiration than Self-sufficient students of Pre-university Colleges.
15. Vocational aspirations of female students influenced by the interaction effect of achievement motivation and social status.
16. vocational aspirations of female students influenced by high achievement motivation and low social status

17. Vocational aspiration of female students is influenced by interaction effect of low achievement motivation and social status.
18. The vocational aspiration of students with arts subject is influenced by high and low achievement motivation of Pre-university College.
19. The vocational aspiration of students with science subject is influenced in high and low social status.
20. The vocational aspiration is different in high and low achievement motivation of Pre-university College Kannada medium students.
21. The vocational aspiration is different in high and low social status of Pre-university College English medium students.
22. The vocational aspiration is different in high and low achievement motivation of aided Pre-University College students.
23. The vocational aspiration of unaided college students influenced by is high and low social status of unaided Pre-University College students.
24. The vocational aspiration of unaided college students influenced by the interaction effect of achievement motivation and personality traits.
25. The vocational aspiration of students belong to GM is influenced in high and low achievement motivation.
26. The vocational aspiration of students with General merit is influenced by social status of Pre-University Colleges.
27. The vocational aspiration influenced by achievement motivation of Pre-University College other backward community (OBC) students.
28. The vocational aspiration if students belong to OBC influenced by social status of Pre-University College other backward community (OBC) students.
29. The vocational aspiration of SC/ST/Cat-I students is influenced by achievement motivation.
30. The vocational aspiration of SC/ST/Cat-I students is influenced social status.

31. The vocational aspiration of students of rural colleges is influenced by achievement motivation.
32. The vocational aspiration of rural students is influenced by the interaction effect of achievement motivation.
33. The vocational aspiration of urban college students is influenced by social status.

Findings of Correlation Analysis

34. Increase in the variables like personality traits, long term involvement, desire to excel regardless of social reward, educational status and vocational status these variables are significantly supporting to increase the vocational aspirations of Pre-university College students.
35. Increase in the variables like educational status and vocational status increases the vocational aspirations of Pre-university College male students.
36. Increase the variables like personality traits, long term investment, success in competition with standard of excellence, desire to excel regardless of social reward, educational status and vocational status increases the vocational aspirations of Pre-university College female students.
37. Increase in the variables personality traits, long-term involvement, desire to excel regardless of social reward and educational status increases the vocational aspirations of Pre-university College arts students.
38. Increase in the variables like educational status and vocational status increases the vocational aspirations of Pre-university College science students.
39. Increase in the personality traits, educational status and vocational status increases the vocational aspirations of Pre-university College Kannada medium students.
40. Increase in the variable like educational status and vocational status increases the vocational aspirations of Pre-university College English medium students.
41. Increase in the variables like personality traits and educational status increases the vocational aspirations of Pre-university Government College students.

42. Variables like desire to excel regardless of social reward and educational status increases the vocational aspirations of Pre-university Aided College students.
43. Increase in variables like educational status and vocational status increases the vocational aspirations of Pre-university Unaided College students.
44. Variables like desire to excel regardless of social reward, educational status and vocational status increases the vocational aspirations of Pre-university General merit students.
45. Variables like desire to excel, regardless of social reward and educational status increases the vocational aspirations of Pre-university other backward (OBC) community students.
46. Increases in educational status increases the vocational aspirations of Pre-university SC/ST/Cat-I students.
47. Variables like personality traits, long term involvement, desire to excel regardless of social reward and educational status increases the vocational aspirations of Pre-university Rural students.
48. Variables like desire to excel, regardless of social reward, educational status and vocational status increases the vocational aspirations of Pre-university Urban students.
49. Increase in the personality traits A (Reserved/ Warmhearted) , E (Obedient/Assertive), and H (Shy/ Adventurous) factors increases the vocational aspiration of the students.
50. Personality factors A, (Reserved/ Warmhearted) B (Less intelligent/ More intelligent) and C (Affected by feelings/ Emotionally stable) increases the vocational aspirations of male students.
51. Increase in the personality factor C (Affected by feelings/ Emotionally stable) increases the vocational aspirations of female students.
52. Increase in personality factors A, (Reserved/ Warmhearted) C, (Affected by feelings/ Emotionally stable) E, (Obedient/Assertive) G (Weaker superego/

Stronger superego)and Q3 (Uncontrolled/ controlled) increases vocational aspirations of students with arts subject.

53. Increase in personality factor E (Obedient/Assertive) increases the vocational aspiration of students with science subject.
54. Increase in personality factor E (Obedient/Assertive) increases the vocational aspirations of students of commerce.
55. Increase in personality factors A, (Reserved/ Warmhearted) C (Affected by feelings/ Emotionally stable)and G (Weaker superego/ Stronger superego) increa es the vocational aspirations of students studying in Kannada medium colleges.
56. Increase in personality factor E (Obedient/Assertive) and G (Weaker superego/ Stronger superego) increases vocational aspirations of students studying in English medium colleges.
57. Increase in personality factors A,) (Reserved/ Warmhearted) E (Obedient/Assertive) and G (Weaker superego/ Stronger superego)increases vocational aspirations of students studying Government colleges.
58. Increase in personality factor F (Sober/ Enthusiastic) increases the vocational aspiration of aided college students.
59. Increase in the personality factor C (Affected by feelings/ Emotionally stable) increases the vocational aspiration of unaided college students.
60. Increase in the personality factor E (Obedient/Assertive) and H (Shy/Adventurous) increases the vocational aspirations of students belong to General merit.
61. Increase in personality factors A, (Reserved/ Warmhearted)C (Affected by feelings/ Emotionally stable)and E (Obedient/Assertive) of increases vocational aspirations of students belong to OBC.
62. Increases the vocational aspirations of studying in rural areas.

63. Increase personality factor Q2 (Group dependent/ Self-sufficient increases the vocational aspirations of students studying in urban areas.

Findings of Regression Analysis

64. Educational status is the highest contributor to predict the vocational aspiration which is followed by social status and achievement motivation in their significance to predict.
65. Achievement motivation the highest contributor to predict the vocational aspirations which followed social status and personality trait and educational status.
66. Educational Status (X8) contributes better than the remaining potent predictors. The next predictor that contributes for predicting the vocational aspirations of the Pre-university College female students is Achievement Motivation (X2). It is observed from the analysis that the Educational Status (X8) and Achievement Motivation (X2) are important in explaining the vocational aspirations of female students.
67. Personality traits (X1) contributes better than the remaining potent predictors. The next predictor that contributes for predicting the vocational aspirations of the Pre-university College arts students is Educational Status (X8). It is observed from the analysis that the Personality traits (X1), Educational Status (X8) and Achievement Motivation (X2) are important in explaining the vocational aspirations of arts students.
68. Social Status (X7) contributes better than the remaining potent predictors. The next predictor that contributes for predicting the vocational aspirations of the Pre-university College science students is Achievement Motivation (X2). It is observed from the analysis that the Social Status (X7) and Achievement Motivation (X2) are important in explaining the vocational aspirations of science students.
69. Personality traits (X1) contributes better than the remaining potent predictors. The next predictor that

contributes for predicting the vocational aspirations of the Pre-university College commerce students is Personality traits (X1). It is observed from the analysis that the Educational Status (X8) and Personality traits (X1) are important in explaining the vocational aspirations of commerce students.

70. Educational Status (X8) contributes better than the remaining potent predictors. The next predictor that contributes for predicting the vocational aspirations of the Pre-university College Kannada medium students is Personality traits (X1). It is observed from the analysis that the Educational Status (X8), Achievement Motivation (X2) and Personality traits (X1) are important in explaining the vocational aspirations of Kannada medium students.
71. Social Status (X7) contributes better than the remaining potent predictors. The next predictor that contributes for predicting the vocational aspirations of the Pre-university College English medium students is Personality traits (X1). It is observed from the analysis that the Social Status (X7), Achievement Motivation (X2) and Personality traits (X1) are important in explaining the vocational aspirations of English medium students.
72. Educational Status (X8) contributes better than the remaining potent predictors. The next predictor that contributes for predicting the vocational aspirations of the Pre-university Government college students is Achievement Motivation (X2). It is observed from the analysis that the Educational Status (X8) and Achievement Motivation (X2) are important in explaining the vocational aspirations of Government students.
73. Educational Status (X8) contributes better than the remaining potent predictors. The next predictor that contributes for predicting the vocational aspirations of the Pre-university Aided college students is Achievement Motivation (X2). It is observed from the analysis that the Educational Status (X8) and Achievement Motivation

(X2) are important in explaining the vocational aspirations of Aided students.

74. Educational Status (X8) contributes better than the remaining potent predictors. The next predictor that contributes for predicting the vocational aspirations of the Pre-university Unaided college students is Social Status (X7). It is observed from the analysis that the Educational Status (X8), Achievement Motivation (X2) and Social Status (X7) are important in explaining the vocational aspirations of unaided students.
75. Social Status (X7) contributes better than the remaining potent predictors. The next predictor that contributes for predicting the vocational aspirations of the Pre-university College GM students is Educational Status (X8). It is observed from the analysis that the Social Status (X7), Educational Status (X8) and Achievement Motivation (X2) are important in explaining the vocational aspirations of GM students.
76. Educational Status (X8) contributes better than the remaining potent predictors. The next predictor that contributes for predicting the vocational aspirations of the Pre-university College OBC students is Personality traits (X1). It is observed from the analysis that the Educational Status (X8), Personality traits (X1) and Achievement Motivation (X2) are important in explaining the vocational aspirations of OBC students.
77. Educational Status (X8) contributes better than the remaining potent predictors. The next predictor that contributes for predicting the vocational aspirations of the Pre-university College SC/ST/CAT-I students is Achievement Motivation (X2). It is observed from the analysis that the Personality traits (X1), Achievement Motivation (X2) and Educational Status (X8) are important in explaining the vocational aspirations of SC/ST/CAT-I students.
78. Educational Status (X8) contributes better than the remaining potent predictors. The next predictor that contributes for predicting the vocational aspirations of

the Pre-university College rural students is Achievement Motivation (X2). It is observed from the analysis that the Educational Status (X8), Achievement Motivation (X2) and Personality traits (X1) are important in explaining the vocational aspirations of rural students.

79. Occupation Status (X9) contributes better than the remaining potent predictors. The next predictor that contributes for predicting the vocational aspirations of the Pre-university College urban students is Educational Status (X8). It is observed from the analysis that the Educational Status (X8), Occupation Status (X9), Personality traits (X1) and Achievement Motivation (X2) are important in explaining the vocational aspirations of urban students.

Discussion and Conclusion

Vocational aspirations in the formative years of life influence the vocational choices in later life, which are supposed to determine individual's success in regard to job satisfaction, productivity, personality adjustment etc.

There are numerous factors, which may affect the vocational aspirations of students.

Achievement motivation emphasizes that (Roe, 1956) "Occupations as a source of need satisfaction were of extreme importance." It had also been a general opinion that an individual who had high need for achievement would indulge in action for fulfillment of motives (may be vocational choice or otherwise). It might be because of ego involvement that brings about increase in drive and intern brings increase in his performance (Kausler, 1951). It was therefore, thought to evaluate whether achievement motivation was related to the aspired vocations. The findings of present study indicated that high achievement motivation had higher vocational aspirations than the low achievement motivation. Therefore it can be concluded that development of achievement motivation should be considered as an important factor in students' life.

Personality is another factor, which influences the vocational aspirations of individual. Every job can be described in terms of the personality characteristics, which makes a person to be happy and satisfied in it. The findings of present study indicated that some of the personality traits increase the vocational aspirations of the individual. Those traits are to be promoted by the counsellors in colleges.

Social status is another important factor which influences the vocational aspiration. The studies of Teahan (1974), Mishra (1975), Brook *et al*. (1974) believed that Social status could not be a determining factor in a aspiration, preference and choice of the vocations. Majority of the researcher, however, considered it to be a potential factor in vocational aspiration (George and Mathew, 1966; Babelon, 1972-73; Roe, 1956). It is common view that Social status may determine the resources in the society conducive to fulfilling the aspirations. The financial aspects of invariably involved in getting the proper training a pivotal factor in job placement. It has also been our experience that, those individuals who belonged to lower Social status are generally neither in position to afford the requisite educational expenses nor are able to devote full attention to their studies. Their services are also required by their fathers to supplement their income. It was therefore considered desirable to examine whether there was any association between vocational aspirations and Social status of the family in this part of country. From this study it was found that students with high Social status had higher vocational aspirations than the low Social status of students. It can be concluded that Social status plays an important role in student's life.

From the present study, it is also clear that, medium of instruction, (Kannada/ English) location (Rural / Urban), type of college (Government, Aided and Unaided), categories to which students belong (GM/OBC/ST/ST/Cat-I), subject specialization (Arts/Science/Commerce) and gender plays an important role in determining vocational aspirations of Pre-university students studying in 1st year.

Educational Implications and Recommendations

On the basis of the findings of the study and the observations made by the investigator during the study, a few recommendations which may help in developing suitable programmes in colleges to improve vocational aspirations have been offered.

1. The study has shown that better the achievement motivation, higher the vocational aspiration. A simple and standardized tool on achievement motivation should be administered to the students when they are in +2 stage to know their achievement motivation. The instructors should take necessary steps to enhance the motivation level of such students who possess low motivation. Motivation in general and achievement motivation in particular can be promote among students through various academic and non-academic activities. Hence the colleges should take interest in developing achievement motivation among students thereby influencing their vocational aspirations.
2. From the findings it is clear that there is some confusion and overlapping among the students about their aspirations for the future occupations. Better and earlier guidance is needed at +2 levels to overcome this kind of confusion. The students' time, effort and money could be better utilized, if the guidance is provided to them at an early stage. Parents should be more understanding and realistic of their student's abilities and potential for excelling in a field which they desire him/her to enter. The students have the major responsibility for getting information about the occupations. It may, finally, be said that Co-operative efforts of the students, the parents and the teachers are required to realistically appraise the students' potential to succeed in specific vocations.
3. The findings showed that social status of parents was observed to be significant predictor of vocational aspirations of students with an increase in the social status of parents; there was an increase in the vocational aspirations of their children. Some suggestions for improving the social status of children are as follows.
   (1) Mid-day meal could be provided for those children who are in need of it.
   (2) Philanthropists and industrialists can come forward to contribute the students those who are in need.

(3) The managements should see that more number of library books to be given to the poor students to cultivate them to take more interest in their study.

(4) The teacher should encourage the students who belong to low social status to utilize their talents so that these students too would aspire for better vocations.

(5) Though the students belong to low social status enter the colleges, the teacher should make an effort to convince that their low social status has nothing to do with their personality and academic achievement. All the teachers should treat the students alike irrespective of their social status background and provide special attention to the children coming from low and middle social status to develop self-confidence in realizing their potentialities in accordance to their vocational aspirations.

4. The Government colleges in general are located in rural areas and a few in urban areas. It is observed that the students attending these colleges either form urban areas or rural are form low social background. As a result, the students attending the Government Colleges and Aided colleges, the study revealed, have low vocational aspirations. This situation should not be continued. This may be because Government colleges are usually poor in their infrastructure facilities. Mostly poor students for low social status attend these Government and Aided colleges. There is an urgent need to provide necessary infrastructure in these colleges. The instructors in Government and Aided colleges should arrange necessary activities to increase the vocational aspirations of the students.

5. An interaction of the researcher with the teachers indicated that the colleges in rural areas are not well equipped in terms of human and physical resources. Hence, adequate attention should be paid to improve the minimum infrastructural facilities, filling up the vacancies of the teachers and providing orientation and refresher courses periodically to rural teachers, consequently one can expect the children in such colleges to develop a taste for better vocational aspirations.

6. Though much is said about guidance and counselling in the colleges, the fact remains that the colleges do not have guidance centres. The counselling work is not attended by any teacher in the colleges. Immediate steps have to be taken up by the Government of Karnataka to establish guidance services in every Pre-University Colleges.

Suggestions for Further Research

Based on the design for the present investigation, the findings that are arrived at and the limitations that are inevitable, certain suggestions are made for further research in the areas, which appear to be promising and fruitful for investigator to explore:

1. The present study has been largely concerned with the 1st year Pre-university students studying in the Dharwad district. There is therefore a need for a similar study perhaps with a wider sample from all over the state of Karnataka.
2. It will be worthwhile if the other variables like aptitude, interest and intelligence could also be included for the investigation to find out their impact on vocational aspirations.
3. The present study is a cross-sectional one, owing to certain practical considerations such as time, personnel resources. There is a need for a longitudinal study also.
4. The follow-up study of a few subjects may be made to see (i) whether the vocational aspirations made during the college level (ii) their actual entry into the several occupations; (iii) the shift, if any, in their vocational need patterns; and (iv) to find the reasons for such shifts.
5. In the present investigation no attempt was made to assess the extent to which the subjects are realistic in their vocational aspirations. It may be useful to probe deep into these aspects. Such a study would yield fruitful insights into the dynamics of vocational choice making and would be useful in providing suitable assistance through vocational counselling to the subjects.
6. Another fruitful area of research for the investigators is to explore the changes in the vocational aspirations of the subjects from grades two to ten.

7. A study may be carried out to assess whether the individuals choose sex-stereotyped jobs.
8. An exclusive study of the vocational aspirations of female subjects may prove to be quite useful.
9. A comparison may be made between the tribal pupils and non-tribal pupils with regard to their vocational aspirations. Similarly a comparison may also be made among different religious.
10. An investigation of participation of teachers in decision-making and influence of peer group on vocational aspirations may be undertaken.

Bibliography

Aaron, P. G., Marihal, V. G. and Malatesha, R. N. (1969) A Common Socio-economic Status Scale for Rural and Urban Areas – *Manual, Monograph No. 3,* Dharwad: Karnatak University.

Abernatty, Thomas and Davis (1968) Student Perceptions of Influence on Career and Educational Decision Making. *Journal of Psychology,* 12 (3), pp. 182-188.

Abiri, J. O. (1977) A Sample of Nigerian Adolescents' Academic and Occupational Aspirations. *West African Journal of Education and Vocational* Measurement. 4 (1), 55-67.

Adams, H. E. (1972) *Psychology of Adjustment.* The Ronald Press Company, USA.

Adkins, D, C. (1964) Statistics: *An Introduction for Students in the Behavioural Sciences.* Charles E. Merrill Books, Inc., Columbus, Ohio.

Aggarwal, Y. P. (1988) *Statistical Methods-Concepts, Applications, and Computations.* New Delhi: Sterling Publishers Pvt. Ltd.

Ali, S. and Ali, M. (1982) An Investigation into the Educational and Occupational Aspirations of Egyptian Preparatory School Pupils in Relation to Home Background, School, Achievement, Sex and parental Aspirations. *Dissertation Abstracts International.* 49(10), p. 257.

Allport, G. W. (1962) *Pattern and Growth in Personality.* New York: Holt, Rinehart and Winston.

Allport, G. W. (1937) Personality: *A Psychological Interpretation.* New York: Holt, p. 48.

Anderson, G. L. (1975) Anxiety, Risk and Socio-economic Class in Relation to Occupational Preference. *Dissertation Abstracts International,* 35 (12-A), 7642.

Andrews, H. A. (1973) Personality Pattern and Vocational Choice: A Test of Holland's Theory with Adult Part-time Community College Students. *Journal of Counselling Psychology*. 20 (5), 482-483.

Andrews, J. D. W. (1967) The Achievement Motive in two Types of Organization. In : Tiwari, A. N. (1984) *Achievement Motivation in Deprived Society*. Agra: Modern Printers.

Angela, D. B. *et al*. (2005) *Occupational Aspirations of Students in Grades Seven to Twelve*. Alberta: The National Consultation on Career Development.

Angyl, A. (1941) *Foundations for Science of Personality*. New York: Common Wealth fund, p. 200.

Anniamma, Mathew and K. Kunhikrishnan (1995) Achievement Motivation in Relation to Level of Aspiration. *Psychological Studies*. 40 (2), 97-100.

Araip-Maritim, E. K. (1984) Sex Differences in the Vocational Aspiration and Sex Role perceptions of Primary School Children in Rural Kenya. *Journal of Social psychology*. 124 (2), 159-164.

Arnoff, J. and Litwin, C. H. (1971) Achievement Motivation Training and Executive Advancement. *Journal of Applied Behavioural Sciences*. 7 (2), 215-229.

Arnstein, E. Ocupational Preference of Israeli Children, *Jerusalem, Vocational Guidance Center Hadassah*, 6 p. (Mimeo).

Atkinson, J. W. (1958) *Motives in Fantasy, Action and Society*. New York: Van Nostrand Reinhold.

Winnick, Atonie Charles (1964) *The psychology of the Unemployed and Marginal Worker*, Washington: D. C. U.S. Department of Labour. P. 18.

Sandford, Aubrey Cecil (1971) An Investigation of the Relationship between Level of Need for Achievement and Employment Intentions Among College Juniors and Seniors at Louisiana State. *Dissertation Abstracts International*, A-31, 9.

Babelon, S. V. (1973) Study of the influences of the socio-professional level of parents and professional choice of children for 9 to 11 years deviance and conformity. *Bulletin de Psychologic*, 26 (1-4), 35-93.

Bailey, L. J. and Stadt, R. (1973) Career Education. pp. 57-94.

Bandura, A., Barbaranelli, C., Caprara, G. V., and Pastorelli, C. (2001) Self-efficacy beliefs as shapers of children's aspirations and career trajectories. *Child Development* 72 (1), 187-207.

Barahal, G. D. (1953) Personality Problems and Vocational Planning. *Personnel and Guidance Journal*. Jan. pp. 224-225.

Bayti, J.L. (1966) Vocational Preferences of Secondary School Leavers. *Rajasthan Board Journal of Education*, 2(4), 7-42.

Becker, H. A. and Murff, R. C. (1978) Did you Know.....Data About Freshman Career Plans. *T.P.G.A. Journal*. 6 (2), 71-81.

Bennett, W. S. and Gist, N. P. (1964) Class and Family Influences on Student Aspirations. *Social Forces*, 43 (2), 167-173.

Berman, G. *et al.*, (1975) Occupational and Educational Goals and Expectations: The Effects of Race and Sex. *Social Problems*. 23(2), 166-181.

Best, J. W. (2000) *Research in Education*. New Delhi: Prentice-Hall of India Pvt. Ltd.

Best, John, W. (2000) *Research in Education*, Prentice-Hall of India Pvt. Ltd., New Delhi.

Bhargava, M. and Dhir, Preeti (1980) A comparative examination of need patterns of aspirant girls within realistic and non-realistic zones. *Perspectives in Psychological Researches*, 3 (1), 25-28.

Bhatia, H. R. (1965) *A Textbook of Educational Psychology*. Asia Publishing House.

Bigler, A. and Liben (2003) Race and the Workforce: Occupational Status, Aspirations, and Stereotyping Among African American Children. Austin: *Developmental Psychology*, Vol. 39, No. 3, pp. 572-580.

Bigler, Averhart and Liben (2003) Race and the Workforce: Occupational Status, Aspirations, and Stereotyping Among African American Children. Austin: *Developmental Psychology*, Vol. 39, No. 3, pp. 572-580.

Bitney, R. H. (1975) An Analysis of Occupational Choice and Selected Personality Characteristics. *Dissertation Abstracts International*, 36 (2-4), 699.

Bleom, Anne, R. (1972) Achievement Motivation and Occupational Choice: A Study of Adolescent Girls. *Dissertation Abstracts International*, 33 (1-13), 417.

Bloom, B. S. (1972) *Taxonomy of Educational Objectives, The Classification of Educational Goals*. London: Longman.

Brook, J. S. *et al*. (1974) Aspiration Levels of and for Children: Age, Sex, Race, Socio-economic Correlations. *Journal of Genetic Psychology*, 121(1), 3-16.

Brook, J. S. Whiteman, M. Peisach, E. and Dentsch, M. (1974) Aspiration levels of and for children: Age, Sex, race, socio-economic Correlates, *Journal of Genetic Psychology,* 124, (1), 3-16.

Brown, H. C. (1973) A Study of the Occupational Aspirations of Juvenile Delinquents. *Dissertation Abstracts International*, 33 (12-A), 6797-6798.

Brown, Harold, C. (1973) A Study of the Occupational Aspirations of Juvenile Delinquents. *Dissertation Abstracts International*, 33 (12-A), 6797-6798.

Bruce Shertzer, Herman J. Peters, (1965) *Guidance*. The Macmillan Company.

Burlin, F. D. (1976) Sex role Stereotyping: Occupational Aspirations of Female High School Students. *School Counsellor*, 24 (2), 102-108.

Calin, L.V.L. (1969) Relationship of Occupational Aspirations of Youth to Selected Social Variable in two Mississippi Countries. *Dissertation Abstract International* - A Vol. 30.

Camp and Rothney, J.W. (1970) Parental Response to Counsellor's Suggestions. *School Counsellor* (3), 200-203.

Cantril, H. (1950) *The why of man's experience*. New York: Macmillan Book Co.,

Carp, F. M. (1949) High School Boys are Realistic About Occupations. *Occupations*, 28, 97-99.

Cassel, R. N. (1998) High School Success and School Accountability Begin with tentative Job Career Plans for each Student. *Education Winter*: 119 (2), 319.

Chadha, S.S. (1982) *Socio-psychological Correlates of Vocational Aspirations*. New Delhi: National Psychological Corporation.

Chadha, S. S. (1983) The Study of Male Students with Unrealistic Vocational Expression, *Indian Journal of Clinical Psychology*, 10 (1), 93-96.

Chandna, Sunanda (1990) Self Concept, Parental Influence, SES and Sex in Relation to Career Choice Attitudes among High School Students, *Indian Educational Review*, Vol. XXV, No.1. August.

Chaplin, J. P. (1982) *Dictionary of Psychology*. New York: Dell Publishing Co., Inc.

Chopra, S. L. (1984) Socio-economic Background and Occupational Aspirations. *Indian Educational Review*, XIX (1), 99-105.

Chown, Sheila, M. (1959) Personality factors in the Formation of Occupational Choice. *British Journal of Educational Psychology*, 29, 23-33.

Clark, Edward, T. (1965) Culturally Disadvantaged Boys' and Girls' Aspirations to and Knowledge of White-collar and professional Occupations. *Urban Education*, 1 (3), 164-174.

Clyton, K. K. (1993) Family influence over the occupational and educational choices of Mexican American Students. *Paper presented at the annual meeting of the American Vocational Association*. Nashville. TN.

Cranbach, Lee. J. (1960) *Essentials of Psychological Testing*. New York: Harper and Brothers.

Crites, O. J. (1969) *Vocational psychology*. New York: McGrew Hill Book Co.

Crow, L. D. (1974) *Psychology of Human Adjustment*. New York: Alfred A Knoof, Inc.

Dabir, D. (1986) A Study of Vocational Aspirations as a Function of Aptitudes and Motivational Patterns among the Boys and Girls studying in IX, X and XI grades in Nagpur District. *In IV Survey of Research in Education*, M. B. Buch (Ed.) New Delhi: NCERT.

David, C. McClelland (1961) *The Achieving Society*, New York: Van Nostrand Reinhold.

David, C. McClelland *et al.* (1953) *The Achievement Motive*. New York: Appleton.

Denga, D.I. (2004) The Influence of Gender on Occupational Aspirations of Primary School children in Cross River state. Nigeria: The African Symposium. *An On-Line Educational Research Journal*, Educational Research Network. 4 (2)

Denga, D. I. (1986) *Career Guidance in Primary and Junior Secondary Schools*, Calabar.

Denga, D. I. and Ali, A. (1989) *Introduction to research methods and statistics in education and social sciences* (2nd ed.) Calabar: Rapid Educational Publishers Ltd.

Denga, D. I. (2001) *Guidance and counselling in school and non-school settings*. Port Harcourt: Dbouble Diamond Publications 74 Aba Road.

Denta, H. M. (1995) Self-awareness and occupational aspirations among elementary school children in Calabar Municipality. An Unpublished Ph.D. Thesis.

Dewey, J. (1940) *Education Today*. New York: Putman's Sons.

Michael Donald (1963) *The Next Generation*. New York: Random House, 99-100.

Donald, E. Super John, O. Crites (1949) *Appraising Vocational Fitness*. New York: Harper and Row Publishers.

Brown Duane and David J. Srebalus (1973) *Fostering Career Development: Selected Readings in Contemporary Guidance*. WM. C. Brown Company Publishers Uubu Que, Lowa, 201-208.

Dunne, Faith, *et al.* (1981) Sex Differences in the Educational and Occupational Aspirations of Rural Youth. *Journal of Vocational Behaviour*, 18 (1), 56-66.

Dutt, N. K. (1978) *Psychological Foundations of Education*. Delhi: Doafa House.

Dyer, W. G. (1958) Parental influence on the job attitude of children from two occupational strata. *Sociology and Social Research*, 42, 203-206.

Dynes, R. R. Clarke, A., and Dinitz, S. (1956) Levels of occupational aspiration. Some aspects of family experience as a variable. *American Sociological Review*, 21; 212-214.

Edwards, A. L. (1965) *Experimental Design in Psychological Research*. USA. Holt, Rinehart and Winston.

Edwards, A. M. (1943) *Comparative occupational statistics for the United States 1870-1940*. Washington D.C.: Government Printing Office.

Elizabeth, B. H. (1974) *Personality Development*. New Delhi: Tata McGraw-Hill Publishing Company Ltd.

Empey, L. T. (1956) Social Class and Occupational Aspiration – A comparison of Absolute and Relative Measurement. *American Sociological Review*, 21, 703-709.

Encyclopedia of Religion and Ethics, James Hassing (1971) Published by Marrison an Gibb Ltd. Edinberg, Vol. 2, pp. 127-128.

English, H. B. and English, A. C. (1962) *A Comprehensive Dictionary of Psychological and Psychoanalytical terms*, David Mc Kay Company Inc., New York.

Erb, Thomas, O. (1983) Career Preferences of Early Adolescents: Age and Sex Differences. *Journal of Early Adolescence*, 3 (4), 349-359.

Esslinger, C. W. (1976) Educational and Occupational Aspirations and Expectations and the Educational, Personal and Family Characteristics of Selected Twelfth Grade Female Students. *Dissertation Abstracts International*, 37 (1-A), 255.

Eysenck, H. J. (1947) *Dimensions of Personality, Ability and Efficiency*. London: Kegan Paul Trench, Trubner and Co. Ltd. Broadway House.

Eysenck, H. S. (1953) *The Structure of Human Personality*. London: Methuen and Co. Ltd. p. 2.

Eysenck, S. J., Arnold, W. J. and Meiler, R. (Ed.) (1972) *Encyclopedia of Psychology*. Great Britain, Britain Search Press.

Ferguson, G. (1979) *A Statistical Analysis in Psychology and Education*. Bombay: Vakils Feffer and Simons Ltd.

Flugel, J. C. (1945) *Man, model and society*, London: Duckworth. 142.

Form, W. H. and Gesch-Wender, J. A. (1962) Social reference basis of job satisfaction. The case of manual workers: *American Sociological Review*, 27, 228-237.

Fowler (2000) Becoming Adult: *Becoming Christian*, San Francisco: Jossey-Bass Publishers, p. 77.

Frank, J. (1935) Individual differences in certain aspects of level of aspiration. *American Journal of Psychology*, 47 91), 119-128.

Funder, D. C. (2001) *The Personality Puzzle* (2nd Ed) New York: Norton, p. 48.

Garret, H. E. and Woodworth, R. S. (1961) *Statistics in Psychology and Education*. Bombay: Vakils, Fetter and Simons Ltd.

Garrett, H. E. (1981) *Statistics in Psychology and Education*. Bombay: Vakils, Feffer and Simons Ltd.

Gaskell, J. (1980) Sex Role Ideology and Aspirations of High School Girls. *Psychological Abstracts*. 63 (1).

Gaur, J. S. and Mathur, P. (1974) The Effect of Level of Intelligence on the Occupational Aspirations of the Higher Secondary School Students in Delhi, *Indian Journal of Psychology,* Jan., 49 (2), 139-148.

Gaur, J. S. and Mathur, P. (1978) Effect of Personality Factors on the Level of Occupational Aspiration of Higher Secondary School Students of Delhi: A Study on Sex Differences, *Asian Journal of Psychology and Education,* 3 (2), 1-14.

Gautam, R.P. (1981) Student's Vocational Preference and their Parents' Occupational Background. *Journal of Indian Education*. 44-53.

George, E. I. And Mathew, V. C. (1966) Vocational aspirations of school leaving pupils. *Journal of the vocational and Educational Guidance,* 126 (4).

Getzels, J.W. and Jackson, P.W. (1960) Occupational Choice and Cognitive Functioning, Career Aspirations of Highly Intelligent and High Creative Adolescents. *Journal of Abnormal Social Psychology*. 61, 113-119.

Gilger (1942) *Declaration of Vocational Interest Occupations*, 20, pp. 276-277.

Gist, N. P. and Bennett, W. S. (Jr.) (1963) Aspirations of Negro and White Students. *Social Forces*, 42, 40-48.

Grace, A.G. (1931) The Relationship of Mental Ability to Occupational Choice of Adults. *Vocational Guidance Magazine*. 10, 354-358.

Gresham, Mary Harley (1993) Occupational Aspiration Expectation Congruence and Self Efficacy in Career Decision-making. *Dissertation Abstracts International*, 53(12), 4209-A.

Grewal (1987) Vocational Environment and Educational and Occupational Choices, *Third Survey of Research in Education*, (Ed.) M.B. Buch, New Delhi: NCERT.

Grewal, J.S. (1973) *Occupational Aspiration Scale*. Agra: National Psychological Corporation.

Gribbons, W. D. and Lohnes, P. R. (1964) Relationships among measures of readiness for vocational planning. *Journal of Counselling Psychology*, 11, 13-19 (a).

Gruen, E. W. (1945) Level of Aspiration in Relation to Personality Factors in Adolescents. *Child Development*, 16, 181-188.

Guilford, J.P. (1967) *The Nature of Human Intelligence*. McGraw Hill, New York.

Gunn, B. (1964) Children's conceptions of occupational and prestige. *Personal and Guidance Journal*, 42, 558-563.

Gupta, V. P. (1979) *Some correlates of Occupational Choices*. Manas, 20 (1), 33-40.

Haller, A.O. and Miller, I.W. (1971) The Occupational Aspiration Scale. *Cambridge Massachusetts*. Schenkman Publishing Co. Inc.

Harnett, S. (1969) Occupational Aspirations of Normal and Mentally Retarded Adolescent. *Dissertation Abstracts*. 29, 11-A

Harvey, M. G. and Kerin, R. A. (1978) The Influence of Social Stratification and Age on Occupational Aspirations of Adolescents. *Journal of Educational Research*, 7(5), 262-266.

Hauson, J. (1965) Ninth Grade Girls Vocational Choices and their Parents' Occupational Level. *Vocational Guidance Quarterly*, 13, 261-264.

Heckausen, H. (1963) *An anatomy of achievement motivation.* Academic Press, New York and London.

Henry, E. Garrett (1926) *Statistics in Psychology and Education.* David McKay Company, Inc.

Hewitt, L. S. (1975) Age and Sex Differences in the Vocational Aspirations of Elementary School Children. *Journal of Social Psychology,* 96 (2), 173-177.

Highland (1998) Why Teachers Must be Career Counsellors Techniques, 73(6) p. 70.

Hodgkins, B. J. and Parr, A. (1965) Educational and Occupational Aspirations Among Rural and Urban Male Adolescents in Alberta. *Albertia Journal of Educational Research*, 11 (4), 255-262.

Hogan, R. (1991) Personality and Personality Measurement in Dunnete, M. D. Hough, L. M. (Eds.) *Hand Book of Industrial and Organizational Psychology* (22, Ed. pp. 327-396) Palo Aeso, CA: Consulting Psychologist Press.

Holden, G.S. (1961) Scholastic Aptitude and the Relative Persistence of Vocational Choice. *Personnel and Guidance Journal*. 40, 36-41.

Holland, J. L., Gott, F. and Goig, G. D. (1974) *Applying a topology to vocational aspiration Centre for social organization of school reports-* Johns Hopkins University, Jun. No. 176. p. 19.

Hoppe, F. (1930) Erfolg and Misserfolg Psychol. *Forsch*, 14, 1-62.

Hoppe, F. (1941) Recent studies of the level of the aspiration. *Journal Psychology Bulletin*, 38, 208-226.

Hoult, P.P. and Smith, M.C. (1978) Age and Sex Differences in the Number and Variety of Vocational Choices, Preferences and Aspirations. *Journal of Occupational Psychology.* 51(2), 119-125.

Howell, Gwendolyn Jenkins, (1989) A Multiple Regression Analysis Using Parental Influence, Self-concept, SES, Race and Gender as Predictors and Career Maturity. *Dissertation Abstracts International.* 50(3), 649.

Hyman, R. *et al.* (1978) Social Class and Parents Range of Aspirations for their Children, *Social Problems*, 25(3), p. 333-344.

Indown, A. I. and Dere, A. O. (1983) Socio-economic Status and Occupational Aspirations of High School Seniors in Nigeria, *Journal of Educational Counselling*, 20 (4), 136-192.

Jackson, M., Meara, M. and Arora, M. (1974a) Father identification, achievement and occupational behaviour of rural youth. *Journal of vocational behaviour*, (Jan.), 4 (1), 85-96.

Jackson, R. M., Meara, M. and Arora, M. (1974b) Father identification, achievement and occupational behaviour of rural youth. *Journal of vocational behaviour*, (Jan.), 4 (3), 349-356.

Jain, K. C. (1965) *Vocational Choices of Ninth Class Students.* Rajasthan University Studies, 6, 55-63.

James, Michael L., *et al.*, (1966) *Guidance and Counselling in Schools.* New York: McGraw-Hill Book Company.

James, F. Adams, (1965) *Counselling and Guidance.* New York: The Macmillan Company.

Jarvis, P. S. and Keeley, E. S. (2003) From Vocational Decision Making to Career Building: Blue Print Real Games, and School Counselling (Special Issues: Career Development and the Changing Work Place). *Professional School Counselling.* 6 (4), Pp. 244-250.

Jeff, W. J. (2003) Toward a Better Understanding of the Relationship between Personality and Individual Job Performance. In Barrick, M. R. and Ryan, A. M. (Eds.) *Personality and Work.* San Francisco: John Wiley and sons Inc. Pp. 83-120.

Jenson, Paul, G. and Kichner Wayne, K. (1955) A National Answer to the Question, "Do Sons Follow their Fathers' Occupations? *Journal of Applied Psychology and Education*, 11 (1), 36-39.

Jersild, A. T. Judith, S. Brook and David W. (1957) *The Psychology of Adolescence.* New York: Macmillan Publication.

Jhaj, Didar, S. and Grewal, J.S. (1976) A Study of Occupational Aspirations and Socio-economic Status of Advantaged and Disadvantages Children. *Indian Journal of Applied Psychology*. 13 (2), 70-73.

John, L. Schmidt and John W.M. Rothney (1955) Variability of Vocational Choices of High School Students. *Personnel and Guidance Journal*. 34(1).

John, W. Atkinson, Norman T. Feather, Robert E. (Ed.) (1966) *A Theory of Achievement Motivation*. Hustington, New York: Kriegar Publishing Company.

Jones, E.S. (1940) Relation of Ability to Preferred and Probable Occupation. *Educational and Administrative Supervisor*. 26, 220-226.

Joshi, M.C. (1963) Intelligence and Levels of Vocational Aspiration. *Journal of Vocational and Educational Guidance*. (6), p.191.

Joshi, M.C. and Srivastava, R.P. (1964) Intelligence and Teaching Attitude. *Guidance Review*. 2(3), 95-103.

Jucknet, M. (1937) Leistung Anspruch Sniveau und. Selbstbewusstsch Psychol. *Forsch*, 22, 89-179.

Kahl, J.A. (1953) Educational and Occupational Aspirations of Common Man Boys. *Harvard Educational Review*. 23, 186-203.

Kaile, H. S. (1989) Intelligence as a Determiner of Occupational Aspiration of School Students. *The Progress of Education*, LXIV, (4), November.

Hariani Kamala, (1970) Educational and Vocational Aspirations and Planning by High School Girls. *Journal of Education and Psychology*, XXVIII (3).

Kao, G. and Tienda, M. (1998) Educational aspirations of minority youth. *American Journal of Education*, 106, 349-384.

Kao, G., and Tienda, M. (1995) Optimism and achievement: The educational performance of immigrant youth. *Social Science Quarterly*, 76, 1-18.

Kausler, D. H. (1951) A Study of the relationship between ego-involvement and learning. *Journal Psychology*, 32, 225-230.

Kesiezie, Kelhoulezo (1992) An Exploratory Case Study of How Socio-economic Factors Influence Occupational Choice of Students in Nagaland. *Dissertation Abstracts International,* 53 (3), 1495-A.

Khan, M. W. (1985) Educational and Vocational Aspirations of Hindu and Muslim School Students: A Comparative Study. *Indian Educational Review,* 20 (4), 67-77.

Klemmack, D. L. and Edwards, J. N. (1973) Women's Acquisition of Stereotyped Occupational Aspirations. *Sociology and Social Research*, 57 (4), 510-525.

Knill, W. D. (1964) Occupational Aspirations of Northern: Saskatchewan Students. *Alberta Journal of Educational Research*, 10 (1), 3-16.

Kriedberg, Gary et.al., (1978) Vocational Role Choice in Second and Sixth Grade Children. *Sex Roles*, 4(2), 175-181.

Krishna, K. P. and Ansari, M. A. (1975) Influence of Risk, n-ach and Personality Factors on Occupational Choices Among College Students. *Journal of Psychological Research*, 19 (1), 32-40.

Kulas, Henry, K. (1974) Relation of Mental Level and Scholastic Standing to Vocational Aspiration Level in Eight Grade Pupils. *Psychologia Wycho, Wawoza*, 17 (5), 643-651.

Kuppuswamy, B.A. (1962) *Manual of Socio-economic Status Scale*. Delhi: Manasayan.

Lipsett, Laurence (1961) Social Factors in Vocational Development. *Personnel and Guidance Journal*. Vol. XL, No.1.

Lawrence, T. (1956) *The Occupational Structure and Education*. New Jersey: Prentice Hall, Inc.

Leonard, A. L. (1977) Occupational Choices and Training Needs: *Prospects for the 1980s*. New York: Praveger Publishers. Inc. pp. 11-18.

Levine, Adeline (1976) Educational and Occupational Choice: A Synthesis of Literature from Sociology and psychology. *Journal of Consumer Research*, 2 (4), 276-289.

Lewin, K. (1935) *A Dynamic theory of personality*. New York: McGraw, Hill Book Co.

Lewin, K., Tamare, F. L. and Seare, S. P. (1944) Level of aspiration (In M. Mc. V. Hunt edition). *Personality and Behaviour Disorders*, 1, Chap. 10, 333-378.

Lim, Yongsoo (1991) Determinants of Career Aspiration and Career Maturity in Korean Male High School Students. *Dissertation Abstracts International*, 52 (3), 893.

Lindgren, H. C. (1973) Leadership and College Grades. *Journal of Social Psychology,* PP. 389 P. 105.

Litting, L. W. (1979) Motivational Correlates of Real to Ideal Occupational Aspiration Shifts Among Black and White Men and Women, *Bulletin of the Psychonomic society*, 13(4), 227-229.

Lois, L. P. (1971) Changes in parental attitudes related to educational and occupational aspiration for OH springs accompanying family life education. *Dissertation Abstracts International*. a, 32 (5).

Looft, William, R. (1971) Sex Differences in the Expression of Vocational Aspirations by Elementary School Children. *Development Psychology*. Vol. 5(2), 366.

Lynd, R. S. (1948) *Knowledge for What? The Place of Social Science in American Culture.* Princeton: University Press.

Lynd, R.S. (1929) *Knowledge for what? The Place of Social Science in American Culture.* Princeton: University Press.

Mahale, M. (1999) Adolescent's Vocational Aspirations and Economic Status of the Family, *The Progress of Education*, LXXIII, (10), May.

Mahatma, C.M. (1969) An Investigation into the Vocational Interest of X Class Students. *Rajasthan Board Journal of Education.* 5(2), P. 16-21.

Mahone, C. H. (1960) Fear of Failure and Unrealistic Vocational Aspiration. *Journal of Abnormal and Social Psychology*, 60, P. 253-261.

Malathi, V. Gopal. (1987) Aspiration, Motivation and Achievement of Pupils Belonging to Rural and Urban Scheduled Castes. *Perspectives in Education*, 3 (2), 105-110.

Marini, Margaret, M. (1978) Sex Differences in the Determination of Adolescent Aspirations. *A Review of Research Sex Roles.* 4(5), P. 723-753.

Marjoribanks, Kevin (1985) School Attitudes and Adolescents Aspirations Ethnic Group Differences. *International Journal of Psychology*, 23 (3), 277-289.

Markus, H. and Nurius, P. (1986) Possible selves. *American Psychologist*, 41(9), 954-969.

Marotz-Boden, Rormona (1978) Parental Aspirations and Expectations for daughters and sons. *Adolescence*, Vol. 13, Pp. 20-25.

Powell, Marvin and Violar Bloom (1962) Development of and Reasons for Vocational Choices of Adolescent's through the High School Years. *The Journal of Educational Research.* 56(3), 56-60.

Mathur, Purnima and Gaur, J.S. (1974) *The Effect of SES on the Level of Occupational Aspirations of the Higher Secondary School Students in Delhi:* An Investigation. Manas. 21(2), 43-51.

Mau, W. C., and Bikos, L. H. (2000) A longitudinal study. *Journal of Counseling and Development*, 78, 186-194.

McCandless, N. J., Lueptow, L. B., and McKee, M. (1989) Family socioeconomic status and adolescent sex-typing. *Journal of Marriage and the Family*, 51 (3), 627-635.

McClelland, D. C. (1961) *The Achieving Society*, New York: The Free Press.

McClelland, D. C. (1965) Achievement and Entrepreneurship: A Longitudinal Study. In Tewari A. N. (1984) *Achievement Motivation in Deprived Society*. Agra: Modern Printers.

McClelland, D. C. *et al*, (1958) *A Scoring Manual for the Achievement Motive*. Princeton, New Jersey: Van Nostrand.

McCrae, R. P. T. Jr. (1989) Reinterpreting The Myers-Briggs Type Indicator From The Perspective of the Five-Factor Model of Personality. *Journal of Personality*. 57. Pp.17-40.

McLaughlin, Gerald, W., *et al.*, (1976) Socio-economic Status and the Career Aspirations and perceptions of Women Seniors in High Schools. *Vocational Guidance Quarterly*, 25 (2), 155-162.

McMahon, M., and Patton, W. (1997) Gender differences in children and adolescents' perceptions of influences on their career development. *The School Counselor* 44, 368-376.

Mcwhirter, Ellen Marie Hawley (1993) A Test Model of Career Commitment and Aspirations of Mexican American High School Girls. *Dissertation Abstracts International*, 54 (1), 92-A.

Meckhausen, H. (1963) *Hoffnung and Furcht in der Leistungs motivation*. Meisenheim Glan, Allegemeine Psychologie in Experimenten, Gottingen.

Mehta, H. P. (1960) Vocational Choice and Adjustment among Graduates of Delhi University. *Journal of Vocational Education Guidance*, 54-63.

Mehta, Mathur, et al., (1987) Influences of Level of Occupational Aspirations of Adolescents. *Indian Educational Review*, 42-60.

Mehta, P. H., Bhatnagar, and Surender Kumar (1985) Sex Differences in Vocational Planning Among Tribal Students of Meghalaya. *Indian Educational Review,* NCERT.

Mehtha, Mathru, et.al., (1987) Influences of Level of Occupational Aspiration of Adolescents. *Indian Educational Review*. 42-60.

Miller, I. W. and Haller, A. O. (1964) A Measure of Level of Occupational Aspiration. *Personnel and Guidance Journal*, 42, 448-455.

Minor, C. A. and Neel, R. G. (1958) The Relationship between Achievement Motive and Occupational Preference. *Journal Counsel Psychology,* 56, P. 57-67.

Misra, S.S. (1975) A Cross Cultural Studies of Status and Vocational Aspirations Among Aboriginal Tribes of Bastar. *Journal of Psychological Researches*. 19(1), p.3.

Morris, J. L. (1966) Propensity of Risk Taking as a Determinant of Vocational Choice: An Extension of the Theory of Achievement Motivation. *Journal of Personality Social Psychology*, 3, 328-335.

Mount, M. K. *et al.* (2005) Higher-order Dimensions of the Big Five Personality Traits and the Big six Vocational Interest Types. *Personality Psychology*, 58 (2) Pp. 447-478.

Mullis, R. L., Mullis, A. K., and Gerwels, D. (1998) Stability of vocational interests among high school students. *Adolescence* 33, 699-708.

Murry (1938) *Exploration in Personality*. New York: Oxford University Press.

Muthayya, B.C. (1962) A Study of Level of Aspiration and Intelligence of High Achiever and Low Achiever in the Scholastic Field. *Journal of Psychological Researches*, 6, 146-149.

National Classification of Occupations (1962) Government of India, Department of Labour, *Employment and Rehabilitation*, Delhi: Controller of Publications.

National Council of Educational Research and Training (NCTE) (1975) *The curriculum for the Ten-Year School, A framework*. New Delhi.

NCERT (1971) Educational and National Development: *Report of the Education Commission 1964-1966*, (Government of India Publications) Calcutta: Sree Saraswati Press, Ltd.

NCERT (1976) *Higher Secondary education and its Vocationalization*. New Delhi.

McClelland (1966): TAT, adaptation. by Prag Mehta in *Achievement Motive in High School boys and Training for (project report)*.

Nelms, Charlie, *et al*., (1982) Job Choice as a Function of Sex and Achievement Scores for High School Students. *Education*, 103(1), 64-67.

Nelson (1963) *The Source of Eagerness in Daily Work Vocational Guidance Querterly*. Cited in Crites, J. O (1969) Vocational Psychology. The Study of Vocational Behaviour and Development. New York: McCraw Hill Book Company, Pp. 327-328.

Nenty, J. (1993) Comparative Analysis of Realization of Occupational Preference Values. *The Progress of Education*, LXVII, (7), February.

O'Brien, K. M. (1996) The influence of psychological separation and parental attachment on the career development of adolescent women. *Journal of Vocational Behaviour*, 48, 257-274.

O'Brien, K. M. and Fassinger, R. E. (1993) A casual model of the career orientation and career choice of adolescent women. *Journal of Counseling Psychology*, 40 (4), 456-469.

Ogawa, K. and Tanaka, K. (1979) The Influence of a Father's Occupation on a Son's Occupational Choice. *Japanese Journal of Educational Psychology,* 27 (4), 272-281.

Olayinka, M. S. (1973) Job aspirations of the youth and the educational provision in Lagos. *West African Journal of Education* 17 (1) 41-49.

Orleans, Edward, l. (1970) Family Interaction, Personality Development and Vocational Choice in Adolescent Males. *Dissertation Abstracts International,* 31 (2-B), 919-920.

Ory, J. C. and Helfrich, I. M. (1978) A Study of Individual Characteristics and Career Aspirations. *Vocational Guidance Quarterly,* 27(1), p. 43-49.

Oxford English Dictionary, Oxford University Press, London, Vol. 1., 1972.

Pal, S.K. (1968) Personality Needs of Engineering, Law, Medical and Teachers Training Students in an Indian Situation. *Journal of Social Psychology*. 6, 74, 135-137.

Pappas, A.V. (1975) Occupational and Educational Aspiration: An Analysis of North Mississippi Post-elementary Pupils. *Dissertation Abstracts International*. 36(7), 4267.

Pappas, A. V. (1976) Occupational and Educational Aspiration: An Analysis and North Mississippi Post-elementary Pupils. *Dissertation Abstracts International*, 36(7-4), P. 4267-4268.

Parks (2000) Big Questions, *Worthy Dreams*. San Francisco: Jossey-Bass, p. XXI.

Passi, B.K. (1970) Patterns of Vocational Aspirations of Higher Secondary School Adolescents in Relation to Sex and Residential Background. *Journal of Education and Psychology.* Vol. XXVIII (2), p. 57-65.

Perrone, A.P. (1964) Factors Influencing High School Senior's Occupational Preferences. *Personnel and Guidance Journal*. 52(10), p. 975-980.

Picou, J.S. (1979) Black-white Variations in a Model of the Occupational Aspiration Process. *Journal of Negro Education*, 42 (2), 117-122.

Picou, J. S. and Curry, E. W. (1971) Structural, Interpersonal and Behavioural Correlates of Female Adolescents' Occupational Choices. *Adolescence*, 8 (31), 421-432.

Pillai, P. G. (1977) Intelligence as Determiner of Occupational Aspiration of High School Students. *Journal of Psychological Researches*. 21(1), P. 81-86.

Plunkett, S.W. and Bamaca-Gomex, M.Y. (2003) The relationship between parenting, acculturation, and adolescent academics in Mexican-origin immigrant families in Los Angeles. *Hispanic Journal of Behavioural Sciences*, 25, 222-239.

Porter, J. R. (1954) Predicting Vocational Plan of High School Senior Boys, *Journal of Personnel Guidance*, 33, P.215-218.

Powell, M. and Bloom, V. (1962) Development of and Reasons for Vocational Choices of Adolescent's through the High School Years. *The Journal of Educational Research*. 56(3), P. 56-60.

Prenter, I. L. and Steward, R. (1972) Educational and Vocational Aspiration of new Zealand Adolescent Girls in Relation to Achievement Motivation. *New Zealand Journal of Educational Studies*, 7(1), P. 38-44.

Qian, Z., and Blair, S. L. (1999) Racial/ethnic differences in educational aspirations of high school seniors, *Sociological Perspectives*, 42, 605-625.

Quereshi and Bhargav (1989) Adjustment Problem of Female Adolescents belonging to Realistic and Non-realistic zones of Aspiration level. *Indian Journal of Psychology*, 64 (1-4), Pp. 83-86.

Ralph, R. Berdie *et al*., (1963) *Testing in Guidance and Counselling*. New York: McGraw-hill Book Company, Inc.

Ramchand, T.S. Sohal (1978) Vocational Aspiration of Students. *Journal of Indian Education*. 21-25.

Rao, G.C. and Pal, K. (1973) A Study of Occupational Values and Preferences of School Going Youth. *Manas*. 20(2), 73-91.

Raynor, J. D. (1978) *In personality, motivation and achievement by Atkinson* J. W. and Raynor, J.D. Hemisphere Publishing Corporation: Washington and London.

Reddy, A. V. (1972) A Study of Vocational Needs of .1m16 Secondary School Pupils in Relation to their Occupational Choices and other Variables. *Unpublished Doctoral Thesis*, Sri Venkateshwara University, Tirupati.

Reddy, A. V. (1978) A Study on Vocational Choices. *Unpublished Thesis*, S. V. University, Thirupati.

Reilly, Janet Zakryk (1975) Birth Order and Vocational Choice Among Eight Grade Pupils. *Dissertation Abstracts International*. 36(7), 51-59.

Rezler, A. (1963) Occupational Values and Occupational Choices of Young Indians. *Guidance Review*, 1 (1), 3-21.

Rhee, Ock (1989) Family Background Variables of Korean Female Adolescents Related to Traditional Versus Non-traditional Occupational Aspirations. *Dissertation Abstracts International,* 50 (6), 91.

Riesman, F. (1972) *The Culturally Deprived Child*. New York: Harper and Row.

Robert, H. (1957) *Occupational Information*. New York: McGraw-Hill Book Company.

Rodman, Hyman *et al*, (1978) Social Class and Parents' Range of Aspirations for their Children. *Social Problems*, 25 (3), 333-344.

Roe, A. (1954) A new classification of occupations. *Journal of counseling Psychology*, 1, 215-220.

Roe, A. (1956) *The Psychology of occupations*. New York: Hohn Willey and Sons. Inc.

Roe, A. (1957) Early determinants of vocational choice. *Journal of Counselling*. (4) 212-217.

Rojewski, J. W. and Yang, B. (1997) Longitudinal analysis of select influences on adolescents' occupational aspirations. *Journal of Vocational Behaviour*, 51, 375-410.

Saha, L. J. (1982) Gender, School Attainment and Occupational Plans: Determinants of Aspirations and Expectations Among Australian Urban School Leavers. *Australian Journal of Education*, 26 (3), 247-265.

Sandefur, G. D. (1998) Race, ethnicity, families, and education. In : H. I. McCubbin and E.A. Thomposon (Eds), *Resiliency in Native American and Immigrant Families. Resilency in Families Series* (vol. 2. pp. 49-70). Thousand Oaks, CA: Sage.

Saxena. S (1985) A Study of Need Achievement in Relation to Creativity, Values, Level of Aspiration and Anxiety. *Journal of Higher Education*, 10(3).

Schoenfeld, Eugen (1959) Status and Career Decision: An Analysis of the time Dimension. *Sociological Quarterly*, 24, 246-256.

Schulenberg, J. E., Vondracek, F. W., and Crouter, A. C. (1984) The influence of the family on vocational development. *Journal of Marriage and the Family* 10. 129-143.

Sewell, W.H., Haller, A.O. and Strauss, M.A. (1957) Social Status and Educational and Occupational Aspiration. *American Review*. 22, 67-73.

Sewell, William, S. and Orenstein, A. M. (1965) Community of Residence and Occupational Choice. *American Journal of Sociology*, 70 (5), 551-563.

Shah and BHargava (1973) *Level of Aspiration Test*. Agra: National Psychological Corporation.

Shah, A. B. Veenu (2000) Vocational Aspirations of Home Science Students. *Indian Journal of Psychometry and Education*, 31, (2), July.

Shailaja, H. M. (1992) Interaction Effect of Intelligence, SES and Sex on Occupational Aspiration of Standard Nine Pupils of Bangalore City. *Fifth Survey of Educational Research*, II, (Ed.) M. B. Buch, New Delhi: NCERT.

Sharma (2003) *Guidance and Counselling*. Meerut: Surya Publication, P. 266.

Shaver, P.F. (1970) Birth order of medical students and the occupational ambitions of their parents. *International Journal of Psychology*, 5 (3), 197-207.

Sherwood, R. A. (1989) A conceptual framework for the study of aspirations. In R. Quaglia (Ed.), *Research in Rural Education*, 6 (2), 61-66.

Shipp, Judy Louire (1997) Differential Effects of the Structure of Opportunity on the Development of Career Aspirations: A Study of project Talent Participants. *Dissertation Abstracts International,* 52 (7), 441.

Shoeib, Aly Mahamaud Aly (1982) An Investigation into the Educational and Occupational Aspirations of Egyptian Preparatory School Pupils in Relation to Home Background, School, Achievement, Sex and parental Aspirations. *Dissertation Abstracts International*. 49(10), 257.

Shoffner, S. M. and Klemer, R. H. (1973) Parent education for the parental role in children's vocational choices, *family co-ordinator*, (Oct.) 22, 94), 419-427.

Sibbison, V. H. (1975) Occupational Preferences and Expectations of Rural High School Males and Females: Background, Grade and Sex-role Correlates. *Dissertation Abstracts International,* 35 (11-A), 7-69.

Singh and Kour (1987) Motive to Avoid and Approach Success: Two Dimensions of the Same Motive: *Asian Journal of Psychology and Education*, Pp. 1-7, 19.

Singh, L. C. (1963) Relationship between Personality and Vocational Choice, *Guidance Review*, 1(2), 9, P. 332-354.

Small, L. (1953) Personality Determinants of Vocational Choice. *Psychological Monographs*, 67, (1, whole No. 351).

Sparling, E.J. (1933) Do College Students Choose Vocational Wisely? *Teachers College Contributions to Education*, No. 561.

Srivastava, S. S. and Palo, S. N. (1970) Occupational Choices of High School Boys in Relation to their Fathers Occupational Level. *Manas*, 17 (2), 119-124.

Srounce, W. F. (1957) On Perception of Occupation. *Journal of Abnormal and Social Psychology,* 54 (1).

Steimel, R. J. and Suziedelis, A. (1963) Perceived Parental Influence and Inventoried Interests. *Journal Counsel Psychology,* 10, 289-295.

Stein, H. (1973) The effects of material employment and educational attainment on the sex type attributes of college females. *Social behaviour and personality*, 1 (2), 111-114.

Stephenson, R. M. (1955) Occupational Aspirations of Plans of 443 Ninth Graders. *Journal of Educational Research*, 49, 27-35.

Stot, L. D. (1989) Relationship between home environment and intrinsic versus extrinsic orientation of higher achieving and lower achieving Puerto Rican children. *Educational Research Quarterly,* 13, 22-36.

Sundararajan, S. (1988) Some Correlates of Occupational Aspirations of Higher Secondary Students in Tamilnadu, *Experiments in Education,* 21 (10), October.

Sundararajan, S. and Lilly Epsy Bai (1990) Socio-Economic Status and Occupational Aspirations of the Higher Secondary Leavers. *The Progress of Education,* 65 (4), 94-96.

Sundararajan, S. and Rajasekhar, S. (1988) Occupational Aspirations of the Higher Secondary Students. *The Progress of Education.*

Sundararajan, S., Kalavathi, N. (1990) Occupational Aspiration of the Higher Secondary Girls in the University of Madras. *Experiments in Education*, 18 (8), August.

Sundararajan, S.; Chandra, R. (1993) Occupational Aspiration of the Matriculation Schools in Salem Town, *Experiments in Education*, 19 (2), October.

Super, D. E. (1957) *The Psychology of Careers.* New York: Harper and Brothers.

Super, D. E. (1957) *Vocational Development: A Framework for Research*. New York: Columbia University Burean of Publications.

Super, D. E. and Crites, J. O. (1962) *Appraising Vocational Fitness*. New York: Harper, p.2, 337-380, 410,408,515.

Teachan, J. E. (1974) The Effect of Sex and Predominant Socio-Economic Class School Climate on Expectation of Success Among Black Students. *Journal of Negro Education*, 43(2).

Teachman, J. D., and Paasch, K. (1998) The family and educational aspirations. *Journal of Marriage and the Family*, 60, 704-714.

Thakral, M.M.S. (1977) A Comparative Study of Locus of Control, General Intelligence and Level of Vocational Aspiration of Scheduled Castes and Non-scheduled Castes High School

Students. *Society for Educational Research and Development*, Baroda. 131.

Tilgher (1962) Work Through the Ages. In Crites, O. S. (1969) Vocational Psychology. *The Study of Vocational Behaviour and Development.* New York: McCraw, Hill Book Company, 327.

Tiwari (1984) *Achievement Motivation in Deprived Society.* Agra: Modern Printers.

Trice, A.D., and Kind, R. (1991) Stability of kindergarten children's career aspirations. *Psychological Reports* 68, 1378.

Trice, A.D., and Knapp, L. (1992) Relationship of children's career aspirations to parents' occupations. *The Journal of Genetic Psychology* 153, 355-357.

Trice, A. D., Hughes, M. A., Odam, C., Woods, K., and McClellan, N. C. (1995) The origins of children's career aspirations: IV. Testing hypotheses from four theories. *The Career Development Quarterly* 43, 307-322.

Trivedi, R. S. and Desai, D. B. (1972) Achievement Motivation Development in High School Pupils, *Journal of Education and Psychology*, 30 (2) pp. 88-92.

Trivedi, R. S. and Desai, D. B. (1972) Achievement Motivation Development in High School Pupils. *Journal of Education and Psychology,* 30 (2) pp. 88-92.

Trow, W. D. (1941) *Phantasy and Vocational Choice Occupation.* 20, 89-93.

Tseng, M. S. (1971) Social Class, Occupational Aspiration and Other Variables. *Journal of Experimental Education*, 39(4), Pp. 88-92.

Tseng, M. S. (1972) Comparison of Selected Familial Personality and Vocational Variables of High School Students and Drop-outs. *Journal of Educational Research* 65(10), pp. 462-466.

U.S. Department of Education (1993) National Center for Education Statistics National Education Longitudinal Study of 1998 second follow up: *Student component data file user's manual*. Washington, DC: Author.

Uzzell, O. (1961) Influencers of Occupational Choice. *Personnel Guidance Journal,* 39, 666-669.

Valadez, J. R. (1998) Applying to college: Race, class, and gender differences. *Professional School Counseling* 1 (5), 14-20.

Vasantha, R. (1966) Vocational Preference of College Students. *Indian Educational Material,* 187-225.

Vasantha, R. (1970) Vocational Preference of College Students. *Indian Educational Material*. 5(3).

Verman, J. N. and Colvin, L. H. (1974) *A guide to psychologists and their concepts*: San Francisco, Freeman and Company.

Vignod, Z. (1972) The Relationship between Occupational Choice and Parental Occupations. *Journal of Educational Research,* 18 (4), 287-294.

Wahl, K. H., and Blackhurst, A. (2000) Factors affecting the occupational and educational aspirations of children and adolescents. *Professional School Counseling* 3, 367-374.

Walberg, H. J. (1989) Student aspirations: National and international perspectives. In : R. Quaglia (Ed.) *Research in Rural Education,* 6 (2), 1-9.

Wall, J., Covell, K., and MacIntyre, P. D. (1999) Implications of social supports for adolescents' education and career aspirations. *Canadian Journal of Behavioural Science* 31, 63-71.

Walter, L. S. (1966) *Occupational Careers*. Chicago: Aldine Publishing Company. Pp. 187-225.

Webster's Third New International Dictionary (1976) *Encyclopedia Britannica,* Inc. G.C. Merrian Co.,

Werrbach, G. B., Grotevant, H. D., and Cooper, C. R. (1990) Gender differences in adolescents' identity development in the domain of sex role concepts. *Sex Roles,* 23 (7-8), 349-362.

Werts, Charles, E. (1967) Career Choice Patterns. *Sociology of Education,* 40 (4), 348-358.

Westaway, M. and Skuy, M. (1984) Self-esteem and the Educational and Vocational Aspirations of Adolescent Girls in South Africa. *South African Journal of Psychology*. 14(4), Pp. 113-117.

Williams, A. P. and Woodward, S. (1983) Factors Related to

Career Aspirations of New Entrants into a Stratified Occupational System. *British Journal of Guidance and Counselling*, 11 (1), 68-81.

Willson, A. B. (1959) Residential Segregation of Social Classes and Aspirations of High School boys. *American Social Review*, 299.

Witty, P.A. and Lehman, H.C. (1931) A Study of Vocational Attitude and Intelligence. *Elementary School Journal.* 31, 735-746.

Wrenn, G.G. (1935) Intelligence and the Vocational Choices of College Students. *The Educational Record.* 16, Pp. 217-219.

Yaegel, J. S. (1977) Certainty of Vocational Choice and the Persistence and Achievement of Liberal Arts Community College Freshman. *Dissertation Abstracts International*, 38 (1-A), 118-119.